Praise for *Managing Customers for Profit*

"Dr. V. Kumar is one of the world's leading experts in customer relationship management (CRM). In this book, he offers practical guidance to managers on how to implement CRM strategies in their own firms. It is a *must have* book for anyone interested in developing profitable and stronger relationships with their customers."

> —*Russ Winer*, Executive Director Marketing Science Institute and William Joyce Professor of Marketing Stern School of Business, New York University

"Not only have I had the opportunity to participate in one of Dr. Kumar's presentations on *Managing Customers for Profit*, but we also followed through with him in bringing the know-how to our company. We definitely see tremendous value in his concepts and strategies described in this book as evidenced by successes seen in other companies. Currently, we are implementing the framework prescribed in his book in India."

> —*Maninder Singh Juneja*, Senior General Manager, Head–Retail Channel Liabilities Group, ICICI Bank Limited, India

"This book is the antidote that marketers have needed to satisfy the pressing demand for accountability. The concepts and metrics are grounded in the realities of customer behavior, while speaking the language of senior management."

> —*George S. Day*, Geoffrey T. Boisi Professor; Professor of Marketing, Co-Director, Mack Center for Technological Innovation, Director, Emerging Technologies Management Research Program

"Marketing leaders face many pressing challenges and opportunities in a rapidly changing global business environment and, as a result, are always on the lookout for fresh insight, new learning, and real-world experiences that they can leverage. Dr. Kumar's new book is a *must read* for marketing managers in B2C- as well as B2B-focused businesses who are looking for a strategic approach to maximizing customer profitability. Kumar's book provides a different and proven model. Marketers should have to read it."

> —*Dennis Dunlap*, CEO, American Marketing Association

"Customer management has become a key business function as organizations seek to complement an understanding of what they do with their brands with a deep knowledge of those they serve: customers. Dr. Kumar's book is an essential resource for those who wish to optimize their customer investments. Strategically, it ties customer-facing activities to the firm's objectives. Operationally, it has an insightful analysis of the activities that will lead to the achievement of those objectives. And in terms of accountability, it has the marketing metrics to calibrate success in execution, including diagnostic information for learning organizations. Dr. Kumar's pre-eminent academic credentials combined with his extensive industry practice are married to make this book of immense value to both academics and practitioners."

> —*John Roberts*, Scientia Professor, Faculty of Business, University of New South Wales, Sydney, Australia and Professor of Marketing, London Business School

"Firms that view their customer base as a portfolio and manage that portfolio most effectively will continue to outperform those that do not... In this important and comprehensive look at how to manage customers for profit, V. Kumar lays out the issues, dispels the myths, and provides templates for success. I recommend you read this book before your competitors beat you to it."

> —*Gary L. Lilien*, Distinguished Research Professor of Management Science and Co-founder and Research Director, Institute for the Study of Business Markets (ISBM), Penn State

"One of the best books in marketing that analyzes and demonstrates how to *simultaneously* manage both customer loyalty and company profitability by targeting and reallocating the four Ps of Marketing."

> —*Jagdish N. Sheth*, Charles H. Kellstadt Professor of Marketing, Goizueta Business School, Emory University

"Today's hyper-competitive financial services marketplace makes it more important than ever to manage our business to maximize the lifetime value of our customer relationships. V. Kumar has been a leading practitioner as well as a pioneer in extending the state of the art in this area. Now with the publication of this book, he has put together a compelling overview of the fundamental theory and key tools required to optimally manage customer relationships."

> —*Jim Pedrick*, Senior Vice President of Strategic Marketing, ING Financial Services

MANAGING CUSTOMERS FOR PROFIT

MANAGING CUSTOMERS FOR PROFIT

STRATEGIES TO INCREASE PROFITS AND BUILD LOYALTY

V. Kumar

First Printing: January 2008

ISBN-10: 0-13-611740-6
ISBN-13: 978-013-611740-7

This product is printed digitally on demand. This book is the
paperback version of an original hardcover book.

Pearson Education LTD.
Pearson Education Australia PTY, Limited.
Pearson Education Singapore, Pte. Ltd.
Pearson Education North Asia, Ltd.
Pearson Education Canada, Ltd.
Pearson Educatión de Mexico, S.A. de C.V.
Pearson Education—Japan
Pearson Education Malaysia, Pte. Ltd.

Vice President, Publisher
Tim Moore

**Associate Publisher and
Director of Marketing**
Amy Neidlinger

Editor
Yoram (Jerry) Wind

Acquisitions Editor
Martha Cooley

Editorial Assistant
Pamela Boland

Development Editor
Russ Hall

**Digital Marketing
Manager**
Julie Phifer

Marketing Coordinator
Megan Colvin

Cover Designer
Chuti Prasertsith

Managing Editor
Gina Kanouse

Project Editor
Jovana San Nicolas-
Shirley

Copy Editor
Keith Cline

Proofreader
Gill Editorial Services

Senior Indexer
Cheryl Lenser

Compositor
Fast Pages

Manufacturing Buyer
Dan Uhrig

Library of Congress Cataloging-in-Publication Data is on file.

Dedicated, with love, to Anita & Rohan, and Prita.

CONTENTS

Foreword

Whilst corporations continue to strive to improve customer loyalty and customer profitability, the conventional customer profitability model offers a great opportunity for enhancement. Based on my experience over the last two decades across three different industries, quite often, the link between customer satisfaction, customer loyalty and customer profitability is tenuous. Secondly, since customer satisfaction and loyalty are measured across the customer base, corrective actions are designed uniformly for all customers. However, neither the customers nor the customer behavior is uniform!

With organizational resources being scarce and improvement of marketing return on investment (ROI) being a key challenge for business managers, it is imperative to have a fresh perspective to customer relationship management (CRM) with customer profitability and the notion that different customers should be managed and satisfied differently as its focus. This profit-based strategy draws upon robust CRM research that lays emphasis on future customer value. The future value of customer profitability can be measured through the customer lifetime value (CLV) metric. Dr. Kumar has developed innovative quantitative approaches to calculate CLV, which can be leveraged for CRM decisions relating to customer acquisition, retention and attrition.

CLV is a powerful tool that could potentially be the source of competitive advantage for organizations and provide the armory to win in the marketplace. This book is recommended for business managers interested in nurturing long-lasting relationships with customers to drive profitable growth.

—*Sangeeta Pendurkar*
   Chief Marketing Officer, HSBC Bank Middle East Limited

Preface

This book is aimed at top/mid-level management of small, medium, and large business-to-business (B2B) and business-to-consumer (B2C) enterprises that have the power and resources to change customer management strategies in their organization. This book also serves as a guide for executives-on-the-rise to understand the importance of customer-oriented strategies.

What constitutes an effective customer management strategy? Is it enhancing customer loyalty, widening the customer base, or maximizing customer profitability? Although conventional wisdom suggests that enhancing customer loyalty and widening the customer base are effective strategies, this book focuses on the profitability angle and establishes that managing customers based on their profitability is the most effective approach to customer management.

This book identifies three paths to profitability a firm can undertake: operational excellence, brand equity, and relationship marketing. If relationship marketing is selected as a path to profitability, managing customer loyalty becomes crucial. While managing loyalty programs, companies have traditionally placed undue emphasis on maximizing customer loyalty. This book adopts a fundamentally different approach toward customer management and demonstrates that stable healthy growth of a company is built on the profitability of customers, not just on their numbers or loyalty. This book also shows that loyal customers are not always profitable, and not all profitable customers are loyal. Therefore, when firms are developing a customer management strategy, they must adopt an approach that closely links loyalty with profitability.

To effectively manage loyalty programs, firms use several customer selection metrics, such as Recency-Frequency-Monetary value (RFM), Past Customer Value (PCV), Share of Wallet (SOW), and Customer Lifetime Value (CLV). This book concludes that CLV outscores other metrics when it comes to profitable customer management. CLV outscores the other metrics in this regard because it is a forward-looking metric and because it factors future customer behavior into current marketing initiatives.

Empowered with CLV, firms can reevaluate and overhaul their existing customer management strategies. This book offers nine strategies to manage customers profitably. These strategies aim to select the right customers, manage them profitably, and retain them through optimal allocation of resources. Furthermore, these strategies demonstrate the benefit of pitching the right products to the right customers at the right time, holding on to profitable customers, encouraging multichannel shopping, increasing brand value for customers, acquiring potentially profitable customers, and identifying customers who provide value through referrals. The knowledge obtained through implementing these strategies can then be leveraged to acquire prospective customers with a higher profit potential.

Although CLV can be an effective tool to measure and manage direct (transactional) contributions made by customers, it overlooks the indirect (referral, word-of-mouth) contributions toward firm profitability. To maximize profit, the crucial contribution made by customer referral behavior has to be carefully monitored and managed. This book introduces Customer Referral Value (CRV) as a metric that firms can use to maximize the indirect contributions made by customers. CLV, used in conjunction with CRV, will enable marketers to implement strategically designed marketing initiatives to profitably manage customer loyalty.

This book identifies organizational and implementation challenges that firms might encounter when adopting a CLV-based approach and suggests appropriate guidelines to overcome such challenges. Firms need to adopt an "interaction-orientation" approach when dealing with customers. By establishing a strong firm-customer relationship, and by treating customers as a resource, managers can effectively implement the CLV-based strategies. Because CLV is a dynamic approach, marketing strategies have to be constantly updated for sustained profitability. This book recommends a balanced approach, keeping in mind the ethical issues involved in collecting and managing customer-level information. This book also outlines issues that firms might potentially face when implementing a CLV-based approach and suggests the necessary strategies to stay ahead of the competition.

Organization of the Book

This book adopts a strategic approach toward profitable customer management and illustrates the strategies needed to manage customers efficiently. It presents techniques to aid in customer-oriented marketing initiatives using the concept of Customer Lifetime Value. The book consists of 15 chapters.

Chapter 1 introduces key concepts of customer management. It describes the different paths to profitability and identifies relationship marketing as the one that leads to profitable customer management. It also discusses the role of loyalty programs in bringing firms and customers closer to each other. Chapter 2 links loyalty with profitability and discusses the drivers of profitable customer loyalty. After establishing the need for managing customers for profit, Chapter 3 reviews the popular metrics used to measure customer loyalty. The concept of Customer Lifetime Value is discussed, as is how to measure CLV. Chapter 4 describes how to build and sustain profitable customer loyalty and calls for a fundamental outlook change to manage customer loyalty. Chapter 5 outlines nine strategies available to managers to maximize CLV. These strategies will help firms decide how to select the best customers (Chapter 5), make loyal customers profitable (Chapter 6), optimally allocate resources (Chapter 7), pitch the right products to the right customers at the right time (Chapter 8), prevent customer attrition (Chapter 9), encourage multichannel shopping behavior (Chapter 10), maximize brand value (Chapter 11), and link acquisition and retention to profitability (Chapter 12). Chapter 13 introduces the concept of Customer Referral Value (CRV), which firms can use to measure the indirect impact (referrals, word-of-mouth) made by customers toward the firm's profit. Chapter 14 discusses potential organizational and implementation challenges when adopting a CLV-based approach, and Chapter 15 covers potential issues that need to be addressed to sustain profitable customer management.

Acknowledgments

I want to thank Andrew Petersen, Denish Shah, Morris George, Bharath Rajan, Magesh Nandagopal, and Saurabh Bhargava for their assistance in the preparation of this manuscript. I also want to thank Archana Muppaka for her assistance in the operational details. I would particularly like to thank Keith Cline and Renu for copy editing the manuscript and Jovana San Nicolas-Shirley for managing the publication process. I also want to thank my coauthors in each of the studies referenced in this book for their contributions. I am also thankful to Martha Cooley for her support in the process of streamlining the content of this book. Finally, special thanks are owed to Peter Fader for making this book happen, and Dave Reibstein and George Day for their encouragement and guidance. I am deeply indebted to the editorial team of Prentice Hall for accepting this manuscript for publication.

About the Author

 **Dr. V. Kumar (VK)** is the inaugural holder of the Richard and Susan Lenny Distinguished Chair Professor in Marketing, and the Executive Director of the Center for Excellence in Brand and Customer Management, in J. Mack Robinson College of Business at Georgia State University. Previously, Dr. Kumar was the ING chair professor of marketing and the executive director of the ING Center for Financial Services in the School of Business at the University of Connecticut. He was recently ranked among the top five marketing scholars worldwide based on his research productivity. Dr. Kumar has been recognized with many teaching and research excellence awards and has published numerous articles in premier journals of marketing, such as the *Harvard Business Review, Journal of Marketing, Journal of Marketing Research, Marketing Science, and Operations Research.* He has won several awards for his research publications in scholarly journals, including the Don Lehmann Award twice for the best paper published in the *Journal of Marketing/Journal of Marketing Research* in a two-year period and the MSI/Paul H. Root Award twice for two different *Journal of Marketing* articles contributing to the best practice of marketing. He has coauthored more than 100 articles, book chapters, and textbooks, such as *Marketing Research, International Marketing Research,* and *Customer Relationship Management: A Databased Approach.* He is currently on the editorial review board of several scholarly journals and has lectured on marketing-related topics in various universities and organizations in the United States, Europe, Australia, and Asia. His current research focuses on international diffusion models, customer relationship management, customer lifetime value analysis, sales and market-share forecasting, international marketing research and strategy, marketing resource allocation, sales promotion, and interaction orientation.

Dr. Kumar is also a consultant to many Fortune 500 firms, for whom he has helped design suitable marketing strategies to identify the most profitable customers. His work with IBM and P&G has been recognized by INFORMS as award-winning entries in the 2006 and 2007 Practice Prize Competition, respectively. Recently, Dr. Kumar was conferred with *two Lifetime Achievement Awards* from the American Marketing Association Special Interest Groups for his contributions to the fields of marketing strategy and interorganizational marketing. He received his Ph.D. from the University of Texas at Austin.

Dr. Kumar can be reached by email at (dr_vk@hotmail.com).

1

Introduction

"Customer is king" is a centuries-old corporate saying. Not much has changed in the current century other than the fact that your company's customer can also be the *most sought after.* Because of advances in technology and globalization, you never know in what form competition will emerge to attract your customers. For example, the incumbent books-retailer leader Barnes & Noble was overshadowed by a then-innocuous Internet-based company, Amazon; IBM was challenged by the new entrant Dell; and American car companies are currently running huge losses at the expense of Japanese and Korean car manufacturers.

A common factor governing the success or failure of any firm is almost always the ability of the firm to service its customers better or offer superior value propositions. So, what's new? It is common wisdom that customer relationship initiatives are *expected* to deliver superior financial performance. However, *reality* often belies *expectation.*

Consider Continental Airlines, for example.[1] In late 1994, Continental had lost an average $960 million per year for the previous four years. Customers were annoyed by the way the airline was being operated—unreliable, dirty, and frequently losing passenger baggage. The Department of Transportation ranked Continental last on the list based on its on-time airline rankings. By March 1995, Continental had moved from last to first in the on-time rankings. In 2000, Continental Airlines was ranked number one in customer satisfaction by J. D. Power and

Associates. An unprecedented recovery! The biggest underlying success factor was Continental's ability to win back customer satisfaction. There was no doubt that Continental had a winning customer management formula. But, was the formula profitable? What about the cost of satisfying the customers? Between 2001 and 2005, Continental Airlines reported an average net loss of about $200 million per year.

In the mid 1990s, Dell Corporation introduced a novel e-commerce business model.[2] The company's strategy of selling directly over the Internet with no intermediaries (such as retail outlets) was the most talked about success story of the early twenty-first century. Dell's revenues and earnings grew by more than 30% year after year, and the company reported a return on invested capital of 243% for 2000. *Fortune* magazine listed Dell as America's third-most admired company. Television audiences in the United States were treated to an extensive advertising campaign by Dell that showed Dell employees putting in long hours in their customer contact centers to service customers. Was Dell's success profitable in the long run? Dell's stock has tumbled more than 40% over the past two years on decreased sales and slimmer profit margins. In March 2007, Dell reported a 33% drop in fourth-quarter profits and warned that growth and profit margins will remain "under pressure" for the next few quarters.

A common underlying theme of these two examples is the importance of sustaining successful customer management initiatives in the long run. In other words, although it might be possible to keep customers happy and loyal in the short run, the greater challenge often lies in achieving that objective with both *growth* and *profits* in the long run.

It may be argued that operational efficiencies are also important. We don't deny that fact. However, operational efficiency cannot hold precedence over customer focus. Consider the case of First USA & Capital One, for example.[3] Both companies are prominent players in the credit card industry. However, what sets them apart is their customer management approach. First USA is "laser focused on operating efficiency and to pass those savings on to customers," according to former Chairman Richard Vague. In contrast, Capital One's primary goal is to "deliver the right product, at the right price, to the right customer, at the right time." This is an interesting paradox between two players of the same industry selling exactly the same product.

First USA transacted its business with little differentiation across its customers. This approach was consistent with its corporate structure, which was organized around products or functions. The company's customer acquisition strategy was based on luring customers from other credit card companies and using affinity partners. The company did not make an investment in archiving customer data. Therefore, it lacked the ability to compute individual customer profitability. Employees were mandated to try to retain all customers irrespective of whether they appeared as good or bad prospects in the long run. In 1999, the bank discontinued the policy of allowing a grace period for late payments and raised late-fee penalties. This policy was applied uniformly across the board, across all customers. Not surprisingly, a mass exodus of customers (both profitable and unprofitable) resulted. The company was later forced to revoke its policy. However, the damage was done.

In contrast, Capital One's primary focus is customers. The company conducts business by microsegmenting its customer base so that each customer can be individually serviced in consonance with the customer's value potential. Furthermore, Capital One set up a customer data warehouse that has an unmatched ability to mine any customer's information in a matter of seconds. For instance, when a customer calls, computers instantly access the full history of the customer and cross-reference it with millions of other customers. If a valuable customer calls to cancel a credit card, the call-routing system automatically rattles out three attractive counteroffers that the customer service representative can use to negotiate. In a nutshell, each customer is treated differently. Capital One's deep commitment to knowing its customer is evident from the fact that in 2000, Capital One ran 45,000 tests on product variants, procedural changes, and customer interactions.

So, what was the financial consequence of these two approaches? As the credit environment worsened, First USA's customer attrition rate grew by 50%, contributing to a 23% decline in revenue in 2000, and the company's first ever loss. On the other hand, Capital One earned 40% more interest income from each customer as compared to First USA, with double the profit margin, despite being half the size.

The bottom line is that the bottom line matters. To manage and sustain profitability, we need to come up with the right marketing strategies, backed by the right marketing metrics. Although there are 50+ important metrics that every executive should know,[4] this book focuses on one particular metric: the *Customer Lifetime Value* (CLV) metric. This book takes an in-depth look at how marketing strategies based on this powerful metric can help manage customer relationship and profitability simultaneously.

Customer Lifetime Value

Customer Lifetime Value refers to the net present value of future profit from a customer. The beauty of the metric lies in the fact that it is *forward*-looking, unlike traditional measures based on past contributions to profit. Hence, it enables marketers to adopt the right marketing activities *today* to increase *future* profitability. Moreover, CLV is the only metric that incorporates all the elements that drive profitability: revenue, expense, and customer behavior. Thus, the metric keeps the focus on the customer (rather than the product) as the driver of profitability. In fact, in recent times, the importance of CLV has evolved from merely being an important metric to a way of thinking and of doing business.

Figure 1.1 shows a typical life cycle curve of a customer. If a manager at time (t) were to make a managerial decision regarding this customer, would it make sense to decide based on the customer's past customer value, or would it make sense to decide based on the customer's future value. If the customer's future revenue is expected to drop as compared to past revenue (as seen in Figure 1.1), it may make sense moving forward to reduce the marketing expenditure for this customer.

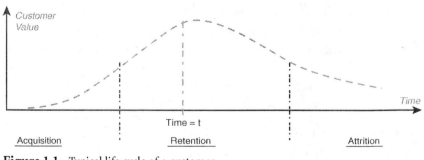

Figure 1.1 Typical life cycle of a customer

Because the metric is forward-looking, the value associated with the CLV is an estimate or a prediction. Therefore, it is imperative that proper methods be employed to measure CLV.

CLV can be measured in two fundamental ways: top down and bottom up.

Top-Down Approach

As shown in Figure 1.2, the top-down approach involves estimating the average customer equity (or lifetime value) of the customer. This can be accomplished by identifying and measuring the drivers of customer equity at the firm or customer segment level. For example, Lemon, Rust & Zeithaml define the drivers of customer equity as comprising the value equity, brand equity, and relationship equity.[5] These drivers are measured based on the customer's objective and subjective assessments of these three drivers of customer equity. The drivers are typically measured using a survey-based methodology because the drivers include subjective assessments of the customer that are not directly observed (such as the customer's attitude toward the firm's brand and the customer's brand awareness). It is practically infeasible to measure these drivers from each customer through a questionnaire. This is particularly true for large firms having millions of geographically dispersed customers. Hence, the drivers are typically measured on a small sample of customers and then extrapolated across the population to arrive at the customer equity at the firm level or the customer segment level.

The customer equity at the firm or the customer segment level can then be divided by the total number of customers of the firm/segment to arrive at the average lifetime value of a customer.

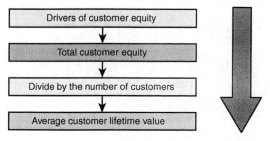

Figure 1.2 Top-down approach to measuring CLV

Another way to compute customer equity using the top-down approach is by applying observed aggregate measures pertaining to customers at the firm level. These measures include the total number of customers of the firm, their growth, the average margin per customer, the average customer retention rate, the average customer acquisition cost, and the discount rate for the firm.[6] Using these measures, firms can easily calculate customer equity at the firm level.

The main benefit of top-down approaches is the ability to measure customer equity without the need for customer-level information for *all* customers of the firm. Such an approach offers a simple way to compute the overall customer equity of a firm. However, a potential drawback is that all customers of the firm (or customer segment level) have the same CLV. Therefore, they are all treated as equal. In reality, customer values can differ significantly within the customer base (or segment). In fact, most firms swear by the Pareto principle (the 80/20 rule). That is, 20% of customers usually provide 80% of the total value to the firm. In such a scenario, it is advisable to adopt a computation method that recognizes the individual-level differences in customer value.

Bottom-Up Approach

As shown in Figure 1.3, the bottom-up approach involves first estimating the lifetime value of each customer of the firm. Thereafter, the individual CLV measures are summed up across the customer base/segments to arrive at the total customer equity at the firm/customer segment level.

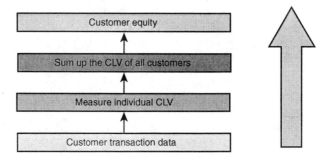

Figure 1.3   Bottom-up approach to measuring CLV

A key requirement of this approach is that it needs data at the customer level. Not all firms may meet this criterion. Further, estimation of CLV for each customer could be time-consuming, especially for large firms with millions of customers. However, the bottom-up approach offers rich customer-level insights (such as individual customer behavior, response to promotion, and individual customer value) that might have otherwise been lost due to aggregation under the top-down approach. Our contention is reinforced by new challenges infused by the changing business landscape of the twenty-first century, as shown in Figure 1.4.

	Traditional Business	Twenty-First Century Business
Philosophy	Sell products	Serve customers
Orientation	Market orientation	Interaction orientation
Management Criteria	Portfolio of products	Portfolio of customers
Strategy Motivation	Increase customer satisfaction	Increase customer profitability
Selling Approach	How many customers can we sell this product to?	How many products can we sell to this customer?
Strategy Outcome	Sales maximization	Customer Lifetime Value maximization

Figure 1.4   Changing business landscape of the twenty-first century

The shift in focus from products to customers has been a significant development of the twenty-first century. State-of-the-art marketing is now concerned with servicing each customer differently. These developments have been accelerated by technological advances. Increase in computation power and reduction in data-storage costs have prompted several companies to set up huge IT infrastructures to archive customer-level data. The proof lies in the ubiquity of grocery cards, retailer credit cards, and point-based loyalty schemes (such as airline frequent-flyer programs). All these measures are a means to a common end: collection of customer-level data in an effort to know the customer better. So, if you don't know your customers, your competition will! Further proof comes from companies that have succeeded in knowing and managing their customers at the individual level. Such organizations have been richly rewarded because of an improvement in both cost and profit efficiencies. For example, Harrah's Entertainment, a prominent casino and gaming resort chain, has consistently outplayed its competition and recorded impressive financial performance despite a weak economy. The critical success factor: superior ability to cater to its customers based on a forward-looking metric.

The concepts covered in this book apply to disparate relationships, regardless of whether the customer is contractual or noncontractual, whether the firm sells a product or a service, or whether transactions with specific customers occur repeatedly or are just one-off (and perhaps with follow-up services). CLV can be measured across all these situations, but how it is measured will vary. Chapter 3, "Customer Selection Metrics," covers CLV measurement issues across various scenarios.

Therefore, the adoption of the CLV metric seems to be not only sufficient but a necessary condition of business in the twenty-first century. Given the increasing focus on customers, this book strongly advocates the bottom-up approach to CLV estimation. The bottom-up approach enforces customer-centricity within an organization, as you will discover in the subsequent chapters of this book. The full potential of the CLV metric is realized when all customer-level marketing strategies of the firm are aligned and integrated with the CLV metric.

Aligning Customer Management Strategies with the CLV Metric

Figure 1.5 illustrates a typical customer life cycle scenario. Based on the location of the customer on the life cycle plot, the firm can extend acquisition, retention, or customer win-back strategies in an effort to speed acquisition, increase revenue during retention, and delay attrition. The net result is a lift in customer value. This is denoted as strategic impact in Figure 1.5.

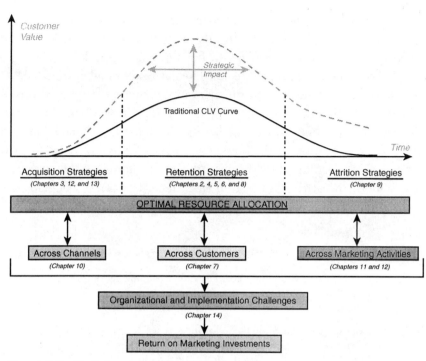

Figure 1.5 Typical customer life cycle scenario

The rest of this book takes an in-depth look at powerful customer-level strategies relevant to virtually any business in the business-to-consumer (B2C) or business-to-business (B2B) domain. With regard to the customer acquisition stage, this book covers how firms can go about acquiring profitable customers, the best metric to use while acquiring customers, and how to use customer referral as a strategic tool to acquire new customers. With regard to the retention stage, this book examines how firms can manage customer value, loyalty, and profitability simultaneously; that is, how can they pitch the right product to the right customer at the right time. With regard to the customer attrition stage, this book discusses dynamic proactive strategies to prevent losing customers. Deployment of these customer-level strategies has resource allocation consequences that lead to greater cost and profit efficiencies. This book talks about reallocation of resources *across different channels* to increase the level of interaction and hence spending per customer. Resource allocation *across customers* helps in the prudent reallocation of limited marketing budgets from low-profit customers to customers who are expected to provide higher profits in the future. Resource allocation *across marketing activities* seeks to balance marketing budgets across acquisition and retention strategies. The net result of all customer-level initiatives is a higher return on marketing activities. However, this is often an impediment in the wake of strategy-implementation challenges at the organizational level. These challenges have been addressed in a separate chapter of the book. The book chapters relevant to each strategy/topic are indicated in parentheses in Figure 1.5. All strategies are state-of-the-art, with a proven track record of unprecedented success when implemented at select Fortune 500 corporations.

Endnotes

[1] The Continental Airlines example is based on the following sources: (a) B. O'Reilly, "The Mechanic Who Fixed Continental," *Fortune,* April 23, 1999: 176–186; (b) Continental Airlines annual reports.

[2] The Dell example is based on the following sources: (a) Rangan V. Kasturi and Marie Bell, "Dell-New Horizons," *Harvard Business Review* Case Study 9-502-022, October 10, 2002; (b) Dell Corporation annual reports; (c) Kelley Rob, "Dell reports steep decline in profits," CNNMoney.com, March 1, 2007.

[3] George Day, "Creating a Superior Customer-Relating Capability," MSI Working Paper Series, Issue One, No. 03-001 (2003): 21–36.

[4] Paul W. Farris, Neil T. Bendle, Philip E. Pfeifer, and David J. Reibstein. *Marketing Metrics: 50+ Metrics Every Executive Should Master* (Prentice Hall, 2006).

[5] Katherine N. Lemon, Roland T. Rust, and Valarie A. Zeithaml, "What Drives Customer Equity," *Marketing Management,* Spring 2003: 21–25.

[6] Sunil Gupta and Donald R. Lehmann, *Managing Customers as Investments* (Prentice Hall, 2006).

2

Maximizing Profitability

Relevant Issues

- Are loyal customers profitable customers?
- What is the link between loyalty and profitability?

Firms, across various industries, have used loyalty programs as a primary tool to build and maintain long-term relationships with their customers. For more than 20 years, the airline industry has been administering loyalty programs. Customers are typically awarded one point for every mile traveled, which they can later redeem for free trips and other offers. The hotel industry is another example of an industry that uses loyalty programs. In this case, customers are rewarded according to the number of days/nights or the number of stays. Over the past ten years, the retail industry has also offered loyalty programs, with customers rewarded for every dollar spent.

Firms tend to cite profitability as the justification for such loyalty programs; they believe that over time, long-term customers tend to spend more, cost less to serve per period, have greater propensity to generate word-of-mouth, and pay a premium when compared to short-term customers. For these reasons, they think loyal customers are more profitable than nonloyal customers, and that by cultivating loyalty alone, a company can increase its overall profitability.[1]

However, a recent marketing study has shown empirical evidence that not all loyal customers are profitable, and not all profitable customers are loyal.[2] The relationship between loyalty and profitability is much weaker, and more nuanced, than proponents of loyalty programs claim.

This finding shows the need for a more accurate measurement of customer behavior and loyalty and its effect on the firm's profitability. So, the question is, are loyal customers profitable? Before we answer this question, the traditional view of loyalty is examined. The following section briefly reviews the evolution of loyalty programs over the years and customer buying behavior.

Loyalty Programs

Traditionally, firms have vied for loyal customers in the belief that they are the most profitable ones. These firms have primarily used loyalty programs as the tool to establish and maintain a strong relationship with customers. Loyalty programs are marketing processes that reward customers based on their repeat purchases. After customers enroll in loyalty programs, they tend to purchase more from the focal company, thereby increasing their own store-switching costs and making them more likely to purchase from the focal firm. In return for their loyalty to the firm, customers are rewarded through various means. In some cases, they accumulate "points" that they can later redeem for products or services, mostly from the focal firm. In other instances, they are given, based on their level of loyalty, special promotions and offers not given to others.[3] For example, Dorothy Lane Market, a small grocery retail chain in the United States, custom targets its coupons and promotions by directly mailing them to its profitable customers instead of offering coupons and promotions through newspapers, which reach all the customers. In addition, the firm offers greater discounts and better promotions to customers who have been more loyal and profitable to the firm (as compared to relatively new customers). This has enabled the firm to successfully reduce its customer churn rate.[4]

Even though loyalty programs are most well known in the business-to-consumer (B2C) setting, loyalty programs do exist in the business-to-business (B2B) setting, but they are usually called something different. For example, the loyalty program administered by a corporate service provider is called a tier of *relationship benefits*. In this type of program, client firms are categorized based on their level of loyalty and the revenue they bring in, and are rewarded accordingly. For example, loyal clients are offered personalized websites to service them; thus, when the client accesses the service provider's website, he is directly led to a specialized website that deals with the specific needs and services of that client.

The use of loyalty programs as an instrument to build customer relationships has been around since the early twentieth century. Sainsbury (UK grocery chain) archives from the 1930s reveal how managers wrote to customers who had not made their usual shopping trip, in an effort to maintain patronage. Later, the store used Green Stamps, which customers enthusiastically supported, despite the need to paste them into books.[5]

Loyalty programs are necessary because consumers have varying degrees of loyalty associated to brands, stores, and companies.[6] A loyalty program provides marketers an opportunity to retain customers with the focal firm by offering a mutually beneficial relationship between the customer and store; the store receives the repeat patronage, and the customer receives some incentives for becoming "behaviorally" loyal. Despite its early presence in marketing, most of the advancements in loyalty programs have occurred in the past 25 years. These advancements include the introduction of frequency reward programs, the promotion of customer clubs, and purchase-based incentives, among others. Figure 2.1 presents a timeline of loyalty programs.

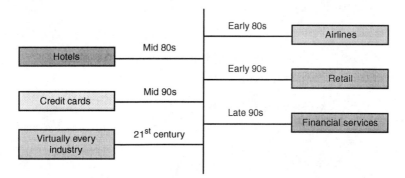

Figure 2.1   Evolution of loyalty programs

Loyalty programs were first in force in the airline industry during the early 1980s. American Airlines introduced its frequent-flyer program, AAdvantage, in 1981. Consumers could earn free flights for every x number of trips they made with American Airlines. This program came into effect to counter the decrease in margin resulting from competition. Soon, United launched a similar program that considered the length of the trip to reward customers. With other players following suit, award programs started to steamroll. By 2002, there were more than 120 million airline frequent-flyer members worldwide, with most residing in the United States (74 million), Europe (24 million), and Asia (21 million).[7] American's AAdvantage is now the largest frequent-flyer program in the world. As of November 2003, it had grown to a membership of more than 45 million.[8]

The hotel industry followed the model established by the airline industry. Marriott was the first hotel chain to launch loyalty programs, in 1983, with its Honored Guest Awards, based on the total number of days/nights per year and the duration of the stay. This sparked a series of loyalty programs from other hotel chains, such as Starwood with its Starwood Preferred Guests Program, Hilton with its Hilton HHonor, and Hyatt with Hyatt Gold Passport. By October 2003, Marriott Rewards had grown to 19 million members and more than 2,700 participating hotels worldwide.[9]

In the early 1990s, grocery stores started implementing loyalty card programs for their customers. These programs were aimed at building customer loyalty by

- Encouraging customers to visit the store more often, and
- Increasing the Share of Wallet (SOW) by encouraging customers to spend more.

In 1995, Tesco launched its Clubcard loyalty card in the United Kingdom.[10] Other popular loyalty cards include the Boots Advantage card, introduced in 1997; the Somerfield Saver card, introduced in 2002; and the Marks & Spencer's &more card, introduced in 2003. In the United States, some of the popular cards include the Albertsons Preferred Savings Card and the CVS/Pharmacy ExtraCare card.

Loyalty programs then reached the casino industry in the late 1990s, with Harrah's launching its Total Rewards program. Since the inception of its rewards program in the late 1990s, Harrah's has increased its share of customers' gaming budgets from 36% to 50%.[11] Casino loyalty programs typically provide a membership card (swipe card) that records all customer transactions (casino games, restaurants, stores, hotel stays). This behavior-tracking technology gives casinos an insight into customer behavior, and in turn helps in designing effective customer relationship strategies.[12] The effect of implementing these loyalty programs on the overall performance of Harrah's is illustrated in Figure 2.2. As you can see, the total revenue has been steadily increasing, and the overall profit also exhibits an upward trend. Other popular loyalty programs in casinos include those of Grand Casinos and the Tropicana.

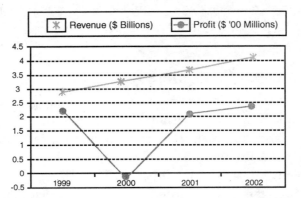

Figure 2.2   Effect of loyalty measures on the performance of Harrah's Entertainment

Recently, cruise lines have joined the loyalty bandwagon. Cruise lines have started rewarding their customers based on the number of days at sea. Customers are rewarded with discounts for selected trips, upgrades when available, advance notice of special promotions, special invitations to captain receptions, and so on, based on their level of loyalty.[13] Customers of Silversea Cruises are rewarded with a free week's cruise if they have sailed for 250 days with the firm. Seaborn offers its customers complementary trips, up to 2 weeks free, if they have sailed for 140 days. Some firms also provide special services to their loyal customers, offering them free laundry service, Internet access, and priority embarkation. Regent Cruise Line offers its highest loyalty customers free pickup from and return to their home/airport. Disney Cruise Line offers its loyal customers advance booking privileges to excursions, specialty restaurants, and so forth. Disney's loyal customers also receive a custom-designed pin set of Mickey and Minnie, a mesh beach bag, and other goodies as rewards for their loyalty.

Companies constantly update their loyalty programs to suit customer needs. According to Gartner Analyst Adam Sarner, U.S. companies spent more than $1.2 billion on customer loyalty programs in 2003.[14] Loyalty programs have become an important relationship-marketing tool used by marketers to identify, award, and retain profitable customers. Therefore, a clear understanding of the goals of a loyalty program is necessary to design and implement effective marketing strategies. In addition, when designing the benefits and incentives of the loyalty program, companies should always consider the profitability of the loyalty program with regard to each customer.

How Do Loyal Customers Really Perform?

In spite of all the time and resources spent on loyalty programs, a question remains: How do loyal customers really perform? The loyalty program of a large U.S. high-tech company was studied to answer this question.[15] This firm had instituted a cost scheme to analyze the effect of its recently initiated loyalty program. This scheme was executed for the next five years, and the company was able to determine the profitability of all its customers in the loyalty program over this period. This scheme, apart from measuring the direct product costs for every customer, also measured the associated costs such as advertising, service, sales force, and other organizational expenses. The loyalty program cost the firm $2 million annually, and the cost-tracking scheme allowed the firm to calculate the overall profitability of its customers. The results were rather surprising. Nearly half of the "behaviorally" loyal customers (customers who regularly made purchases for a minimum of two years) studied barely generated a profit. On the other hand, nearly half of the highly profitable customers were short-term customers, customers who bought a large number of high-margin products in a short time before they stopped buying from the firm.

Are Loyal Customers Profitable?

To address this issue, the relationship between how long customers stay with a firm and the firm's profitability was studied for four different companies: a high-tech corporate service provider, a U.S. mail-order company, a French grocery retailer, and a German direct brokerage firm.[16] Table 2.1 shows the results. If a strong relationship exists between loyalty and profitability, one would expect a strong positive correlation. A perfect correlation between these two factors (indicated by $r = 1$) would mean that managers could make predictions with certainty about a customer's level of profitability based on the loyalty of each customer. The weaker the correlation between the two factors (that is, the closer the r value is to 0), the weaker the relationship between customer loyalty and customer profitability.

From the results shown in Table 2.1, you can see that the association between loyalty and profitability is moderate at best and weak at worst. The correlation coefficients were found to be 0.45 for the grocery retailer, 0.30 for the high-tech corporate service provider, 0.29 for the direct brokerage firm, and 0.20 for the mail-order company.

Table 2.1   Correlation between Loyalty and Profitability

Companies Studied	Correlation between Loyalty and Profitability (r)
Corporate service provider	0.30
Grocery retailer	0.45
Mail-order company	0.20
Direct brokerage firm	0.29

This study provides an overall glimpse of the relationship between the duration of a customer's tenure with the firm and the firm's profitability. But, several myths pertain to loyal customers, especially the three main myths widely held by proponents of customer loyalty:

- Loyal customers cost less to serve.
- Loyal customers are willing to pay more for products.
- Loyal customers serve effectively in marketing the company's products.

Each myth was tested by looking at data from the four companies mentioned previously. Customers from each company who had started to do business at the same time were selected, and their purchase behavior was tracked over a period of four years.[17] This study also included how these companies approached these customers over time and what level of service was given to them. The following sections discuss the detailed results of this study.

Myth 1: Loyal Customers Cost Less to Serve

One of the widely held beliefs is that loyal customers, even though they can be expensive to acquire, turn out to be profitable in the long run because the acquisition cost is spread out over a large number of future transactions. This belief is based on the assumption that these customers will be profitable in their future transactions. Another more reasonable argument linking loyalty to reduced cost is that as the customers become acclimated to the company's products and transaction process, they will need less attention, and hence will consume fewer operational resources (in turn making them more profitable). For example, a loyal customer who buys software products from a specific firm will need less customer support; perhaps the customer will have access to the online store and other less-expensive resources to solve his problems without needing the intervention of a customer support technician.

Based on studying the four companies, no evidence supported these arguments. The cost of maintaining a relationship with a customer (which includes, apart from the transaction costs, the cost of marketing communications through email, direct mail, telephone, and so on) varies widely within a given company. In some cases, this cost varied by a factor of 100 or more. But, none of the loyal customers in all four companies studied were found to be consistently cheaper to manage when compared to short-term customers. Actually, evidence to the contrary was found in the case of the high-tech service provider, where the loyal customers were found to be more expensive to manage. This finding is not very surprising. It is widely known that in the B2B setting, long-term customers tend to be less profitable because long-term or experienced customers generally tend to purchase in high volumes and demand deeper volume discounts and more personalized service. In fact, the high-tech corporate service provider, to win over its top 250 clients, had developed a customized website for each client to receive personalized service from special sales and service teams. Maintaining the website and the special teams cost the firm $10 million annually.

This trend is also reflected in the other industries studied. In the case of the mail-order catalog firm, it took about the same amount of marketing spending to generate a comparable level of sales for long-term customers as it did for short-term customers. (It took about 6 cents of marketing spending to generate $1 in sales.) The reason for this was when a long-term customer migrates to a less-expensive channel (for example, ordering products using the company's website rather than through a brick-and-mortar store), that customer expects lower prices, and this offsets the cost savings realized by making the customer use a cheaper communication channel. A similar trend was observed in the case of the grocery retailer and brokerage firm. This study showed that loyal customers expect something in return for their loyalty, and in turn, this behavior might make their relationship with the firm less profitable than expected over the long term.

Myth 2: Loyal Customers Are Willing to Pay Higher Prices for the Same Products

Another widely held belief is that loyal customers are so used to purchasing from the focal firm or brand that they are willing to pay a premium to get the same product than a less-loyal customer. It is argued that customers stay long enough with a firm because of the high cost associated with switching to a different supplier. Therefore, they are willing to pay a higher price (up to a reasonable level) to avoid switching.

This belief might be relevant to a certain extent in the B2C setting, where customers who are more familiar with the transaction process of a particular firm might be willing to pay more in a given transaction for the same products they could get elsewhere at a cheaper price. For example, customers who are used to ordering from a particular catalog might be averse to switching and might pay a little more to buy a given set of products from this catalog retailer rather than another retailer who discounts the products. However, this trend is very unlikely in the corporate setting, where clients might bargain for lower prices in return for greater purchase frequency.

The evidence from the high-tech service provider proves that loyal customers are not always willing to pay higher prices. The long-term customers of this firm paid somewhere between 5% and 7% less, based on the product category, than the relatively new customers. In addition, contrary to expectation, the same trend was replicated in the B2C setting. The customers in a B2C setting also expect to get something in return for their loyalty. For example, in the case of the mail-order firm, in a particular product category long-term customers paid as much as 9% less when compared to newer customers.

This shows that loyal customers are far more price sensitive when compared to newer customers, both in the B2B and B2C settings. This could be because loyal customers are a lot more familiar with the various product offerings and can therefore better assess the quality and value of the products. Also, they are more aware of the reference prices, causing them to react more cautiously when compared to relatively new customers when the price seems high. This behavior was evident in the mail-order company, where loyal customers will mostly opt for a cheaper product alternative when compared to more recently acquired customers, who have a much lower familiarity with the firm. Overall, customers tend to be more sensitive to any form of price differentiation, and it is very difficult for firms to implement such strategies for any duration. Recent surveys report that customers expect lower prices in return for their loyalty to the firm. U.S. telecom firms are one example where firms offer special discounts in the beginning and raise prices at a later stage, only to experience low rates of customer retention.

Myth 3: Loyal Customers Effectively Market the Company

Managers have a high expectation that loyal customers act as effective marketers of the company and its products. Many managers argue that by investing in loyalty programs, they could benefit from the new customers that the loyal ones bring to the firm. To test this belief, a series of surveys were administered to the customers of a French grocery retailer to measure the extent of their passive and active word-of-mouth marketing. Passive word-of-mouth marketers named the focal firm when asked to recommend a grocery retailer, and active marketers spontaneously shared information with family or friends about the positive experience with the company. The customers' actual loyalty to the firm was measured by analyzing their previous purchase behavior, such as the products purchased, the frequency of purchase, and the product categories they purchased from. Apart from this, the "attitudinal loyalty" of customers was also measured by querying the customers on how loyal they feel toward the firm, how satisfied they are with the firm, and whether they are considering switching to a different firm.

This study showed that the link between the loyalty of customers and their propensity to act as word-of-mouth marketers for the firm was not strong. But, some interesting results were revealed when customers' behavior loyalty and attitudinal loyalty were considered separately. It was found out that customers who scored high on both behavioral loyalty and attitudinal loyalty were 54% more likely to be active word-of-mouth marketers and 33% more likely to be passive word-of-mouth marketers when compared to customers who scored high based only on behavioral loyalty only. Similar studies of customers from the high-tech service provider also reflected this trend. Customers who scored high on both attitudinal and behavioral loyalty were 44% more likely to be active word-of-mouth marketers, and 26% were more likely to be passive word-of-mouth marketers. This study holds important lessons for managers. To identify effective word-of-mouth marketers, they need to look at both the attitudinal and behavioral loyalty of their customers, instead of focusing only on their purchasing behavior. You can find a more detailed discussion about attitudinal and behavioral loyalty in Chapter 6, "Managing Loyalty and Profitability Simultaneously." Apart from the myths discussed here, various other myths about loyalty and the benefits of customer loyalty[18] misguide managers when making and executing their marketing decisions. Firms should approach these loyalty myths with caution and avoid all the pitfalls inherent in them when implementing strategic decisions.

Debunking the Myths

To clearly understand the relationship between loyalty and profitability, customers from four firms (as discussed previously, a high-tech service provider, a grocery retailer, a mail-order catalog firm, and a direct brokerage house) were segmented based on the longevity of their relationship with the firm and their level of profitability. As shown in Figure 2.3, the customers from all these firms were segmented into four groups based on their loyalty and profitability, and their contributions to overall profit were determined. The results show an interesting scenario. As you can see, a sizable number of long-term customers (Segment 4) from all four firms yield only marginal profit, whereas a large number of the short-term customers (Segment 1) are highly profitable. Customers in Segment 1 are the main cause for driving down the correlation between loyalty and profitability. Because this trend is observed in all four industries, it is clearly demonstrated that the belief "all loyal customers are profitable" is just a myth.

	Segment 1	Percentage of Customers	Segment 2	Percentage of Customers
High Profitability	High-tech service provider	20%	High-tech service provider	30%
	Grocery retail	15%	Grocery retail	36%
	Mail-order	19%	Mail-order	31%
	Direct brokerage	18%	Direct brokerage	32%
	Segment 3	**Percentage of Customers**	**Segment 4**	**Percentage of Customers**
Low Profitability	High-tech service provider	29%	High-tech service provider	21%
	Grocery retail	34%	Grocery retail	15%
	Mail-order	29%	Mail-order	21%
	Direct brokerage	33%	Direct brokerage	17%
	Short-Term Customers		Long-Term Customers	

Figure 2.3　Association of profitability and loyalty of customers

Source: W. Reinartz and V. Kumar, "The Mismanagement of Customer Loyalty," *Harvard Business Review* 80(7), 2002: 86. Printed with permission from the Harvard Business School Publishing.

To test the belief that "loyal customers are willing to pay more for the same product," we studied customer spending behavior in a European grocery retailer. The customers were segmented into four quartiles based on how long they had shopped with the retailer, and the average price paid by each quartile across various product categories was determined. As you can see from Figure 2.4, very little difference exists between the average price paid by customers in the top and the bottom loyalty quartile. This clearly debunks the myth that "loyal customers are willing to pay more for the same products."

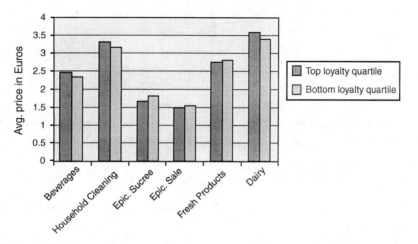

Figure 2.4   How much more are loyal customers willing to pay?

Where Do Firms Go Wrong?

In spite of the overwhelming presence of loyalty programs in virtually every industry, firms implementing them have tended to overlook certain important limitations, often to the detriment of company profitability. Instead of building long-term profitable customer relationships, these programs have become a major drain on the marketing resources of firms, resulting in an overall reduction in profitability. One major limitation that has often been ignored is the cost of implementing loyalty programs. These programs were implemented across all customers, irrespective of whether they were profitable. One standout example of firms following such a strategy is the early loyalty programs introduced in the airline industry. Earlier, customers were rewarded based on the miles they traveled with a given airline, regardless of the price they paid. This resulted in the economy-class traveler and the first-class traveler being awarded the same number of points. Such a strategy often resulted in the airline spending more on the economy-class customer than what that customer brought in as profit from the sale of the ticket. Only recently has this trend in airline loyalty programs been corrected. Now, airline customers are rewarded based on what they spend, using a fare tier-class structure rather than just the number of miles traveled.

An example of a failed loyalty program in the airline industry is the loyalty program launched by Latin Pass. Latin Pass, a frequent-flyer consortium of ten Latin American airlines, ran a promotion in 2000 awarding one million miles to customers who visited ten Latin American countries and utilized hotel and rental car partners within a certain timeframe. Latin Pass had to terminate the promotion earlier than planned when 50 people qualified for rewards in three months and generated costs of up to $10,000 per qualified customer. This demonstrates the pitfalls in executing loyalty programs without considering the cost involved in implementing them.

Another example of a failed loyalty program is the one introduced by Safeway. Safeway, a U.K.-based grocery retail chain, introduced its ABC (Added Bonus Card) loyalty program in 1995. Safeway abandoned the program in 2000, claiming that it was unable to use the information generated by the program to generate enough incremental sales to justify the program's high cost. Instead, Safeway is focusing on weekly promotions and improved customer service.

The Problem with Measuring Loyalty

One of the main problems in implementing loyalty programs is using outdated metrics to measure a customer's value. Loyalty metrics are used by firms to rank order their customers based on their loyalty to the firm and their past purchasing behavior. Some of the traditionally used metrics are Recency-Frequency-Monetary value (RFM), Share of Wallet (SOW), and Past Customer Value (PCV). (An elaborate discussion of various loyalty metrics is presented in Chapter 3, "Customer Selection Metrics.") Firms use this rank ordering of customers to direct appropriate marketing strategies to them. The problem arises when they choose the wrong customers based on these faulty metrics. Traditional metrics assume that past customer behavior will be replicated in the future. In reality, this is not the case, particularly in a noncontractual setting. The traditional metrics do not give any recommendation as to what specific marketing strategies need to be taken to maintain a customer's relationship. To overcome these drawbacks, we use the forward-looking Customer Lifetime Value (CLV) metric to measure and manage customer loyalty. CLV accurately predicts customer's future behavior based on his/her past purchasing behavior and gives a CLV score for every customer. Managers can design detailed marketing strategies based on the CLV scores of the customers. (Chapter 3 contains a full discussion of the various ways to calculate the CLV of customers.)

When to Stop Investing in a Customer

Making objective marketing decisions becomes difficult if firms cannot accurately predict what the customer's future spending behavior is going to be. This problem becomes particularly relevant when firms use traditional metrics such as RFM, SOW, and PCV (Past Customer Value) to measure a customer's value. Because these metrics assume that the customer is going to continue his/her purchasing behavior in the future, they misjudge the customer's worth and purchase lifetime with the firm. This presents a skewed picture to the managers, causing them to implement suboptimal marketing campaigns. The managers continue to invest in a large number of customers who have ceased to purchase from the firm and have no intention of returning to the firm. This drains the firm's limited marketing resources and ignores the opportunity to invest in more profitable customers. (In the case of the high-tech service provider, about 40% of its customers were not worth chasing because they were unlikely to make a purchase in the future. In spite of this, the firm continued to invest in them.)

To study the effect of retaining unprofitable customers on a firm, the customers of a general merchandise catalog retailer were segmented into four groups based on their level of loyalty and profitability[19]. As you can clearly see in Figure 2.5, both segments of customers start out to be profitable, and they generate comparable profits until month 20. After that, customer 1 maintains his/her current profitability level, whereas customer 2 becomes less and less profitable. At this point (month 20), the firm can greatly benefit from using a forward-looking metric to assess its customers. If the firm assumes that customers are going to continue their past purchasing behavior into the future, the managers will keep allocating an equal amount of resources to both customer 1 and 2. Clearly, customer 2 is not worth pursuing.

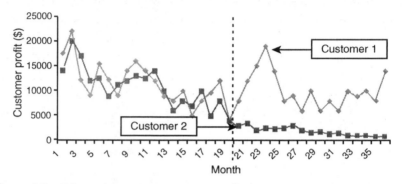

Figure 2.5   When to lose a customer: a case study

If the firm can accurately predict the purchasing behavior of its customers, it can custom target its profitable customers with promotions and messages. The use of a forward-looking metric such as CLV will save the firms from incurring such losses, helping managers invest their marketing resources more wisely and ensuring a larger return on investment (ROI) for each marketing campaign.

Conclusion

Firms are often mistaken when they believe that loyal customers are profitable. These firms are just as wrong when they believe that by creating loyalty programs they can make their customers more "behaviorally" loyal, with higher profit to follow. The reality shown in the examples in this chapter proves otherwise. Loyalty does not automatically ensure profitability, and the relationship between loyalty and profitability is more complex than is often perceived. In addition, firms regularly use outdated loyalty metrics to measure the value of their customers, and these lead managers to implement flawed marketing strategies that drain the firm's resources. By accurately predicting the value and relationship duration of a customer via a forward-looking metric such as CLV, firms can generate profit by targeting customers who are actually going to add to the firm's profit in the future (regardless of whether these customers are behaviorally loyal or just short-term customers who buy a lot now and switch to another firm later). This chapter does *not* conclude that loyalty programs are a waste. Instead, to be more effective, loyalty programs must be tailored with a metric that measures the future profitability of customers. To do this, managers need a metric such as CLV to tie in with their loyalty programs, to understand the incentives necessary to entice all their customers to make future purchases.

Endnotes

[1] Frederick F. Reichheld and W. Earl Sasser Jr., "Zero Defections: quality comes to services," *Harvard Business Review*, 68(5) 1990: 105–11.

[2] W. W. Reinartz and V. Kumar, "The Mismanagement of Customer Loyalty," *Harvard Business Review* 80(7) 2002: 86.

[3] V. Kumar and W. J. Reinartz, *Customer Relationship Management: A Databased Approach* (New York: John Wiley & Sons, Inc., 2006).

[4] M. L. Young and M. Stepanek, "Trends: Loyalty Programs," *CIOInsight*, December 1, 2003 (available at www.cioinsight.com/article2/0,3959,1458960,00.asp).

[5] J. Passingham, "Grocery Retailing and the Loyalty Card," *Journal of the Market Research Society* 40(1) 1998: 55–67.

[6] P. Kotler, *Marketing Management*, 11th edition (New York: Prentice Hall, 2004)

[7] www.webflyer.com

[8] www.webflyer.com

[9] www.marriottnewsroom.com

[10] J. Yehia, "House of Cards," *MediaWeek*, May 3, 2005.

[11] T. Hoffman, "Harrah's Bets on Loyalty Program in Caesars Deal," *ComputerWorld*, June 27, 2005.

[12] J. Barsky and L. Nash, "Casinos Lead Hotels in Loyalty-Program Strength," *Hotel & Motel Management*, February 17, 2003.

[13] A. Bleecker and S. Bleecker, "Cruise Lines Offer Perks for Frequent Passengers," *The Hartford Courant*, March 18, 2007: F7.

[14] M. L. Young and M. Stepanek, "Trends: Loyalty Programs," *CIOInsight*, December 1, 2003 (available at www.cioinsight.com/article2/0,3959,1458960,00.asp).

[15] W. W. Reinartz and V. Kumar, "The Mismanagement of Customer Loyalty," *Harvard Business Review* 80(7) 2002: 86.

[16] Ibid.

[17] Ibid.

[18] T. L. Keiningham, T. G. Vavra, L. Aksoy, and H. Wallard, *Loyalty Myths: Hyped Strategies That Will Put You Out of Business and Proven Tactics That Really Work* (John Wiley & Sons, 2005).

[19] W. Reinartz and V. Kumar, "On the Profitability of Long Lifetime Customers: An Empirical Investigation and Implications for Marketing," *Journal of Marketing*. Vol. 64(4) 2000: 17–35.

3

Customer Selection Metrics

Relevant Issues

- How can we measure a customer's worth?
- How do we incorporate future purchase behavior in calculating a customer's worth?

Various customer selection metrics are available for measuring and managing loyalty. These metrics help companies to measure the value of customers and prioritize them based on their contribution to overall profits. This enables the firms to allocate a higher proportion of resources to the customers who are expected to generate greater profit. Several metrics are currently available. Practitioners in the mail-order industry predominantly use the Recency-Frequency-Monetary value (RFM) metric, whereas high-tech firms tend to use Share of Wallet (SOW) to implement their marketing strategies. Past Customer Value (PCV), used in the financial services industry, is another metric. Customer Lifetime Value (CLV) is an advanced metric that is widely gaining popularity across all sectors and industries. The forward-looking CLV metric, used to predict customers' future behavior, is applied when designing and implementing marketing strategies for the present, with the goal of maximizing profitability.

This chapter describes how various metrics, including the CLV, are computed for noncontractual but repeated transactions scenarios (the most common relationship in the market). This chapter also discusses other scenarios, such as contractual transactions and one-time purchases with add-on services.

Traditional Metrics

Traditionally, the metrics used for resource allocation were RFM, SOW, and PCV. These methods are backward-looking and do not consider if a customer is going to be active in the future. These methods only consider the observed purchase behavior and assume that the future will be the same as the past for each customer. A detailed description of these metrics is provided in the following section.

RFM (Recency-Frequency-Monetary Value)

RFM is a widely used customer selection metric that stands for Recency-Frequency-Monetary value. It is mainly used in the mail-order and catalog industries, where predicting the future purchase behavior of customers is crucial, and it has been estimated that 71% of the firms use RFM in their direct marketing efforts.[1] This technique uses past customer information to evaluate and predict customer behavior and customer value, as follows:

- Recency is a measure for the time elapsed since a customer last placed an order with the company.

- Frequency is a measure of how often a customer orders from the company in a certain time period.

- Monetary value is a measure of the amount that a customer spends on an average transaction.

To compute the RFM score, it is necessary to first determine values for each of the different variables for each customer and then add them together based on the relative weights of the metrics. These relative weights can be determined directly by managers or by using simple regression techniques. To understand how businesses compute an RFM score and use it strategically in marketing campaigns, consider the following example.

ABC Sportswear, a catalog seller of sportswear, has the budget to contact one of its two customers. The company has the purchase behavior data for each of these two customers over a period of five months (January through May). Both the frequency and the dollar value of the transactions are shown in Tables 3.1 and 3.2, respectively. At the beginning of June, ABC Sportswear wants to select the best customer on whom it can invest its limited marketing budget.

Table 3.1   Dollar Amount Spent by Each Customer

Customer	January	February	March	April	May
1	200	50	80	100	200
2	300	200	0	25	45

Table 3.2   Purchase Frequency of the Customers of ABC Sportswear

Customer	January	February	March	April	May
1	3	1	2	1	1
2	2	1	0	1	2

To figure out which customer to market to, ABC Sportswear computes the RFM score of each customer; the customer with the higher RFM score will be selected for its marketing campaign. To compute the RFM score, ABC Sportswear determines the relative weights of the three variables Recency, Frequency, and Monetary value to be 50%, 20%, and 30%, respectively (see Table 3.3).

Table 3.3   Table for Calculating the RFM Scores

Recency =	**20 Points If Purchased within the Past Month**
	10 points if purchased 2 months ago
	3 points if purchased 3 or 4 months ago (count only once)
	That is, if the customer has purchased both 3 and 4 months ago (February and March), the Recency point is 3 (not 6).
	2 points if purchased 5 or more months ago
Relative weight	50%
Frequency =	**3 Points for Each Purchase within the Past Six Months**
Relative weight	20%
Monetary Value =	10% of $ Volume of Purchase within the Past Six Months
Relative weight	30%

The RFM scores of the two customers are calculated using the data from Table 3.3 and are presented in Table 3.4.

Table 3.4 Customers Rank Ordered Based on Their RFM Scores

	RFM Scores
Customer 1	41.2 (Rank 1)
Customer 2	38.2 (Rank 2)

Based on these scores, Customer 1 has a higher (41.2) RFM score than Customer 2 (38.2). Because RFM is a relational measure, a higher ranking means that you are a better customer. So, ABC Sportswear decides that Customer 1 will likely be a better target for its marketing resources than Customer 2.

Share of Wallet

Share of Wallet (SOW) indicates the degree to which a customer meets his or her needs in the category with a focal brand or firm.[2] SOW is used widely in retail businesses such as supermarkets and in financial companies mainly to identify whether consumers are loyal to a specific store or whether they shop around at different stores. For example, one consumer might shop 100% of the time at the same grocery store, whereas another consumer might choose to shop equally across four different stores, giving each store a 25% SOW. This metric provides business-to-business (B2B) companies with an idea of what portion of the marketing budget is being spent with that firm. For example, a technology firm knows that if a business customer is spending 100% of its IT budget with them that the business customer is behaviorally loyal and relies specifically on that firm for all its IT needs.

SOW can be estimated either at the individual level or at the aggregate level. With respect to a customer scoring metric, it is almost exclusively measured at the individual level because measures at the aggregate level do not give managers enough information about individual customers to make actionable strategies. At an individual customer level, SOW indicates the degree to which a customer meets his or her needs in a specific category with a focal brand or firm. The individual SOW is computed by dividing the value of sales (S) of the focal firm (j) to a buyer in a category by the SOW (the total amount spent by the customer in that category across all the firms) of the same customer in a time period. SOW is measured in percentages.

$$\text{Individual SOW} = S_j / \sum_{j=1}^{J} S_j \qquad\qquad \text{Equation 3.1}$$

where,

    S = sales to the focal customer

    j = firm

$$\sum_{j=1}^{J} = \text{sum of the value of sales made by all firms} \qquad \text{Equation 3.2}$$
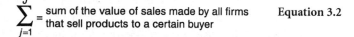
      that sell products to a certain buyer

For instance, consider the two customers from ABC Sportswear used in the RFM example in the previous section (purchase data in Table 3.1). The total dollar amount spent by these two customers in the five-month period (January through May), and the overall amount they spent on sportswear (total spending at ABC Sportswear and their competitors), is shown in Table 3.5. The calculated SOW for each customer is also shown.

Table 3.5   SOW Data on Two Customers of ABC Sportswear

	Amount Spent in ABC Sportswear from Jan–May ($)	Total Amount Spent on Sportswear in the Same Period ($)	SOW
Customer 1	630	2,000	31.5%
Customer 2	570	1,000	57%

By simply dividing the amount spent at ABC Sportswear by the total amount spent on sportswear during that time period, ABC Sportswear can figure out each customer's SOW. You can see that Customer 1 has a lower SOW than Customer 2. Here, ABC has to choose a customer with a higher SOW because customers who spend a higher percent of their wallet with a firm are more likely to continue to stay loyal to that firm (that is, be repeat purchasers). Even though a customer with a low SOW might show great potential for future growth, that customer spends most of his or her budget elsewhere. Such a customer is more likely to be a brand-switcher (nonloyal), making it difficult to guarantee a repeat purchase. Therefore, ABC Sportswear chooses Customer 2 as the better customer to target using its limited marketing budget.

Past Customer Value

The Past Customer Value (PCV) model is built on the assumption that the past profitability of the customer indicates the level of future profitability. This model extrapolates the results of past transactions into the future, to obtain a measure of the customer's future value. The value of a customer is determined based on the total contribution (toward profit) made by the customer in the past. Because the various products and services are bought at different points in time by the customer, the contributions from past transactions should be adjusted for the time value of money. The cumulative contribution until the present period represents the PCV of a customer. PCV can be computed using the following formula:

$$\text{PCV of a customer} = \sum_{t=1}^{T} GC_{it} * (1+r)^t \qquad \text{Equation 3.3}$$

where,

i = number representing the customer

r = applicable discount rate (for example, 15% per annum or 1.25% per month)

T = number of time periods prior to the current period when the purchase was made

GC_{it} = gross contribution of transaction of the ith customer in time period t

The gross contribution made by each customer is given in Table 3.6. The PCV score for the two customers (from the original ABC Sportswear example) is calculated based on the formula given in equation 2 (assuming the discount rate as 1.25% per month). Table 3.7 shows the results of these calculations.

Based on the PCV scores, ABC Sportswear decides that Customer 1 has the greater potential for profitability because the PCV score for Customer 1 ($196) is higher than for Customer 2 ($180). Therefore, in this case, ABC Sportswear chooses Customer 1 as the ideal customer for its current marketing campaign.

Table 3.6 Total Dollar Amounts Spent and the Gross Contribution Made by the Customers (Assuming Gross Contribution = 30% * Purchase Amount)

	Jan	Feb	March	April	May
Customer 1					
Total Spent ($)	200	50	80	100	200
GC ($)	60	15	24	30	60
Customer 2					
Total Spent ($)	300	200	0	25	45
GC ($)	90	60	0	7.5	13.5

Table 3.7 PCV of the Customers

	Past Customer Value (PCV), as of June
Customer 1	$196
Customer 2	$180

(For computational details, please refer to www.drvkumar.com/mcp)

The Need for a Forward-Looking Metric

Based on the three commonly used scoring metrics (RFM, SOW, and PCV), ABC Sportswear has conflicting decisions. If ABC were to use RFM or PCV, it would select Customer 1 as the optimal customer for an upcoming marketing campaign. However, if ABC were to use SOW, it would select Customer 2 as the optimal customer for an upcoming marketing campaign. So, which, if any, is the best metric?

When managing customer loyalty to achieve maximum profitability, it is not sufficient to just track customer data and transactions. It is imperative to predict future customer behavior and accommodate this prediction when designing marketing strategies. Metrics such as RFM, PCV, and SOW score customers based on their past purchasing behavior and create an index as to which customers are most desirable, making the key assumption that past buying is symmetrical to future buying. In addition, each of the metrics makes other key assumptions that do not reflect marketplace reality.

The RFM metric is based on rank ordering existing customers based on their purchasing history. Although it does uncover some aspects of customer buying behavior (RFM) that do have an impact on future buying behavior, the actual score does not reveal any key information to marketers, such as whether a customer is loyal, when a customer is likely to buy next, or how much profit a customer is likely to give.

The SOW metric has its significant shortcomings, too. Although it does uncover the level of loyalty a customer has with the firm, which the RFM score does not, it suffers from the lack of ability to explain when a customer is likely to buy next and how profitable a customer will be in the future. In addition, if SOW is the only metric used for marketing resource allocation, it tells nothing about the SOW. Because of this, a small firm ($100,000 in spending) with a 90% SOW would be considered a better prospect for marketing resources than a large firm ($1 million in spending) with a 50% SOW.

The PCV metric was used to try to answer the question of how much a customer provides in profit. However, in calculating the future value of the customer, it makes the assumption that the past spending behavior of the customer is going to continue in the future, and the past pattern is a good predictor of future behavior. In the rapidly changing market scenario, this could prove to be a costly error. Based on this metric, the firm would be in no position to accommodate for market shifts, changes in product offerings, and so forth. Also, although it does look at profitability directly, unlike RFM and SOW, it does not give the marketer any information about when to market in the future.

This leads us to the quest for a forward-looking metric that overcomes these drawbacks posed by the traditional metrics, to help firms to accurately measure customer behavior and manage customers profitably. We have found a solution to this problem in the Customer Lifetime Value (CLV) metric. Unlike other traditional measures that include only past contributions to profit, the merit of CLV rests on the fact that it is a forward-looking metric. CLV assists marketers to adopt appropriate marketing activities today, to increase future profitability. In addition, the computation can be used to include prospects, not just current customers (as used by the RFM, SOW, and PCV metrics). Further, CLV is the only metric that incorporates into one all the elements of revenue, expense, and customer behavior that drive profitability. This metric also manages to score over other metrics by adopting a customer-centric approach, rather than a product-centric one, as the driver of profitability. The following section explains the concept of CLV and discusses how CLV can be measured.

Introducing Customer Lifetime Value (CLV)

Traditionally, it was assumed that loyal customers are always desirable because they are more profitable for the firm. Although this might be true in a contractual setting, where there is no repeat cost to entice customers into buying, the case of a noncontractual setting presents a different picture.

In a noncontractual setting, it might be difficult to ascertain the duration for which the customer has been associated with a firm. In the absence of a contract that guarantees future revenue generation, it is difficult to predict for how long the customer is going to stay with the firm. In such a scenario, predicting the lifetime duration of a customer by observing buying patterns and other explanatory factors assumes importance. Further, the poor correlation between loyalty and profitability as exhibited by the traditional metrics creates the need for firms to use a customer value metric such as the CLV to ensure that valuable (as opposed to simply loyal) customers will be profitable customers. CLV considers the total financial contribution—revenues minus costs—of a customer over his or her entire lifetime with the company and therefore reflects the future profitability of the customer. So, CLV can be defined as follows:

> The sum of cumulated cash flows—discounted using the weighted average cost of capital (WACC)—of a customer over his or her entire lifetime with the company

Calculating the CLV can be the basis for formulating and implementing customer-specific strategies for maximizing customers' lifetime profits and increasing their lifetime duration. In other words, CLV helps the firm to treat each customer differently based on his or her contribution, instead of treating all the customers in a similar fashion. Calculating CLV helps the firm to know how much it can invest to retain the customer so as to achieve positive return on investment. A firm has limited resources and ideally wants to invest in those customers who bring maximum return to the firm. This is possible only by knowing the cumulated cash flow of a customer over his or her entire lifetime with the company, or the lifetime value of the customers. After the firm has calculated the CLV of its customers, it can optimally allocate its limited resources to achieve maximum return. The CLV framework is also the basis for purchase-sequence analysis and customer-specific communication strategies. CLV can be considered as the metric that guides the allocation of resources for ongoing marketing activities in a firm adopting a customer-centric approach.

Although a "true" CLV implies the measuring of a customer's value over his or her lifetime, we compute the CLV of a customer over a three-year time period for most applications. Of course, you might now wonder why three years. First, no one truly knows how long a customer is going to live. Second, given that future cash flows are discounted heavily, the contribution beyond three years might be quite small. Third, the predictive accuracy of the models we use can also decline over longer forecasting times. Fourth, a major purpose of computing CLV is for resource allocation; resources have to be allocated today based on the customer's value in the near future. The exceptions to this three-year measurement period are for the auto industry (we suggest 20 years for the future time horizon, to include at least 3 purchases) and the insurance industry (we suggest 7 to10 years, so that the firm can recover the acquisition costs, which can take up to 7 years).

The calculation of CLV for all customers helps firms to rank order customers based on their contribution to the firm's profit. This helps firms develop and implement customer-specific strategies that can maximize customer lifetime profits and lifetime duration. Figure 3.1 illustrates the approach for measuring CLV.

Given the limited resources, it is natural that firms invest only in those customers who provide the maximum return. In this regard, calculating CLV helps the firm to know how much it can invest in retaining the customer in order to achieve positive return on investment. This is possible only by knowing the cumulated cash flow of a customer over his or her entire lifetime with the company or the lifetime value of the

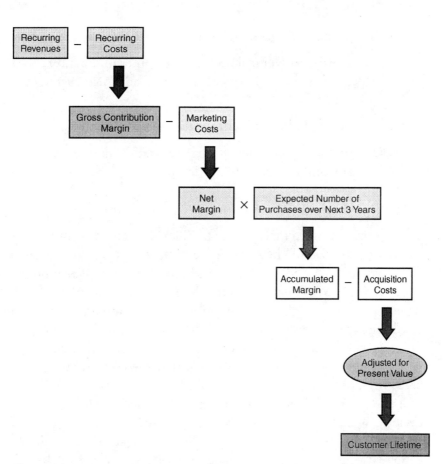

Figure 3.1 CLV measurement approach

customers. Based on the calculation of CLV, firms can optimally allocate their limited resources to achieve maximum return by developing and implementing appropriate strategies. The CLV is thus considered as a metric that guides the allocation of resources for marketing activities in a firm by adopting a customer-centric approach.

Specifically, CLV assists firms to decide the following:[3]

- Which customers should be provided with preferential and sometimes personal treatment
- Which customers to interact with through inexpensive channels such as the Internet or the touch-tone phone

- The timing of contacting the customer with an offer

- Which prospect will make a better customer in the future, and is therefore worthwhile to acquire now, and which customer to let go of

- What kind of sales and service resources to allocate

- On monitoring customer activity, to readjust the form and intensity of their marketing initiatives

CLV Measures

It has been established that whereas traditional metrics do not take into account the probability of being active in the future and the costs, the CLV approach incorporates both these aspects in the calculation. If a manager wants to evaluate marketing resource allocation plans that are targeted at improving the long-term value of customers, appropriate control measures have to be put in place. This means that looking at profit on a per-transaction basis does not suffice. Managers want to have an idea about how the value of a client has evolved over time. The general term that has been used to describe the long-term economic value of a customer is *lifetime value*. In very simple terms, CLV is a multi-period evaluation of a customer's value to the firm. It assists managers in allocating resources optimally and developing customer-level marketing strategies. The lifetime value of a customer can be calculated either at an aggregate level or at an individual level.

Aggregate Approach

According to this approach, the average lifetime value of a customer is derived from the lifetime value of a cohort or segment or even the firm. Three approaches are available to compute the average CLV.

In the first approach, the sum of lifetime values of all the customers is calculated. The value referred to as the customer equity (CE) of a firm is calculated as follows:

$$CE = \sum_{i=1}^{N} \sum_{t=1}^{T} CM_{it} \left(\frac{1}{1+d} \right)^{t}$$

Equation 3.4

where,

> CE = customer equity of the customer base in $ (sum of individual lifetime values)
>
> CM = average contribution margin in time period t (after taking into account marketing costs)
>
> d = discount rate
>
> i = customer index
>
> t = time period
>
> N = number of customers for which the CE is being estimated
>
> T = number of time periods for which the CE is being estimated

Now, from where do we get this information? The contribution margin (CM) and the duration (T) are derived either from managerial judgment or come from actual purchase data. The discount rate (d) is a function of the cost of capital of the firm and can be obtained from the financial accounting function. The average CLV could then be calculated by dividing CE by the number of customers.

In the second approach, the average CLV of a customer is calculated from the lifetime value of a cohort or customer segment.[4] The average CLV of a customer in the first cohort, or Cohort 1, can then be expressed as follows:

$$Average\ CLV = \sum_{t=1}^{T} \left[\frac{(GC-M)}{(1+d)^t} r^t \right] - A \qquad \text{Equation 3.5}$$

where,

> r = rate of retention
>
> d = discount rate or the cost of capital for the firm
>
> t = time period
>
> T = number of time periods considered for estimating CE
>
> GC = average gross contribution
>
> M = marketing cost per customer
>
> A = average acquisition cost per customer

Case Study

The purchase behavior of a cohort of 100 customers in a financial services firm, NSE Inc., was observed over a period of 3 months starting January 2005. The average gross contribution from this group of customers in the next month (April 2005) is projected to be $500. The marketing cost and acquisition cost per customer is $45 and $60, respectively. The discount rate is 15% per year, or 1.25% per month. The retention rate for this cohort is 0.75. Assuming that the discount rate, retention rate, and gross contribution are constant over time, the average CLV of a customer belonging to this cohort over the next three time periods is determined as follows:

$$CLV = \frac{455}{(1.0125)^1} * (0.75)^1 + \frac{455}{(1.0125)^2} * (0.75)^2 + \frac{455}{(1.0125)^3} * (0.75)^3 - 60 = \$712 \quad \text{Equation 3.6}$$

This approach considers only the average gross contribution (GC), the average acquisition cost per customer (A), and marketing cost (M) per customer for calculating the CLV. Although the retention rate (r) is the average retention rate for the cohort and is taken to be constant over a period, the case in reality may suggest otherwise. This is so because customers may choose to discontinue the relationship with the firm at different points in time, and hence the retention probabilities would vary across customers. Therefore, the retention probabilities will have to be factored in while calculating CE. Recently, the assumption of using a constant retention rate has been relaxed.[5]

In the third approach, the CE of the firm is first calculated as the sum of return on acquisition, return on retention, and return on add-on selling.[6] Following this, average CLV can then be calculated by dividing CE by the number of customers.

One of the important applications of computing average CLV is to evaluate competitor firms.[7] In the absence of competitors' customer-level data, firms can deduce information from published financial reports about approximate gross contribution margin, marketing, and advertising spending by competing firms to arrive at reasonable estimates of average CLV for competitors. Such an exercise would help the firm to know the profitability of the competitors' customers. The average CLV approach can also be used to evaluate the market value of the firm. It has been demonstrated that for high-growth companies, aggregate CLV of a firm or CE may be used as a surrogate measure of a firm's market value.[8]

However, average CLV has limited use as a metric for allocation of resources across customers. This is because the average CLV metric does not capture customer-level variations in CLV, which is the basis for developing customer-specific strategies. Also, calculating the aggregate CLV does not allow corrective measures to be implemented at the segment level or the individual customer level. Therefore, it is necessary to calculate the CLV of individual customers to design individual-level strategies.

Individual-Level Approach

As mentioned previously, CLV, at an individual level, is calculated as the sum of cumulated cash flows—discounted using the WACC—of a customer over his or her entire lifetime with the company. It is a function of the predicted contribution margin, the propensity for a customer to continue in the relationship, and the marketing resources allocated to the customer. In its general form, CLV can be expressed as follows:

$$CLV_i = \sum_{t=1}^{T} \frac{(\text{Future contribution margin}_{it} - \text{Future cost}_{it})}{(1+d)^t} \qquad \text{Equation 3.7}$$

where,

  i = customer index

  t = time index

  T = number of time periods considered for estimating CLV

  d = discount rate

The calculation of CLV includes determining the future contribution margin and future costs, both of which are adjusted for the time value of money. The calculation of contribution margin and future costs are given in the following section. The components required to calculate CLV are discussed next.

P (Active)

To calculate the future contribution from a customer in a noncontractual setting, firms should know the probability of the customer being active with the firm at future time periods. In such circumstances, *P* (Active) is used. It refers to the probability that the customer continues to be active in a subsequent time period. Calculation of this probability at an individual level is essential for CLV calculation at an individual level. This is because each customer is likely to have different purchase patterns and inactive periods. Figure 3.2 illustrates this point.

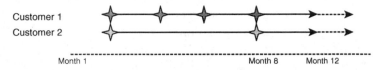

Figure 3.2   Variation in inter-purchase time

Source: V. Kumar, G. Ramani, and T. Bohling, "Customer Lifetime Value Approaches and Best Practice Applications," *Journal of Interactive Marketing,* 18(3) 2004: 60–72

Given the customer's past purchasing behavior, one can predict the probability of individual customers being active in subsequent time periods using a simple formula.

$$P \text{ (Active)} = (T/N)^n \qquad \textbf{Equation 3.8}$$

where,

n = number of purchases in the observation period

T = time period of the most recent purchase

N = current time period for which *P* (Active) needs to be determined

In Figure 3.2, the "stars" indicate purchases made by a customer. Therefore, for Customers 1 and 2, the *P* (Active) for month 12 is as follows:

P (Active) for Customer 1 in month 12 = $(8/12)^4$ = 0.197, where $n = 4$

P (Active) for Customer 2 in Month 12 = $(8/12)^2$ = 0.444, where $n = 2$

In the preceding example, it is interesting to note that a customer who has bought four times in the first eight months and has not bought in the past four months has a lower probability of buying in the twelfth month, when compared to a customer who has bought only twice in the same period of eight months. This is because it can be seen that Customer 1 has been making one purchase every two months and has failed to maintain his purchase frequency by not making a purchase in the tenth and the twelfth month. Whereas, even though Customer 2 has made fewer purchases overall, Customer 2 makes a purchase every six months and hasn't missed any purchase occasions. This indicates that Customer 2 is more likely to be active in the future, and hence he is assigned a greater P (Active) value.

A few limitations apply to the use of this approach to calculate P (Active). First, this model is applicable only to those situations in which a customer has a fixed SOW in a given time period. Therefore, the more the customer buys early on, the less is available for future time periods. Also, the model penalizes higher frequencies of buying because any fraction raised to a higher power (which is the frequency of buying) results in a lower probability. These limitations can be relaxed if the focus is on modeling the expected inter-purchase time (explained later in this book).

Average Monthly Gross Contribution

Firms ascertain the average gross contribution margin (AMGC) by deducting the average cost of goods sold from the average monthly revenue from a customer. This is calculated based on the customer's past purchases. This is obtained for all customers (i) and for the time period (t) for which the lifetime value is being estimated. To arrive at the present value of the future contribution, the AMGC of the customers is adjusted with a discount rate (d), for the number of time periods (n).

Net Present Value (NPV)

The net present value (NPV) of the expected gross contribution (EGC) can be calculated by taking the product of the P (Active) of customers at period n and the discount-adjusted AMGC for all customers (i), and adding this quantity over all future time periods (T). This is calculated as follows:[9]

$$\text{NPV of } EGC_{it} = \sum_{t=1}^{T} P(Active)_{it} \times \frac{AMGC_{it}}{(1+d)t} \qquad \text{Equation 3.9}$$

where,

$AMGC_{it}$ = average gross contribution margin in period t based on all prior purchases

i = customer index

t = period for which NPV is being estimated

T = number of periods beyond t

d = discount rate

$P (Active)_{it}$ = probability that customer i is active in period t

The following case study demonstrates the calculation of the NPV at the individual customer level.

Case Study

Consider the spending pattern of the two customers of ABC Sportswear from the previous sections. Refer to Table 3.6 for the spending patterns of the two customers over a five-month period (January through May). The AMGC of Customer 1 is calculated as follows:

$$AMGC_1 = \frac{(200+50+80+100+200)}{5} = 126 \qquad \text{Equation 3.10}$$

Table 3.8 shows the AMGCs of Customer 1 and Customer 2.

Table 3.8 AMGC of the Customers

	AMGC
Customer 1	$126
Customer 2	$114

The probability of the customer being active, $P (Active)$, is calculated for the following three months (June, July, and August) using the formula given in Equation 3.8, and the values are shown in Table 3.9.

Table 3.9   Probability [P (Active)] of the Customers Being Active in Future Time Periods

	June	July	August
Customer 1	0.40	0.19	0.10
Customer 2	0.48	0.26	0.15

The NPV of EGC for June, July, and August for Customer 1 can be calculated as follows, based on the data available in Tables 3.8 and 3.9. Assume the discount rate is 15% per year, or 1.25% per month.

$$NPV of\ EGC_1 = 0.40^* \frac{126}{(1.0125)^1} + 0.19^* \frac{126}{(1.0125)^2} + 0.10^* \frac{126}{(1.0125)^3} = \$85 \quad \text{Equation 3.11}$$

Table 3.10 shows the NPVs of Customers 1 and 2.

Table 3.10   NPV of EGC of the Customers

	NPV of the EGC
Customer 1	$85
Customer 2	$99

Calculating CLV

To calculate the lifetime value of a customer, the acquisition (A) and the marketing costs (M) incurred at future time periods have to be deducted from the NPV of EGC of a customer. The marketing costs at future time periods should be discounted with the appropriate discount rate (d) to arrive at the present value of these costs. The discounted marketing costs (M) and the acquisition cost (A) are then subtracted from the NPV of EGC to arrive at the CLV of a customer. If the marketing costs are accounted at the beginning of a given time period and the gross contribution at the end of a time period, we can express CLV as follows:

$$\text{CLV of customer } i = \sum_{t=1}^{t} P(Active)_{it} \times \frac{AMGC_{it}}{(1+d)^t} - \sum_{t=1}^{T} M_{it} \times \left(\frac{1}{1+d}\right)^t - A_i \qquad \text{Equation 3.12}$$

where,

$AMGC_{it}$ = average gross contribution margin in period t based on all prior purchases

i = customer index

t = period for which NPV is being estimated

T = future time period

d = discount rate

$P(Active)_{in}$ = probability that customer i is active in period n

M = marketing costs of the firm

A = acquisition costs of the firm

Components of CLV

The components of the cost and future contribution margin that determine the calculation of CLV are as follows:

- **Marketing cost (M).** Marketing cost refers to the costs of programs that service customer accounts, increase the value of existing relationships such as loyalty or frequent-flyer programs, and attempt to "win back" lost customers. In general, it includes development and retention costs. A major component of these costs is the cost of marketing through various channels of communication such as direct mail, email, and face-to-face interactions. The calculation of marketing costs becomes straightforward when firms decide the channel of contact, the number of contacts, and the cost involved in contacting each customer. Such an exercise would help firms in developing customer-specific communication strategies.

- **Discount rate (d).** Because the value of money is not constant across time, and because money received today is more valuable than money received in future time periods, the gross contribution and marketing costs have to be discounted, to arrive at the present value of money. This is done by dividing the cash flow in time period t by $(1 + d)^t$ where d is the discount rate. The discount rate (d) depends on the general rate of interest and is normally proportional to that of a Treasury bill or the interest that banks pay on savings accounts. It can also vary across firms depending on the cost of capital to the firm.

- **Time period (*t*).** The number of future time periods (*t*) refers to the natural "lifetime" of the customers. The word *lifetime* possesses different connotations when considering one-time purchases (such as a house) and regular purchases (such as groceries). Another important aspect is the estimation of duration while making marketing decisions. For most businesses, it is reasonable to expect that customers will return for a number of years (*t*); however, there are no strict guidelines to decide the value of *t*. For instance, a direct-marketer of general merchandise may consider a four-year time span as the maximum; in other cases, only two years might be considered as the maximum while developing marketing decisions. After all, beyond a certain time period, any calculation and prediction may become difficult because of the presence of uncontrollable factors such as customer attrition (customers switching to a different firm or product) and new competitors, among others.

Advanced Model for Measuring CLV

When a firm is using P (Active), managers must address certain concerns. For example, under P (Active), it is assumed that a customer will not come back to the firm after choosing to discontinue that relationship. With such customers referred to as "lost for good," this approach systematically underestimates CLV.[10] This could be overcome by using the "always-a-share" approach, which takes into account the possibility of a customer returning to the firm after a temporary dormancy in a relationship.[11] By incorporating such an approach while predicting the frequency of a customer's purchases, managers would have a better view of future customer activity.

A more advanced model for calculating CLV models the inter-purchase time (quantified by *frequency)* rather than P (Active). The inter-purchase time is modeled by fitting a distribution over the past inter-purchase behavior of the customer and by determining the expectation value of this distribution. Using *frequency* rather than P (Active) accounts for customers who are dormant for a particular period of time (as frequently for purchases such as automobiles or computers) and who then come back to the firm. This provides a more realistic and robust prediction of customer purchasing behavior. This advanced model involves predicting three parameters that can be plugged into calculating CLV:

- Future customer activity (*frequency*)

- Future marketing costs (MC)

- Gross contribution margin from each customer (GC)

The method used here for predicting the future customer activity is to predict the frequency of a customer's purchases given past purchases. This model is based on the assumption that customers are most likely to reduce their frequency of purchase or exhibit a period of long dormancy before terminating a relationship. This assumption is based on the reasoning that a decline in the frequency of purchase is either due to splitting of loyalty between companies or due to the customer ceasing to buy a particular product because of falling demand or outdated products. In this framework, CLV is measured by predicting the purchase pattern (frequency of purchases) over a reasonable period. This time period (customer lifetime) varies from industry to industry. (Typically, for example, automakers can expect customers to make a purchase every five to seven years, whereas computer manufacturers can expect customers to make a purchase every one or two years.) It is prudent to predict the purchasing pattern of customers over a fixed time period instead of in perpetuity because

- Uncertainty explodes for longer time periods. Over longer time periods, customers' needs change, their position in the family cycle changes, they might switch jobs, and therefore they may have different requirements.

- Product offerings are changing due to technological advancements and based on customer needs.

- CLV predictions need to be updated based on a rolling-time horizon to accommodate changes in other environmental factors.

Based on the predictions of contribution margin, purchase frequency, and variable marketing costs, the CLV function can be calculated. In one of the studies, the drivers of the purchase-frequency model (*frequency*) for the customers of a B2B firm were as follows:[12]

- Number of product purchase upgrades
- Cross-buying behavior of customers (across product categories)
- Ratio of number of customer-initiated contacts to total contacts (customer initiated and supplier initiated)
- Product return behavior
- Frequency of web-based contacts
- Frequency of customer contacts (in-person, direct mail, and telephone) by the firm
- Average time between two customer contacts

Similarly, the drivers of the gross contribution margin (*GC*) model can be listed as follows:

- Customer's contribution margin from the previous year
- Total number of customer contacts across all channels
- Total quantity purchased across all product categories

Two methods can be used to forecast the future marketing cost ($MC_{i,l,m}$):

- The first method assumes that the past cost will continue in the future, if there is not much change in marketing costs at the customer level over the years.
- The second method considers the future marketing cost as a function of current purchase activity and current marketing cost.

Based on the input derived from these models, the lifetime value of a customer can be calculated as follows:

$$CLV_{it} = \sum_{t=1}^{T_i} \frac{GC_{i,t}}{(1+r)^{t/frequency_i}} - \sum_{l=1}^{n} \frac{\sum_m MC_{i,ml}}{(1+r)^l}$$

Equation 3.13

$$\underbrace{\hphantom{\sum_{t=1}^{T_i} \frac{GC_{i,t}}{(1+r)^{t/frequency_i}}}}_{\text{PV of Gross Contribution}} \quad \underbrace{\hphantom{\sum_{l=1}^{n} \frac{\sum_m MC_{i,ml}}{(1+r)^l}}}_{\text{PV of Marketing Cost}}$$

where,

CLV = Customer Lifetime Value

$GC_{i,t}$ = gross contribution from customer (i) in purchase occasion (t)

$MC_{i,l,m}$ = marketing cost for customer (i) in communication channel (m) in time period (l)

where,

$MC_{i,l,m} = c_{i,m,l}$ (unit marketing cost) $* x_{i,m,l}$ (number of contacts)

$frequency_i = 12/expint_i$ (where, $expint_i$ = expected inter-purchase time for customer [i])

r = discount rate for money

n = number of years to forecast

T_i = number of purchases made by distributor (i), until the end of the planning period

The measurement of CLV for each customer enables managers to optimally allocate resources so that CLV can be maximized. Therefore, the model considers purchase frequency and the gross contribution margin of customers as a function of marketing resource variables. Based on the customer responsiveness to marketing actions (provided by the purchase-frequency and the gross contribution margin models), resource allocation strategies that can maximize CLV are developed.

In the preceding model, $x_{i,m,l}$ gives the number of customer contacts made in a particular channel during a given time period. This includes in-person contacts initiated by the sales team and direct-mail and telephone contacts. The marketing cost incurred in such contacts is given by $c_{i,m,l}$. The frequency factor (*frequency$_i$*) helps in forecasting the purchase frequency in the following years. The term $GC_{i,t}$ predicts the gross contribution margin made by a customer in each future purchase occasion. Similarly, future marketing cost ($MC_{i,l,m}$) is also generated for each customer. Although this CLV model is a significant advancement beyond earlier customer value models, continuous effort is being made to improve the CLV measurement model. For example, there are two issues related to calculating CLV that are relevant and need to be addressed: endogeneity and heterogeneity. If you fail to account for these statistical issues, the actual measurement of CLV might be biased.

Endogeneity is a statistical issue in the CLV model that relates directly to causation. This CLV model predicts the three parameters (frequency, MC, and GC) independently, meaning that it does not take into account whether it is current MC that leads to future GC or whether it is potentially current GC that leads to future MC. This issue has a relatively straightforward solution and requires only that all three parameters be simultaneously obtained.[13]

Heterogeneity is a statistical issue in the CLV model that relates directly to customer profiles. If we assume that different customers respond differently to marketing messages, it is therefore not ideal to have the same weights on all coefficients in the GC model relating to marketing communications. The solution to this problem is also fairly straightforward. If you allow regression weights to be different for each customer, you will get more accurate results for each customer.[14]

The CLV model will continue to improve, especially because of increasingly available customer data and the competitive market. However, having a reliable model, such as the one described earlier, as a basis for measuring CLV is the key to establishing optimal marketing strategies (detailed in the following chapters). When you understand how to implement this model, you can then determine how best to measure CLV for different firms. The following case study provides a numeric demonstration of calculating CLV for a B2B firm, based on the inputs from these models.

Case Study

The calculation of CLV for customer (i) is explained based on the data collected from a B2B firm. The unit cost ($c_{i,m,l}$) for different channel contacts such as telesales and a salesperson are $30 and $600, respectively. The number of such contacts ($x_{i,m,l}$) through different channels is shown in Table 3.11. The predicted frequency and predicted gross contribution margin from a customer in each purchase occasion in the next two years are also given in Table 3.11.

Table 3.11 Predicted Gross Margin over Time

Time Period	June 2004	September 2004	June 2005	December 2005
Predicted gross contribution margin ($)	20,000	22,000	31,000	23,800

Time period (l) = 2 years

Frequency of purchase = 2 purchases per year

Unit cost of telesales = $30

Number of predicted contacts through telesales = 25 in year 1 and 20 in year 2

Unit cost of salesperson = $600

Number of predicted sales contacts by salesperson = 10 in year 1 and 15 in year 2

Discount rate (r) = 15%

The CLV score can be calculated for this data as follows:

$$CLV_i = \frac{20000}{(1.15)^{0.5}} + \frac{22000}{(1.15)^{0.75}} + \frac{31000}{(1.15)^{1.5}} + \frac{23800}{(1.15)^2} \left.\right\} \text{PV of Gross Contribution}$$

$$-\left\{ \left(\frac{600^* 10}{1.15} \right) + \left(\frac{600^* 15}{(1.15)^2} \right) + \left(\frac{30^* 25}{1.15} \right) + \left(\frac{30^* 20}{(1.15)^2} \right) \right\}$$

$$= \$68,465$$

Equation 3.14

As you can see from the CLV calculations, the lifetime value of a customer depends to a great extent on whether the customer is going to be active in future time periods. This is especially important in a noncontractual setting because the customer has the freedom to leave the relationship at any time.

In a contractual relationship, you must estimate two sources of revenue/contribution margin: the regular monthly contribution from the customer for the relevant time period, and the additional contribution from the add-on services/products that the customer is predicted to buy in the relevant period. The information about which products/services may be added can come from the use of choice and purchase timing models described in Chapter 8, "Pitching the Right Product to the Right Customer at the Right Time." The CLV model can be revised as follows:

$$CLV_i = \sum_{t=1}^{T} \frac{BaseCM}{(1+r)^t} + \sum_{t=1}^{T} \frac{\hat{p}(Buy_{it}=1)^* \hat{CM}_{it}}{(1+r)^t} - \frac{\hat{MC}_{it}}{(1+r)^t} \qquad \text{Equation 3.15}$$

where,

CLV_i	= lifetime value for customer i
$\hat{p}(Buy_{it})$	= predicted probability that customer i will purchase in time period t
$\hat{CM}_{it}$	= predicted contribution margin provided by customer i in time period t
$\hat{MC}_{it}$	= predicted marketing costs directed toward customer i in time period t
t	= index for time periods; quarters in this case
T	= marks the end of the calibration or observation time frame
r	= monthly discount factor; 0.0375 in this case (15% annual rate)
Base CM	= predicted base monthly contribution margin

Similarly, if it is a one-time transaction but with the opportunity for add-on products/services, the information for which products/services are likely to be added can come from the choice/timing model described in Chapter 8. As for the prediction of the one-shot purchase of a significant item, you can use a logistic regression model (described in Chapter 9, "Preventing Attrition of Customers") or the choice model (described in Chapter 8), combined with a regression-type model for predicting the quantity of that purchase. Finally, you can use the models suggested for any service-oriented businesses.

After the CLV has been computed, firms must look ahead to maximize it, to reap the full benefits of the metric. The following chapters discuss the various strategies firms can use to maximize CLV.

Conclusion

Some of the most popular metrics currently in use, such as the RFM, SOW, and PCV, are inherently backward-looking. In other words, they do not account for future customer behavior that is critical for making customer management decisions. The CLV metric illustrated throughout this chapter overcomes this fundamental drawback. Furthermore, the CLV metric is the only metric that incorporates all the elements that drive profitability: revenue, expense, and customer behavior. This enables managers to efficiently measure and manage customer value.

Endnotes

[1] The DMA 2005 Customer Prospecting and Retention Report, at www.the-dma.org/research/customer_prospectingexecutivesummary.pdf.

[2] V. Kumar and W. J. Reinartz (2006), *Customer Relationship Management: A Databased Approach* (New York: John Wiley & Sons, Inc., 2006).

[3] V. Kumar, G. Ramani, and T. Bohling, "Customer Lifetime Value Approaches and Best Practices Applications," *Journal of Interactive Marketing* 18(3) 2004: 60–72.

[4] P. D. Berger and N. I. Nasr, "Customer Lifetime Value: Marketing Models and Applications," *Journal of Interactive Marketing* 12 1998: 17–30. Also see V. Kumar, G. Ramani, and T. Bohling, "Customer Lifetime Value Approaches and Best Practices Applications," *Journal of Interactive Marketing* 18(3) 2004: 60–72.

[5] David A. Schweidel, Peter S. Fader, and Eric T. Bradlow, "Understanding Service Retention Within and Across Cohorts Using Limited Information," *Journal of Marketing*, Volume (70) 2007.

[6] R. C. Blattberg, G. Getz, and J. S. Thomas, *Customer Equity: Building and Managing Relationships as Valuable Assets* (Boston: Harvard Business School Press, 2001).

[7] S. Gupta and D. R. Lehmann, "Customer as Assets," *Journal of Interactive Marketing* 17(1) 2003: 9–24. Also see V. Kumar, G. Ramani, and T. Bohling, "Customer Lifetime Value Approaches and Best Practices Applications," *Journal of Interactive Marketing* 18(3) 2004: 60–72.

[8] S. Gupta and D. R. Lehmann, "Customer as Assets," *Journal of Interactive Marketing* 17(1) 2003: 9–24.

[9] W. J. Reinartz and V. Kumar, "The Impact of Customer Relationship Characteristics on Profitable Lifetime Duration," *Journal of Marketing* 67(1) 2003: 77–99.

[10] R. T. Rust, K. N. Lemon, and V. A. Zeithaml, "Return on Marketing: Using Customer Equity to Focus Marketing Strategy," *Journal of Marketing* 68 2003: 109–127.

[11] R. Venkatesan and V. Kumar, "A Customer Lifetime Value Framework for Customer Selections and Resource Allocation Strategy," *Journal of Marketing* 68(4) 2004: 106–125.

[12] Ibid.

[13] V. Kumar, Rajkumar Venkatesan, Timothy Bohling, and Denise Beckmann, "The Power of CLV at IBM," forthcoming, *Marketing Science*.

[14] Rajkumar Venkatesan, V. Kumar, and Timothy Bohling, "Optimal CRM Using Bayesian Decision Theory: An Application for Customer Selection," forthcoming, *Journal of Marketing Research*.

4

Managing Customer Profitability

Relevant Issues

- How do we build and sustain profitable customer loyalty?

- What are the drivers of profitable customer loyalty, and how do they help in managing customers?

To implement effective marketing initiatives, firms should have a good understanding of how their actions affect their relationship with the customer and how they affect profit. Customers have different preferences and different goals with the company. Some are long-term customers, and some transact only in the short term. Some are more profitable to the company than others. Their frequency of transaction with the company varies widely. Some buy only through certain channels (such as catalogs), and some customers are comfortable buying through multiple channels. Some customers buy all their products from a specific category with the company, and some come to the company for specific needs. How can the company measure and understand how its individual marketing actions are affecting the purchasing behavior of such a diverse group of customers?

The answer to that question lies in using profitable customer loyalty (also known as CLV, Customer Lifetime Value) as the primary tool to design and implement marketing initiatives. As described in the preceding chapter, firms can classify and manage customers based on their CLV. Because CLV captures their past behavior, their projected future behavior, and the marketing costs incurred to maintain them,

CLV can serve as an important guide in deciding whom to follow and how to approach the customers. It can also guide managers in understanding how their actions influence customer behavior, and in analyzing the effectiveness of their marketing initiatives. For example, if a firm changes its mailing strategy and follows a more selective approach, it can monitor how this particular action affects the CLV of its customers. The change in CLV can give a direct measure of the strategy's effectiveness, and it can guide firms to make a final decision regarding continuing, abandoning, or modifying this strategy.

The guiding rule in making these strategic decisions is simple: Do the actions taken by the company maximize CLV? If yes, continue with the strategy; if no, abandon or modify the current methods.

After you decide to utilize the CLV, the next step is to clearly understand the factors that drive a profitable relationship with the customer and how they affect the CLV. Understanding this relationship will benefit the company in two ways:

- It gives a better understanding of the structure of a profitable customer relationship.

- It helps managers take proactive measures to maximize a customer's lifetime value.

Typical CLV Drivers

CLV drivers are the main factors that affect the lifetime value of a customer. These drivers determine the nature of the relationship between the firm and the customer, and they help estimate the level of profitability and the CLV of each customer. The drivers of CLV can be broadly classified into the following categories:

- **Exchange characteristics.** The exchange characteristics broadly include all the variables that affect and influence the customer-firm relationship, such as the customer spending level, cross-buying behavior, purchase frequency, product returns, marketing contacts made by the firm, and loyalty instruments.

- **Customer characteristics.** Demographic variables, such as location of the customer, age, income levels, and so forth, constitute customer heterogeneity. Classifying customers based on their demographic and psychographic indicators can help firms segment customers and effectively manage the customer-firm relationship.

- **Product characteristics.** This consists of the type of products offered, the timing since product acquisition, and the typical lifetime associated with the product.

- **Firm's marketing actions.** This constitutes the number of marketing messages, offers, promotions, individual visits by salespersons and so on, and the frequency and timing of these contacts.

A Specific B2B Case Study

The exchange characteristics are predominantly the same for the majority of the cases in the B2B and the B2C setting. (The drivers that reflect the customer characteristics could vary in these circumstances.) A typical list of CLV drivers used in a B2B setting follows here and is also illustrated in Figure 4.1. Other CLV drivers will have to be considered in other contexts.

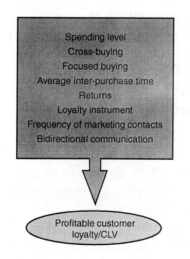

Figure 4.1 Typical CLV drivers

- **Spending level.** This conveys the average monthly spending level in a given period of time. This factor has a positive effect on the customer's lifetime value; that is, the greater the spending level of a customer, the greater his/her CLV. When we understand whether this affects the CLV, the next question is this: How much influence does this have on a customer's CLV? A recent study showed that when the average monthly spending level increased by just $10, the likelihood of termination of the relationship went down by 33%, on average.[1] This is not surprising, because if the customer spends a large share of his/her wallet on the company, it is more unlikely that the customer will switch to a different firm.

- **Cross-buying.** This refers to the degree to which customers buy products from a large number of available products or categories offered by the firm. For example, in the case of a department store, one customer might just buy casual wear and shoes; whereas another customer might buy formal wear, accessories, shoes, casual wear, and children's clothing. The latter customer demonstrates a greater scope of interaction with the firm. The greater the cross-buying behavior, the greater the CLV is for the customer on average. This is because when the customer engages with the firm across various departments, it demonstrates the level of comfort the customer has with the firm's offerings and indicates a strong customer-firm relationship. And, these customers are less likely to terminate their relationship with the firm. For every additional department the customer purchases from, the risk of losing the customer is reduced by about 66%.

- **Focused buying.** This represents the level of purchase made by a customer within a single category. The more heavily a customer purchases from within a single category/department, the lower the customer's lifetime value. This is consistent with the cross-buying effect noted previously; that is, the more spread out the customer's buying pattern across different categories, the greater the CLV and the lower the risk of losing the customer. For example, a customer may buy a particular product (shoes, for example) on a regular basis from a retailer, and it could be reasoned that there is nothing wrong with a customer being comfortable with buying a single product repeatedly throughout the customer's lifetime. But, because there is only a limited interaction with the firm, there is a greater risk of the customer losing interest in the product, leading to the termination of the relationship, and hence a lower CLV.

- **Average inter-purchase time.** This refers to the average number of days between two purchases. This factor has an inverted U-shaped relationship with the customer's lifetime value; that is, the CLV tends to be smaller when the inter-purchase time is either too long or too short. Customers with an intermediate inter-purchase time have the greatest CLV. This might sound counterintuitive, because one might expect customers who make the most frequent purchases to be the most profitable. But, in reality, sustaining this high purchase frequency over a long period of time is not possible given the finite resources, particularly in the general merchandise category. Therefore, such customers end up terminating their relationship with the firm more often than not. For example, a customer may buy shoes and clothes from a retailer. It is unlikely that the customer who makes several purchases within a very short period of time will continue to do so over extended periods. Such items are purchased in a continuous, regularly spaced cycle. This customer might be stocking up on the merchandise that should last for a long time and is unlikely to come back to the firm. There is a lower limit for the average purchase time, too. Customers who don't make a purchase over long periods of time are more likely to have switched to a competitor or stopped using the product altogether, and hence have a low CLV.

- **Returns.** This refers to the number of products the customer returns between two purchase periods. This has an inverted U-shaped relationship with the CLV. Too few or too many returns indicate that the customer is a low-CLV customer. An intermediate number of returns indicates a healthy relationship with the firm. This might sound counterintuitive. But returns provide firms with an opportunity to interact with the customers and satisfy their needs. Also, higher returns indicate that customers are comfortable using the venues open to them and find it an efficient way of transacting with the firm. If the firm has a no-hassle return policy, more customers will be motivated to get more involved with the firm. This opportunity could be turned into a positive reinforcement by making this a positive experience for the customer. Also, because the degree of returns depends on the degree of spending, it could mean that the customer is spending more with the firm. But, too many returns can be harmful to the firm and indicate that the return opportunities have not been exploited properly.

- **Loyalty instrument.** It indicates the status of the customer with the firm. Does the customer own a loyalty card; and if so, at what level (in the B2C setting)? Is the customer a premium service member, based on the revenue contribution made by the customer in the previous years (in the B2B setting)? Customers typically use the loyalty instrument to receive discounts and accumulate points to be redeemed for a special gift at a later date. Issuing of a loyalty card or usage of any other loyalty instruments has a positive impact on the profitability of the customer. By acknowledging that the customer is valuable to the firm, the firm reduces the propensity of the customer to quit the relationship and increases the possibility that the customer will return to the firm to fulfill other needs.

- **Frequency of marketing contacts.** This refers to the number of times a customer is contacted through the various communication channels (telephone, direct mail, direct contact by sales personnel, and so on) between two observed purchases. This factor has an inverted U-shaped effect on the CLV. Too few or too many marketing contacts are not helpful. Marketing efforts are very effective in preventing customers from terminating their relationship and in reminding them about the firm and offering promotions to make them come back to the firm. Therefore, making too few marketing contacts is detrimental to the firm's relationship with the customer. Also, marketing contacts can be very effective in targeting selective product promotions to the customers. Sometimes, however, marketers overdo this, and thus cause a deterioration or termination of the relationship. Overcontacting customers can lead to the customers completely ignoring future promotions and offers and terminating the relationship. Therefore, firms should optimize their marketing initiatives and maximize CLV.

- **Bi-directional communication.** This refers to the ratio of the number of customer-initiated contacts to the total number of customer contacts made (both customer and firm initiated) between two purchases. Bidirectional communication strengthens the customer-firm relationship, indicating customer involvement and increasing the interdependence between firms and customers. This is particularly so in the case of a B2B setting, where customers can initiate contacts with the suppliers to fulfill their training requirements or to get an appraisal about a new product and so on. The greater the bidirectional communication, the greater the profitability.

As stated in Chapter 1, "Introduction," several pathways can lead to an increase in customer equity. A top-down approach would be implemented with the aim of increasing customer equity by using drivers such as *brand equity, value equity,* and *relationship equity.* By maximizing these drivers, the firm can maximize customer equity. Another way to approach this issue, as recommended in this chapter, is to adopt a bottom-up approach, where the various CLV drivers (discussed previously) can be used to increase the lifetime value of customers and thus maximize customer equity. The CLV drivers discussed here are closely linked to the drivers of customer equity such as *brand, value,* and *relationship equity.* For example, a customer's past spending level relates to the *brand equity* driver. The past purchasing activity relates to the *value equity* of the firm, and the cross-buying behavior relates both to the *value* and *relationship equity.* Firms can adopt either approach based on their standing and level of customer-level data and so forth. If a firm doesn't have extensive data about its customers and their purchasing behavior, adopting a top-down approach through maximizing customer equity through *brand, value,* and *relationship equity* is ideal. Whereas, when the firm has customer-level data available, it can adopt the bottom-up approach and maximize CLV through the CLV drivers.

A B2C Case Study in the Retailing Industry

To study the significance of various drivers and to quantify their effect on CLV in a B2C setting, a study was carried out involving a major retailer that sold apparel, shoes, and accessories for both men and women.[2] A large sample of more than 300,000 customers was taken from the firm's customer database for this study, and their individual CLV scores were calculated (based on the techniques outlined in Chapter 3, "Customer Selection Metrics"). As expected, a wide distribution of CLV scores was obtained from these customers.

Traditionally, the retailer used several measures to identify customer loyalty, such as the regularity of purchase, the frequency, and the tenure of the customer with the firm. The regularity of purchase is a measure of how often the customer buys from the firm. Frequency refers to the inter-purchase time, and tenure refers to the total duration during which the customer has transacted with the firm. A correlation study was done to test the effect of these measures of loyalty on the observed future profitability of the customers. Table 4.1 reports the results. Intuitively, one would expect loyal customers to be profitable, and would therefore expect a strong positive correlation between loyalty and profitability. As you can see from the table, the correlation is very weak between the regularity and frequency of purchase and the future profitability of the customer. Also, it is clear that firms cannot rely on traditional loyalty metrics such as RFM (Recency-Frequency-Monetary value method, described in Chapter 3) to manage their customers because only a weak correlation exists between the RFM scores of the customer and the future profitability. If the firms use the traditional metrics, they might end up investing marketing resources in and cultivating relationships with the wrong customers. Firms should adopt a forward-looking metric such as the CLV to identify profitable loyal customers and invest their resources toward such customers.

Table 4.1 Does Loyalty Drive Profitability? Correlation between Profitability and Different Measures of Loyalty

	Regularity	Frequency	RFM	Tenure
CLV	$r = -0.09$	$r = 0.17$	$r = 0.19$	$r = 0.44$

Next, the customers were segmented into ten deciles based on their CLV scores, with the customers in the top two deciles constituting high-CLV customers, the customers in segments three through five constituting medium-CLV customers, and the customers in the bottom five deciles constituting the low-CLV customers. Figure 4.2 shows the segmentation of customers based on their CLV score. This study brought to the fore several interesting insights about customer profitability. It was observed from this study that the top 20% of customers accounted for 95% of profit, and the retailer was actually losing money with 30% of customers. This is because, as you can see in Figure 4.2, several customers in low-CLV segments have negative CLV scores.

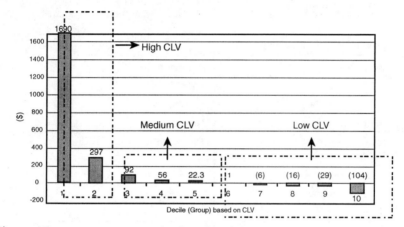

Figure 4.2   Customer segmentation based on their CLV scores

Based on this customer segmentation, a customer profile analysis was done for the low- and high-CLV customers, and some interesting group-level differences were observed. Table 4.2 gives the typical profiles of a high- and low-CLV customer for this specific retailer. This analysis showed that the most profitable customers were professionally employed and married women in the 30 to 49 age group. They had children and a high household income. High-CLV customers typically were members of the store's loyalty program, lived closer to the store, and shopped through multiple channels. In contrast, the typical low-CLV customer was a low-income, unmarried male customer in the 24 to 44 age group, primarily a single-channel shopper, lived farther away from the store, and did not own a home. Doing such profile analyses can help firms put a face on the CLV score of a customer and help them to effectively manage their customers.

Based on this study, customers were segmented based on their CLV scores (high and low CLV) and their profit potential. Several segment-specific marketing strategies were recommended to the firm. Table 4.2 shows the customer segmentation and Figure 4.3 shows the marketing strategies adopted. As shown in this figure, minimal spending should be allotted to the customers with low CLV scores and low profit potential. In the case of customers with high CLV scores and low profit potential, the current level of spending should be maintained.

Table 4.2 Profile Analyses of High- and Low-CLV Customers: A Retailing Case Study

Typical High-CLV Customer	Typical Low-CLV Customer
Gender: Female	Gender: Male
Age: 35–54 years	Age: 25–34 years
Marital status: Married	Marital status: Single
Presence of children	No children present
Estimated household income: $125,000+	Estimated household income: < $50,000
Stays closer to retailer	Stays farther away from retailer
Loyalty card member	Not necessarily a loyalty card member
Mail-order shopper	Single-channel shopper
Shops frequently in upscale stores	

In the case of low-CLV, high-potential customers, they should be encouraged to cross-buy from different product categories and higher-valued products. In the case of customers with high-CLV and high-profit potential, firms should take measures to simulate interest among customers by cross-selling across different product categories and promoting higher-value purchases (see Figure 4.3).

The next step of this study included finding the effectiveness of the various drivers of CLV and their impact on maximizing the CLV score of a customer. For this part of the study, only the high-CLV customers were considered. Figure 4.4 shows the results of this study. The results show the increase in the CLV of a customer given a 15% increase in any of the

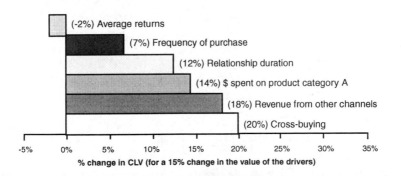

	Simulate more interest through cross-selling and higher-value products
High CLV	Maintain current level of marketing
Low CLV	Minimal marketing spend
	Invest to encourage cross-buying and spending in higher-value goods

High
CLV

Maintain current level
of marketing

Simulate more interest
through cross-selling
and higher-value
products

Low
CLV

Minimal marketing
spend

Invest to encourage
cross-buying and
spending in higher-
value goods

Low-Profit
Potential

High-Profit
Potential

Figure 4.3   Marketing actions taken by the firm based on the CLV score

categories of the drivers. The retailer could use the information from these results to implement appropriate marketing programs. For example, if a firm knows that increasing the number of categories a customer purchases from (cross-buying) by 15% generates a 20% increase in the CLV score for that customer, given all else being equal, a firm can try to induce cross-buying behavior by offering specific promotions for customers to buy across different product categories.

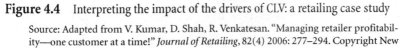

(-2%) Average returns
(7%) Frequency of purchase
(12%) Relationship duration
(14%) $ spent on product category A
(18%) Revenue from other channels
(20%) Cross-buying

-5%   0%   5%   10%   15%   20%   25%   30%   35%

% change in CLV (for a 15% change in the value of the drivers)

Figure 4.4   Interpreting the impact of the drivers of CLV: a retailing case study

Source: Adapted from V. Kumar, D. Shah, R. Venkatesan. "Managing retailer profitability—one customer at a time!" *Journal of Retailing*, 82(4) 2006: 277–294. Copyright New York University.

The key drivers of the CLV are (1) Cross-buying, (2) Multichannel shopping, (3) Selling a specific product, (4) Relationship duration, (5) Frequency of purchase, and (6) Average number of returns. The relative impact of each of these drivers of CLV is described in detail:

- **Impact of cross-buying.** As shown in Figure 4.4, if the cross-buying behavior of high-CLV customers is increased by 15%, their CLV goes up by 20%. This shows that if the customer purchases from more product categories from the retailer, the future profitability of the customer increases. This underlines the importance for firms to build strong relationships with customers both in terms of the value of purchases and the number of product categories purchased from.

- **Impact of multichannel shopping.** If customer spending through other channels (such as web and catalog) is increased by 15%, the CLV score for the customers goes up by 18%. These results show that regular store customers who also buy through alternative channels have a greater lifetime value for the firm. Multichannel shopping gains particular significance with the growth of the Internet and firms increasingly offering products through their websites. Apart from providing added convenience to shoppers, multiple channels also serve to increase revenue and decrease cost for firms by moving customers to low-cost channels and offering a wide range of products that could not be offered in brick-and-mortar stores.

- **Impact of selling a specific product.** A 15% increase in the spending on product category A increased the CLV of the customers by 14%. This CLV driver could serve as a tool for firms to simultaneously manage product profiles and customers. If a retailer wants to know how introducing a new product or changing an existing product profile will affect customer value, the firm can use this method to analyze the situation. In this case, there seems to be a causal relationship between purchasing of product A and the high CLV of the customer.

- **Impact of relationship duration.** As shown in Figure 4.4, if the customer's relationship duration is increased by 15%, the CLV score goes up by 12%. This shows that it is important for retailers to retain their high-value (CLV) customers. But, firms should not attempt to retain all customers. As pointed out previously in this book, not all loyal customers are profitable. Therefore, firms should adopt strategies to retain profitable customers and build loyalty and profitability at the same time. (Chapter 6, "Managing Loyalty and Profitability Simultaneously," discusses this strategy in more depth.)

- **Impact of frequency of purchase.** If the customer's purchase frequency is increased by 15%, the CLV score of the customers goes up by 7%. This result highlights the fact that even though purchase frequency is an important driver of CLV, it has the least positive effect on the CLV score as compared to the other drivers.

- **Impact of average number of returns.** With a 15% increase in the average number of returns made by customers, their CLV score goes down by 2%. However, the relationship between product returns and CLV is more complex than what is suggested by this result. In limited numbers, product returns could indicate a healthy relationship with the customer, because it shows that the customer is willing to communicate with the firm and connect with its channels. However, too many product returns could be damaging to the firm, because it shows that the episodes of product return have not been exploited properly to build a relationship with the customer.

As shown in Table 4.3, 15 stores of the retailer were rank ordered based on the sum of the lifetime value of the customers and their past revenue. As shown in the table, the rank order of the stores based on their lifetime value differs significantly from the rank order based on past revenue. A similar discrepancy was observed when the past and future revenues of the customers were compared. This clearly shows that firms cannot rely on past store performance. Instead, they have to rely on their customer portfolio and its future value. As pointed out earlier, on average around 30% of customers have a negative lifetime value. Stores need to exercise greater caution as to whether they are acquiring and retaining the right customers. The manager can look up the CLV score of a customer to decide on the level of spending on that customer and still remain profitable. For example, the manager should not spend more than $92 per customer (on average) in Decile (Group) 3 (refer back to Figure 4.2) to ensure a profitable lifetime duration with the customer. In acquiring new customers, managers can refer to the profile of a typical high-CLV customer and look for new customers with similar profiles and prioritize resources on these customers. This approach can be used to evaluate relatively new customers, to make marketing decisions about existing customers, and to allocate marketing resources across various customers.

Table 4.3 Measuring Store Profitability

Store	Store Revenue ($)	Revenue Rank	Expected Store Profitability Based on CLV	Profitability Rank
1	20,196,138	1	3,304,942	4
2	11,870,392	2	1,731,856	9
3	9,761,732	3	−4,471,439	14
4	8,705,402	4	7,635,066	1
5	6,487,945	5	2,579,805	7
6	6,314,190	6	−5,816,329	15
7	5,085,694	7	4,660,984	2
8	4,510,125	8	2,759,272	6
9	4,357,225	9	2,526,916	8
10	4,311,662	10	3,577,310	3
11	4,189,061	11	185,066	12
12	3,880,850	12	1,031,893	11
13	3,856,373	13	1,117,543	10
14	3,777,840	14	3,053,192	5
15	3,757,544	15	−348,419	13

This case study helps identify various CLV drivers, such as cross-buying, product returns, multichannel shopping, and so on. Other firms can customize these drivers and add new ones according to their business context, and then test them as to how they affect the lifetime value of customers. This gives firms an invaluable tool on which to base their day-to-day marketing decisions, and it increases the potential for implementing the firm's decision through manipulation of the drivers.

The results obtained from this case study have several strategic implications, as follows:

- The performance of store managers can be evaluated based on CLV scores of the store.

- Store-based decisions can be made to maximize CLV:

    - Stores should target the type of customers each store should have to maximize CLV.

    - Stores should tailor strategies to address a specific set of customers based on their CLV scores.

Conclusion

At any given moment, firms need to make several marketing and strategic decisions regarding their customers and products. The CLV framework provides firms with an effective and centralized method to consistently make the right decisions. As recommended in this chapter, firms should always aim to maximize their CLV, and all decisions should be based on this criterion. And by understanding the drivers of CLV that define the customer-firm relationship, and by taking appropriate measures to maximize the CLV using these drivers, firms can ensure profit maximization and success in the future.

Endnotes

[1] W. Reinartz and V. Kumar, "The Impact of Customer Relationship Characteristics on Profitable Lifetime Duration," *Journal of Marketing* 67(1) 2003: 77–99.

[2] V. Kumar, D. Shah, and R. Venkatesan, "Managing retailer profitability—one customer at a time!" *Journal of Retailing* 82(4) 2006: 277–294.

5

Maximizing Customer Profitability

Relevant Issues

- Why do we need a Customer Lifetime Value (CLV)-based approach to manage customer profitability?
- What are the strategies that can be used to maximize CLV?

The previous chapters described the concept and measurement of CLV and how various factors affect the lifetime value of a customer. The next step is to use strategies based on CLV to maximize customer profitability. This chapter identifies several strategies that can be used to maximize customer profitability.

The Wheel of Fortune

A full understanding of each customer's lifetime value will enable a firm to maximize its own value by maximizing the number, scope, and duration of such value-creating customer relationships. In this chapter, we discuss a set of strategies that can be used by firms to maximize their CLVs. These strategies can be broadly classified into "across-customer" strategies and "within-customer" strategies. By using CLV as a cornerstone to design and implement these strategies, firms can ensure profit maximization.

Across-customer strategies include

- Efficient customer selection by targeting customers with high profit potential

- Managing existing sets of customers and rewarding them based on their profit potential

- Investing in high-profit customers to prevent attrition and ensure future profitability

Within-customer strategies aim at maximizing profits by either increasing revenue or reducing cost or by doing both. The within-customer strategies include multichannel shopping (revenue maximization), optimal allocation of resources (cost reduction), and managing the purchase sequence of the customers (revenue maximization and cost reduction). Maximizing the brand value is another key within-customer strategy.

Figure 5.1 lists these cutting-edge marketing strategies that can be used in maximizing CLV. I call it the Wheel of Fortune. Implementing these

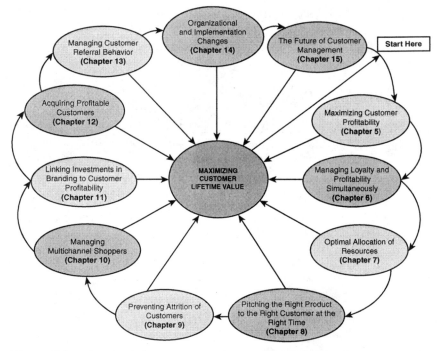

Figure 5.1   The Wheel of Fortune: Strategies Used for Maximizing CLV

strategies is a cyclical process. The knowledge acquired in implementing these strategies should be used as the basis for deciding which customer to pursue in the future and how to select the most profitable set of customers.

As illustrated in Figure 5.1, the CLV maximization cycle starts with selecting the right customers based on future profitability. The strategies that follow this aim at efficient management and retention of customers. The next step is to manage loyalty and profitability of these customers simultaneously. The return on investment (ROI) from the limited marketing resources can be maximized by optimally allocating resources to profitable customers and contacting them through the most effective communication channels at the most appropriate time with the right message.

The next strategy involves pitching the right product to the right customer at the right time. This can be achieved by predicting the purchase sequence of the customers and adapting the marketing initiatives accordingly. Also, preventing the attrition of customers is an important step in retaining the most profitable customers. This could be achieved by obtaining a good understanding of the spending patterns and intervening at the right time to prevent the customer from terminating the relationship with the firm. With the coexistence of online stores, catalog-based businesses, and physical store locations, managing customers in the multiple channels is an important strategy. By encouraging customers to buy from multiple channels and by encouraging them to use the lower-cost channels to make their transactions, firms can maximize profit.

The next strategy is the one used by firms to link a customer's brand value to the customer's profitability. By following this strategy, firms can identify areas for improving brand value and optimally allocate resources to improve the brand value and improve customer profitability.

The last strategy links the acquisition and retention of customers to profitability. By targeting the right customers and retaining customers with high profit potential, firms can ensure future profitability. The experience (or information) obtained by implementing these strategies is taken into account while making future decisions about customer selection and other strategies, thus ensuring a dynamic process that can be exploited to maximize profit. A brief introduction to all these strategies follows.

Customer Selection[1]

The first step in implementing a successful marketing strategy is to select the right customers. Customer selection is a crucial step for several reasons. First, the marketing budget of a firm is limited, and managers have to make choices as to where and on whom they should spend the limited resources available to them. Second, not all customers are equally profitable. As shall be established in future chapters, an overwhelming share of profit is generated by a small percentage of customers. This necessitates targeting those customers with high profitability, and this is the basis of the customer selection strategy.

Traditionally, firms rank order customers based on their profits and prioritize their resources based on this ranking. As described previously, several customer selection metrics have been used by companies for this purpose, such as RFM (Recency-Frequency Monetary value), SOW (Share of Wallet), PCV (Past Customer Value), and CLV (Customer Lifetime Value). As shown in the previous chapters, of these metrics, the forward-looking CLV metric is the most successful in predicting future customer profits.

The performance of the traditional metrics versus the CLV metric in customer selection has been compared numerous times, with CLV always offering higher levels of profitability. For example, in a recent study, customers from a large high-tech services company were rank ordered from best to worst according to each metric. The total revenue, costs, and profits from the top 15% of the customers were compared. The total observation period of the study was 72 months (6 years). The customers were rank ordered according to each metric based on the data obtained from the first 54-month period. The total revenue and the profit generated by the top 15% of customers under each metric were observed over the next 18 months. Table 5.1 shows the results from this study.

Table 5.1 Comparison of Metrics for Customer Selection

Using the First 54 Months of Data to Predict the Next 18 Months of Purchase Behavior (for the Top 15% of the Customers)

	CLV	RFM	PCV
Average revenue	30,427	21,201	21,929
Gross value	9,184	6,360	6,579
Variable costs	107	100	95
Net value	9,077	6,260	6,484

It is clear from Table 5.1 that the net value generated by the customers who were selected based on the CLV score is about 45% greater than that generated through customers selected through other traditional metrics. This shows that using CLV to select customers is far more effective than using the traditional metrics. These findings provide substantial support for the usefulness of CLV as a metric for customer scoring and customer selection.

Managing Loyalty and Profitability Simultaneously[2]

Often, managers fall into the trap of believing that loyalty is the true measure of customer profitability. As explained in the previous chapters, the link between loyalty and profitability is a lot more complex and subtle. By directing all their marketing resources to achieve and maintain loyalty, managers are not only pursuing the wrong customers, but also ignoring customers with high-profit potential. This strategy clarifies the relationship between loyalty and profitability and provides managers with the required framework to manage loyalty and profitability at the same time. In implementing this strategy, the difference between behavioral and attitudinal loyalty is highlighted. Behavioral loyalty refers to the loyalty of customers as reflected through their immediate purchase behavior. Attitudinal loyalty refers to the higher-order, long-term relationship of the customer with the firm. Traditionally, firms relied solely on behavioral loyalty as a measure of a customer's loyalty. But, as explained later in this book, this gives a skewed and often unreliable measure. This strategy explains how "true" loyalty could be measured and what role behavioral loyalty and attitudinal loyalty play in attaining profitability.

The first step in implementing this strategy is to segment customers based on their loyalty and profitability to the firm. Several measures of loyalty and profitability can be used for this purpose. Customers are segmented into cells based on their loyalty and profitability levels, and different strategies are directed toward each set of customers to maximize their loyalty and profitability.

After the customers have been segmented, the next step is to build a loyalty program that aims at maximizing the overall profitability of the firm. This strategy presents a framework that can be used to build such a loyalty program. The framework suggests several steps that can be used to build and sustain profitable customer loyalty.

All customers are not equally profitable. Always remember this when putting a loyalty program in place. A firm's loyalty program should be able to reward customers depending on their level of profitability. For loyalty programs, a two-tiered approach is recommended. The tier 1 rewards are aimed at all customers based on their current and past purchase behavior. This tier 1 reward is a simple, explicit way of rewarding customers and attracting new customers. Tier 2 rewards are aimed at influencing the future purchase behavior of customers. Tier 2 rewards are more selective and reward customers to influence their behavioral and attitudinal loyalty.

Implementing this strategy will enable firms to build and sustain profitable customer loyalty. This chapter provides a comprehensive framework to approach this problem and suggests several steps that can be used to build a more robust and profitable loyalty program.

Optimal Allocation of Resources[3]

Firms are often constrained by limited marketing resources. This poses a challenge because these resources cannot be allocated to all their customers. Ideally, firms should be investing only in customers who are profitable. However, many companies continue to spend resources on a large number of unprofitable customers. They either invest in customers who are easy to acquire but are not necessarily profitable or try to increase the retention rate of all their customers, thereby wasting limited resources. One reason for this is that these firms have not identified who their most profitable customers are and how resources should be spent on them to maximize profitability.

This strategy makes detailed recommendations about optimal allocation of resources to individual customers. The first step is to identify the most profitable customers and the customers who are most responsive to marketing efforts. The second step is to figure out the right mix of different channel contacts for each customer. This depends on how responsive each customer is to these channels of communication (email, direct mail, telephone, direct visit by a salesperson) and how cost-effective these channels are.

The next step in implementing this strategy is to decide how frequently the customer should be contacted and what the inter-contact time should be. Also, the various factors that affect customer behavior—such as upgrading (to a higher product category) and cross-selling (in a different category) and so on—need to be analyzed. Therefore, by carefully monitoring the purchase frequency of customers, the inter-purchase time, and the contribution toward profit, managers can determine the frequency of marketing initiatives to maximize CLV.

This strategy suggests that it is unwise to inundate all customers with marketing initiatives. It has been shown that such an approach only alienates customers and makes them less responsive to such efforts. A more measured approach is recommended, where each customer's responsiveness to each channel of communication is considered and a carefully designed strategy is implemented to allocate the limited marketing resources.

Pitching the Right Product to the Right Customer at the Right Time[4]

Companies are constantly trying to predict customer buying behavior. In such an exercise, the most common method used by companies involves two steps:

1. Estimating the probability that a customer will choose to purchase a particular product

2. Estimating the probability that a customer will make a purchase at a particular time

Most firms stop at the first step, which limits their ability to accurately predict the timing of purchases. However, even those companies that follow the process may not be successful. In a multiproduct firm, it is not easy to predict what product a particular customer is going to buy next. But, from the firm's point of view, this is a very valuable piece of information because the firm can then decide the message and timing of the customized communication strategy. An ideal contact strategy is one that allows the firm to deliver a sales message relevant to the product likely to be purchased in the near future by a customer. This could be achieved by accurately predicting the purchase sequence.

Understanding the purchase sequence calls for analyzing past customer purchases and estimating the likelihood of future purchases to design optimal contact strategies. Some questions that need to be answered are as follows:

- In which product category is the customer likely to make a purchase?

- At what intervals and during which time period will the customer make a purchase?

- How much is the customer likely to spend? (In other words, how profitable is the customer likely to be?)

This strategy describes a model that helps to analyze and answer the preceding questions and predicts the purchase sequence of each customer. After these questions have been answered, the next step is to design an optimal allocation strategy aimed at efficiently contacting customers to induce them to make the next purchase. When tested in a business-to-business (B2B) setting, 85% of the customers predicted by this model to make a purchase actually went on to do so. In comparison, only 55% of the customers predicted by the traditional model actually made a purchase. When this strategy was implemented in the B2B setting, an increase in ROI of 160% was observed. Therefore, this strategy suggests that efficient management of the purchase sequence not only increases revenue by accurately predicting and preempting a customer purchase, but also minimizes cost by reducing the frequency of customer contacts.

Preventing Customer Attrition

An efficient customer retention strategy that leads to profit maximization requires holding on to those customers with high profit potential. Scientific models, such as the dynamic churn models, are used to predict which customer is likely to leave the company and suggest proactive actions for companies. These models empower managers to execute timely, customer-specific marketing interventions that result in an increase in ROI.

When implementing a customer retention strategy, managers face questions such as when to intervene, how to intervene, and through which channel to intervene. While developing a framework, it should be remembered that each customer may have potential for some level of future profit. When designing an intervention strategy, the first step is to study the customer's quitting tendencies. After we identify the potential value through the computation of CLV, we can then create a value proposition at the time of intervention that would not exceed the CLV. This way, the retained customers are still expected to be profitable in the future.

After deciding on the need to intervene and identifying the customers to be intervened with, firms must identify when to intervene. To prevent customer attrition, a proactive intervention strategy is necessary to address those customers who show a strong need for intervention. The dynamic churn model, when implemented with an Internet service provider (ISP) firm, saved more than 30% of the customers who were showing signs of leaving the firm. This savings resulted in an incremental ROI of about 10, based on the saving of customers and retaining them for at least one more year. This strategy of intervening with customers who exhibit potential to churn can result in higher profits for firms.

Managing Multichannel Shoppers[5]

Due to the arrival of complex distribution systems for various industries and sectors, and the growth of web-based sales, firms are spreading themselves across various channels to appeal to diverse customer segments. For example, customers purchase in some retail stores such as Macy's and JCPenney through brick-and-mortar stores, through the Internet, or through mail-order catalogs. Each of these channels services a different set of customers and provides varying levels of service. This leads to reduction in service cost, resulting in an increase in profitability.

The study referred to in this section demonstrated that in a B2B setting, multichannel shoppers are more profitable than single-channel shoppers. Specifically, multichannel shoppers differ from single-channel shoppers by providing higher revenue and having a deeper relationship, a higher SOW, and a higher likelihood of being active. By implementing this strategy in the B2B firm, it was found that customers who shopped through all three channels generated three times the revenue when compared to single-channel shoppers. Also, the likelihood of staying active for those who shop through three channels was about four times more when compared to single-channel shoppers. Multichannel shoppers initiate more contacts with the firm, have longer tenure, purchase more frequently, and are more receptive to contacts through multiple communication channels. Further, the study showed that there exists a nonlinear relationship between returns and multichannel shopping, and that there is a positive enticement toward multichannel shopping when customers are contacted through various communication channels.

Understanding customer behavior in each channel can help managers to migrate low-value customers to low-cost channels and thus reduce cost. For example, if a customer who predominantly buys by ordering from the catalog over the telephone can be migrated to buying from the firm's website, the cost of servicing the customer could be significantly reduced. This strategy identifies the drivers of multichannel shopping and how it influences channel adoption. Further, a conceptual framework that identifies the customer-level characteristics and supplier factors that may influence purchase behavior across multiple channels is provided.

These results show that by effectively managing the purchase pattern of customers across various channels, firms stand to gain from the cost reduction and customer retention. This strategy illustrates how firms can harvest these benefits by managing multichannel shopping.

Linking Investments in Branding to Customer Profitability[6]

A typical dilemma faced by any corporate board is whether to invest in building brands or to invest in building the customer base. Which of these routes will ensure maximum profitability? The answer is probably to invest in both. Also, it would be difficult to estimate how investing in brand building contributes toward attaining higher profitability. A key way to address these issues is to establish a link between brand value and CLV to manage individual customer brand value. This results in maximizing the CLV. This strategy explores the link between Individual Brand Value (IBV) and CLV, and it offers insights about bridging the gap between IBV and CLV.

Brand equity and customer equity have traditionally been viewed as two separate marketing assets. However, building a brand through traditional approaches does not necessarily achieve growth in the CLV. Measurements on components of an individual's brand value are suggested so that a firm can identify how its customers value the brand. This framework enables a firm to optimize a customer's lifetime value, thereby allowing simultaneous growth in brand equity and customer equity. Based on these results, the firm can redesign its communication strategies to cater to the needs of such customers. In one of the implementations, after the brand value was linked to CLV, the scores of the components of the brand value were improved to yield a higher CLV.

Acquiring Profitable Customers[7]

The strategies listed previously are aimed at selecting the right customers, managing them profitably, and retaining them through the optimal allocation of resources. The knowledge acquired in implementing these strategies could be used to acquire prospective customers with high profit potential. This approach to link acquisition and retention of customers to firm profitability is a key contribution of the CLV-based approach.

While making direct marketing investment decisions, many marketers still overemphasize short-term cost over long-term gain, leading to companies pursuing customers who are cheap to acquire and cheap to retain without essentially being profitable. Conventionally, most companies use customer acquisition and retention rates to measure their marketing performance. This approach could diminish returns to the firms because they might be spending more on acquiring and retaining a customer than on what the customer brings in as revenue. Further, different groups of customers require different levels of acquisition/retention spending to maintain their relationship.

The CLV approach recommended in this book suggests optimizing the acquisition/retention costs and directly links such efforts to overall profitability. This strategy helps firms to decide which customers are worth chasing and which dormant customers should be pursued to come back to the firm. Firms should use customer profiles to identify the customers who are most likely to be profitable. This can be achieved by identifying customers with similar characteristics as existing high-CLV customers and by adopting an appropriate marketing strategy. After the customer behavior of a catalog retailer was observed, customers were segmented based on their cost of acquisition and cost of retention. It was found that the largest segment (32%) was made up of customers who were easy to acquire and retain. But they accounted for only 20% of the total profit. On the other hand, 40% of the total profit came from the smallest group of customers (15%), who were expensive to acquire but cheap to retain. Therefore, linking acquisition and retention to profitability helps the firm to target and retain profitable prospects and customers. This demonstrates the importance of the efficient allocation of the marketing budget across acquisition and retention initiatives to maximize profitability.

Viral Marketing Strategies[8]

Although the CLV metric has been shown to outperform all other behavioral metrics such as RFM or SOW, it does have one main limitation as a complete measure of a customer's value. Even though all customer relationship management (CRM) programs collect data on transactions and demographics, they fail to measure data on customer attitudes. And, even if they do collect data on customer attitudes, such as in the form of surveys, these attitude measurements are often left out of the estimation of CLV.

It is clear that not only can customers contribute to the firm through their own transactions (direct profit), but they also have an impact on the transactions of other customers through word-of-mouth and referrals (indirect profit), and both can increase the value of that customer to a firm. A recent study showed that less behaviorally loyal customers tend to have a stronger impact on referring new customers when compared to more behaviorally loyal customers. It was also shown that the referral process is not only able to bring in customers without excessive marketing expense, it is also able to bring in customers who are not likely to join through traditional advertising and promotions by the company. While designing a marketing strategy to target our highest-value customers, we need to consider the actual value that each customer can bring to the table in terms of both direct and indirect profit.

There are two approaches for maximizing customer profitability: maximizing CLV and managing customer referral behavior. The concept of Customer Referral Value (CRV), which is defined as the value of the referral behavior of a specific customer, is introduced in implementing this strategy. This metric enables managers to measure and manage customer referral behavior. This dictates that customers be valued based on their indirect impact on the firm's profits, through savings in acquisition costs and the addition of new customers by way of customer referral.

Implementation/Interaction Orientation[9]

When implementing these strategies, firms need to fundamentally reorient their marketing approach. Traditionally, firms had a "product-centric" approach, and managers were focused on making and selling superior products. In this process, the entire focus remained on the products. For firms to maintain future profitability, a "customer-centric" approach becomes imperative. In this approach, the timely interaction between the customers and the firm, and effective management of this interaction, is recognized as a major source of competitive advantage. We define this interaction between the firm and the customer, which helps in developing organizational resources for successful customer management strategies, as interaction orientation.

In the interaction-oriented approach, marketing activities are conducted with the customer. The customer is viewed both as a source of business and as a resource for the firm. The power of customer-to-customer linkages is recognized and nurtured as a customer empowerment component.

The various components of the interaction-oriented approach are as follows:

- Customer capacity is the belief that the individual customer is the unit of every marketing action or reaction.

- Interaction response capacity is the degree to which a firm can provide successive products or services based on the previous feedback by a specific customer and all other customers.

- Customer empowerment is the extent to which customers connect with the firm and other customers, collaborating and sharing information, praise, and criticism about the firm's products and services.

- Customer value management is the extent to which a firm is able to quantify and calculate the individual customer value and reallocate its resources to higher-value customers based on this evaluation.

By adopting these measures, firms can customize their products and services by better understanding the needs of their customers. This leads to increased customer satisfaction, generates positive word-of-mouth, and leads to acquiring and retaining profitable customers.

The Future of Customer Management

Traditionally, the focus of implementing customer management (CM) strategies was to reduce cost and to an extent make customer management more efficient. But firms have started to realize that CM strategies can not only help retain loyal customers, but can also help businesses grow their revenue and profit.

Firms should realize that CM is not an end in itself, but a means to an end. Firms should employ "customer-centric" strategies to reap the full benefits of CM strategies.[10] By doing so, firms will be able to successfully implement CM strategies in lucrative business scenarios, set reasonable expectations for returns, and evaluate and understand new business opportunities that will arise.

When implementing an interactive marketing approach, firms need to assess individual customers, including their needs, wants, and ways and means of communication. They must also assess lifetime value and profitability. This assessment will involve establishing a department that identifies the necessary components and interfaces for delivery of products/services to the customer. The department also appoints monitors and measures the impact on any change in the firm's consumer base.

In the future, a firm that can accurately assess customer feedback and market trends through an interactive marketing approach will be able to respond to market changes and customer needs within a day (or perhaps even the instant a customer walks in). Such a response requires that the right systems be in place to effectively control and capture all relevant customer data. If the right information system is in place, the data can be processed in real time, and relevant information for the ideal marketing strategy can be provided instantly. Therein lies the future of customer management: You have a marketing plan for each and every customer—to make these customers even more profitable as soon as the purchasing information is updated.

The Power of CLV and the Wheel of Fortune

The strategies listed in this chapter are an integral part of a comprehensive customer management approach recommended in this book. Even though these strategies can yield great results when implemented separately, they work best when implemented as a whole. The knowledge acquired from implementing each strategy can be used to improve on other strategies, and this information can be collectively used to refine future marketing initiatives. All these strategies are powered by CLV and derive the benefit of using a forward-looking metric to evaluate a customer's worth to the firm. Because the CLV takes into account the customer's past and future purchasing behavior, it gives an accurate picture of a customer's worth to the firm and thus enables managers to design and modify their marketing strategies accordingly. Each of the strategies mentioned in this chapter is discussed in detail in the following chapters.

Conclusion

While CLV has proven to be a superior metric, the challenge is maximizing it. As demonstrated in this chapter, there are nine strategies that could effectively manage customers profitably. These strategies aim to select the right customers for future targeting, identify and segment customers with the highest potential for profits in the future, optimally allocate marketing resources to customers across channels to maximize CLV, pitch the right product to the right customer at the right time, prevent attrition of high value customers, identify and target the customers for multichannel shopping, allocate the right amount of marketing resources to build a profitable branding strategy, identify the optimal marketing resources to acquire and retain profitable customers, and identify customers who provide value through customer referrals. Managers may implement these strategies to maximize the firm profits.

Endnotes

[1] R. Venkatesan and V. Kumar, "A Customer Lifetime Value Framework for Customer Selections and Resource Allocation Strategy," *Journal of Marketing* 68(4) 2004: 106–125.

[2] W. Reinartz and V. Kumar, "The Mismanagement of Customer Loyalty," *Harvard Business Review,* July 2002: 86–97.

[3] R. Venkatesan and V. Kumar, "A Customer Lifetime Value Framework for Customer Selections and Resource Allocation Strategy," *Journal of Marketing* 68(4) 2004: 106–125.

4   V. Kumar, R. Venkatesan, and W. Reinartz, "Knowing What to Sell, When, and to Whom," *Harvard Business Review,* March 2006: 131–137.

5   V. Kumar and R. Venkatesan, "Who Are the Multichannel Shoppers and How Do They Perform?: Correlates of Multichannel Shopping Behavior," *Journal of Interactive Marketing* 19 (Spring) 2003: 44–62.

6   V. Kumar, M. Luo, and V. R. Rao, "Linking an Individual's Brand Value to the CLV: An Integrated Framework," Working Paper, University of Connecticut.

7   W. Reinartz, J. Thomas, and V. Kumar, "Balancing Acquisition and Retention Resources to Maximize Profitability," *Journal of Marketing* 69 (January) 2005: 63–79.

8   V. Kumar, J. Andrew Petersen and Robert Leone, "How Valuable is Word of Mouth?," *Harvard Business Review* 85(10) 2007: 139–146.

9   V. Kumar and Girish Ramani, "Interaction Orientation: The New Measure of Marketing Capabilities," forthcoming, *Journal of Marketing.*

10 Denish Shah et al., "The Path to Customer Centricity," *Journal of Service Research* 9(2) 2006: 113–124.

6

Managing Loyalty and Profitability Simultaneously

Relevant Issues

- Should we build customer loyalty?
- How do we choose the right customers?
- How do we avoid choosing the wrong customers?
- How do we manage profitable customer loyalty?

As discussed in the previous chapters, selecting customers purely based on their loyalty is not a prudent approach. To administer efficient reward programs, it is necessary to distinguish between the behavioral and attitudinal loyalty of customers and to alter existing programs to improve each measure. Also, segmenting customers based on their profitability and adopting segment-specific strategies are essential. This results in the efficient allocation of resources (and thus leads to an increase in profitability). This chapter provides a framework that allows firms to classify and manage customers based on their profitability and longevity.

Behavioral and Attitudinal Loyalty

Conventionally, customer loyalty has been defined as a behavioral measure (that is, the loyalty of a customer as obtained from his purchasing behavior). A majority of the existing loyalty programs reward customers based on their behavioral loyalty: The more you spend, the greater the reward. As discussed in the previous chapters, customers should be rewarded based on their profitability, not just on their behavioral loyalty alone. Even if you incorporate this aspect of customer profitability into your loyalty programs, it is still incomplete because the current loyalty programs are not forward-looking; that is, customers are rewarded based on their current and historical purchasing behavior, and the programs do not consider the future profit potential of the customers. That brings up the first question answered in this chapter: Is it possible to design a loyalty program that can reward customers "today" based on their "future" profitability?

To answer that question, we first have to understand the deeper question: What is "true" loyalty? *Truly loyal customers* have been defined as customers "who feel so strongly that you (the company) can best meet their relevant needs that your (the company's) competition is virtually excluded from the consideration set; these customers buy almost exclusively from you (the company)."[1] This observation implies that to build and sustain "true" customer loyalty, it is necessary to include the attitudinal behavior of customers that drives customer behavior.

What is attitudinal loyalty? *Attitudinal loyalty* indicates a higher-order and long-term commitment of a customer toward the firm. This commitment cannot be inferred from just observing the purchasing behavior of customers.[2] In addition, customers who exhibit attitudinal loyalty have a greater propensity to display certain behaviors, such as having a greater likelihood of future purchase or being more likely to recommend the focal firm to their friends and acquaintances.[3] These customers could provide unprecedented customer growth to the company through word-of-mouth publicity or referral behavior. A loyalty program that doesn't factor in both the attitudinal and the behavioral aspect doesn't maximize the potential for profitability, because it is clear that

- Behavioral loyalty by itself cannot be a measure of true loyalty.

- Behavioral loyalty can be an unreliable predictor of customer profitability.[4]

Customer Segmentation

The first step in this process is to segment customers based on their loyalty and profitability diversity. Several measures can be used for this purpose. Figure 6.1 illustrates one such measure; customers are segmented into four groups based on their expected future profitability and on the prediction as to how long they are expected to stay with the firm (duration). After they have been segmented into one of the four cells, a different loyalty strategy is then applied to each cell. Just from this segmentation alone, it is clear that the relationship between loyalty and profitability is more complex than previously believed.[5] Some customers are very loyal but not profitable at all (Cell 4); others are short-term customers and highly profitable (Cell 2). Therefore, because the customers in each cell differ significantly in their behavioral motivations, a different loyalty approach is taken toward each segment of customers to maximize their profitability.

	Short-Term Customers	Long-Term Customers

High Profitability	**BUTTERFLIES** — Cell 2
	• Good fit of company offering and customer needs
	• High profit potential
	• Action:
	  – Aim to achieve transactional satisfaction, not attitudinal loyalty
	  – Milk the accounts as long as they are active
	  – Key challenge: cease investment once inflection point is reached
		TRUE FRIENDS — Cell 3
		• Good fit of company offering and customer needs
		• Highest profit potential
		• Action:
		  – Consistent intermittently spaced communication
		  – Achieve attitudinal *and* behavioral loyalty
		  – Delight to nurture/defend/retain

Low Profitability	**STRANGERS** — Cell 1
	• Little fit of company offering and customer needs
	• Lowest profit potential
	• Action:
	  – No relationship investment
	  – Profitize every transaction
		BARNACLES — Cell 4
		• Limited fit of company offering and customer needs
		• Low profit potential
		• Action:
		  – Measure size and Share of Wallet
		  – If Share of Wallet is low, specific up-selling and cross-selling
		  – If Size of Wallet is small, strict cost control

Figure 6.1 Managing loyalty and profitability simultaneously

Source: W. J. Reinartz and V. Kumar, "The Mismanagement of Customer Loyalty," *Harvard Business Review* 80(7) 2002: 86. Printed with permission from the Harvard Business School Publishing.

Source: V. Kumar and D. Shah, "Building and Sustaining Profitable Customer Loyalty for the 21st Century," *Journal of Retailing*, 80(4) 2004: 326. Copyright New York University.

- **Cell 1: strangers (low-profitability and short-term customers).** The set of customers who are not loyal to the firm and bring in little or no profit are called strangers. These customers have very little fit between the company's offerings and their own needs; therefore, they have very little profit potential. They have to be identified very early on, and any investment toward building a relationship with them should be avoided. Profit should be made from every transaction with these customers because it is likely that the current transaction with these customers could be their last.

- **Cell 2: butterflies (high-profitability and short-term customers).** These profitable, but transient customers can be very profitable, but often do not exhibit traditional behavioral loyalty. Butterflies are very prevalent in many industries. These customers tend to buy a lot in a short time period and then move on to new firms after making those transactions. These customers avoid building a long-term relationship with any single firm. For example, many direct-brokerage firms call such customers "movers" (those who spend large amounts and trade often but switch to a different firm when they find a better deal).

One mistake often repeated when managing these customers is to continue to invest in them even after they stop purchasing from the focal firm. Such efforts to retain butterflies are mostly futile. In a study conducted in various industries, it was observed that attempts to convert butterflies into loyal customers rarely succeeded, and the conversion rate was less than 10% in each industry. So, firms should stop treating butterflies as potential "true believers" and instead adopt a more prudent approach: Enjoy their profits while they last and stop investing in them at the right moment when they switch. This usually involves adopting a short-term, hard-sell strategy through intensive promotions and mailing campaigns that involve promotions for products in other categories (cross-selling). Note that even though this is a good approach toward butterflies, it might irritate loyal customers. The corporate service provider studied uses this strategy with very good effect.[6] The firm telephones those customers it has identified as butterflies four or five times shortly after their most recent purchase, and depending on the product category, contacts them with just one direct mailing 6 to 12 months later. If these communications yield no result, the firm completely stops communicating with these customers.

- **Cell 3: true friends (high-profitability and long-term customers).** Customers who are both loyal and profitable are called true friends. These customers buy steadily and regularly (not too intensively) over time. True friends are generally satisfied with existing arrangements with the firm, as reflected in their loyalty and profitability. They are usually comfortable engaging with the firm's processes. For example, for the mail-order company in that study, it was found that customers had a tendency to return goods at a high rate, indicating that they had a high level of comfort engaging in both buying and returning products. Care should be taken in building relationships with these true friends, because these customers have the highest potential to bring long-term profitability. However, this does not necessarily mean inundating these customers with marketing communications and promotions. In the case of the mail-order catalog firm in that study, it was observed that intensifying the contact level by increasing the mailings and so on was more likely to have a negative impact on the loyal and profitable customers than to increase sales. When flooded with excess mailings, customers tend to ignore all of them, throwing out everything without even looking at the mailings. However, when sent the right number of promotions, they are more likely to look at the material and respond to it.

Firms should find new ways to cultivate and reward loyalty of true friends, which will in turn maximize their profitability and convert them into true believers. In the case of the grocery chain in that study, several measures were taken to reward customers based on their loyalty, and the results were reflected in increased sales and attitudinal loyalty. It was observed that customers who scored high on both attitudinal and behavioral measures of loyalty were 120% more profitable when compared to customers who just exhibited behavioral loyalty. This pattern is not only relevant in the business-to-consumer (B2C) setting, but also holds good in the business-to-business (B2B) setting. In the case of the corporate service provider, it was observed that the customers who exhibited both attitudinal and behavioral loyalty were 50% more profitable when compared to customers who just demonstrated loyalty through behavior alone.

Firms can take a range of measures to reward the loyalty of their customers, and more important, make them feel rewarded for loyalty. The grocery chain lets loyal customers participate in optional emailings of special promotions. Also, it allows these loyal customers special access to many of its company-sponsored events and seasonal promotions.

- **Cell 4: barnacles (low-profitability and long-term customers).** These customers, if managed unwisely, could prove to be a severe drain on company resources. The size and volume of the transactions made by these customers are too low to justify the cost incurred in marketing and maintaining their accounts. They are comparable to the barnacles attached to the hull of a ship; they only create additional drag. If managed in the right manner, they could become profitable in the future.

The primary step in designing a strategy for these customers is to evaluate the size and share of their wallet. If the problem is the small *size* of their wallet, these customers are not valuable enough to continue pursuing. If the problem is identified as small *Share* of Wallet, these customers have the potential to spend more, and they should be pursued and induced to purchase more. This task of tracking the spending pattern of customers to evaluate their value is made much simpler by the advancements in computer and database technology. The French grocery chain in this study was able to track the purchases of individual customers and obtain impressively reliable estimates about their share and Size of Wallet in specific product categories. Based on this information, the company can easily classify the potentially profitable customers and offer them specific promotions to induce them to buy more from the company (in both the previously purchased product categories and unrelated product categories).

A Framework for Building and Sustaining Loyalty

To take action and build an effective loyalty program, it is first necessary to learn how to segment your customers, as discussed in the preceding section. Then, after this segmentation has been completed, you must build a loyalty program with an overall objective of achieving maximum profitability. This section discusses a framework that firms can use to build and sustain customer loyalty (see Figure 6.2). To implement the framework, three fundamental objectives must be fulfilled:

1. Build and enhance behavioral loyalty.

2. Cultivate attitudinal loyalty.

3. Link loyalty to profitability.

These fundamental objectives can be used to represent a tiered reward system. In the following sections, these objectives are explained in detail, and several operational guidelines are given for implementing a profit-oriented, tiered reward system.

Building and Enhancing Behavioral Loyalty

As discussed in the earlier sections of this chapter, to achieve true loyalty of the customers, it is necessary to enhance both their behavioral and attitudinal loyalty. Customer loyalty of any form is meaningful to the firm only when it is reflected in the purchasing behavior. Enhanced purchasing behavior leads to an increase in the direct and tangible returns to the firm, as compared to attitudinal behavior, which may be expressed in terms of long-term commitment and trust, but need not translate into actual purchase behavior. So, pure attitudinal loyalty of customers, without being linked to behavioral loyalty, may only provide limited returns to the firm. Therefore, it is crucial for the firm to build behavioral loyalty before cultivating attitudinal loyalty.

Most loyalty programs implemented by firms today are aimed at rewarding the behavioral loyalty of the customers, and most of the loyalty programs are represented at the aggregate level of customer behavior.

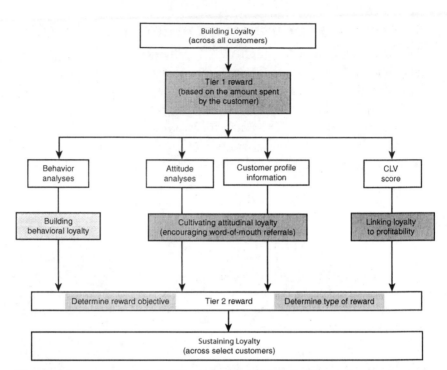

Figure 6.2 Framework for building and sustaining profitable customer loyalty

As illustrated in the previous chapters, rewarding customers based on just their aggregate purchase behavior is skewed and misses several key points. For example, in a traditional loyalty program, two customers who spend $100 in a department store get the same reward irrespective of how their spending pattern is distributed across high-profit and low-margin products, or how they buy from different product categories. Even if one of them buys predominantly low-margin products or sale items, this customer gets rewarded based only on his/her overall spending. To design an effective loyalty program, both the purchase behavior and the profitability aspect of the customers have to be investigated. The following questions must be asked to design a loyalty program: Did the customer buy all the products from a single category/department, or did he/she buy from different departments and product categories? The answer to this question gives insight about the customer's future purchasing behavior. Does the customer frequently buy low-margin or high-margin products? Does the customer predominantly buy sale items or full-price items or both? The answers to these two questions help firms understand how profitable the customer is likely to be in the future.

It is clear that even customers spending the same amount in revenue can have very different future profitability and purchase behavior. Hence, customers should be segmented based on these two dimensions: profitability and purchasing behavior. Figure 6.3 shows how the customers can be segmented on these dimensions.

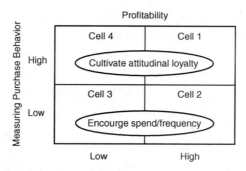

Profitability

	Cell 4	Cell 1
High	Cultivate attitudinal loyalty	
	Cell 3	Cell 2
Low	Encourge spend/frequency	

Measuring Purchase Behavior

Low   High

Figure 6.3   Purchase behavior analyses

Source: V. Kumar and Denish Shah (2004), "Building and Sustaining Profitable Customer Loyalty for the 21st Century," *Journal of Retailing* 80(4) 2004: 317–330. Copyright New York University.

When segmenting customers based on their purchasing behavior, remember that this measure varies across industries and product categories. For example, a multiproduct firm such as a financial services firm will be concerned about the degree of cross-buying across various product categories, whereas a single-product, single-price vendor such as Amtrak will be more concerned about the frequency of buying and will use that as a measure of purchasing behavior. Irrespective of the measure of purchasing behavior used, it is crucial to compare, contrast, and analyze the purchasing behavior against the profitability of the customer. Such analyses would result in a framework that could be used to make informed marketing decisions and interventions. This framework can be used to recognize a very strong purchasing behavior, as represented in Cell 1, or to initiate corrective actions to increase the purchasing behavior of customers in Cell 2 (such as sending promotions to encourage cross-buying, or increasing the profitability of customers in Cell 4). Cell 3 represents either new customers or customers with low revenue potential. The new customers could be induced to spend more with the firm by being offered upfront incentives; these customers should be monitored before investing further in them. Customers with low revenue potential should be managed through low-cost marketing channels, such as email promotions, web-based customer service, and so on.

Cultivating Attitudinal Loyalty

The importance of attitudinal loyalty was discussed in the previous sections, and concerns about the attitudinal loyalty of customers should play an integral part when designing a loyalty program. Firms should be able to understand the customer's attitude toward the firm and should be able to measure customer attitudes in a meaningful way. Aspects about customer attitudes can be measured by conducting surveys at the customer level. Other measures, such as customer feedback and focus groups, can also be used. Managers should consider the fact that information from surveys reflects one particular set of customers in the given timeframe. Hence, surveys conducted at various timeframes across various customer segments can be used to compile a comprehensive picture of customer attitudes.

Attitudinal loyalty has to be "cultivated," and this should involve going above and beyond the standard marketing interventions generally used by firms. Attitudinal loyalty may often result in a long and fruitful relationship between the firm and the customer. Just as firms use behavioral loyalty to ensure profitability, attitudinal loyalty can be used to build an invisible exit barrier for their customers. This is particularly significant in noncontractual settings, where switching costs are low.[7] To design an effective approach to cultivate attitudinal loyalty, firms need to know their customers well (and beyond just the information present in the customer's purchasing history). Detailed customer profile information that contains data about customer heterogeneity and other demographic information should be used to predict the future profitability of a customer.

Linking Loyalty to Profitability

Any marketing initiative should be aimed at maximizing the profitability of the firm. This also holds true for loyalty programs. Customer loyalty programs that have been implemented without an eye on the profitability aspect have led to disastrous results. One example is the ABC Card program introduced in 1995 by the UK-based grocery chain Safeway. This program was implemented without being linked to profitability, and this resulted in the operation and communication costs outweighing the benefits from the program. This led to the program being scrapped in 2000.[8]

One effective way to establish the link between loyalty and profitability while designing these loyalty programs is to use the CLV metric. As described in the previous chapters, CLV is a forward-looking metric that predicts the future profitability of the customer based on the current available data. By using CLV, firms can identify the customers who are most valuable and spend the limited marketing resources on them. Also, by understanding which customers are least profitable in the long run, firms can limit the marketing intervention in these cases. Further, strategies and the effective use of CLV are discussed in detail in the following chapters. In the following sections, strategies are proposed that can be used to define the customer loyalty framework.

Operationalizing the Framework

A two-tier rewards strategy is proposed to effectively operationalize the framework. The two tiers are classified based on the desired results and the level of differentiation. Challenges involved in implementing this strategy include the following:

- The ability to discriminate customers based on their purchasing behavior, attitude, profile, and profitability potential, without alienating the customers

- The ability to build and sustain loyalty without sacrificing customer profitability

The detailed exploration of the two-tier strategy follows:

Tier 1 Rewards

Tier 1 rewards are aimed at achieving the following strategic objectives:

- **A baseline rewards approach.** Reward all customers based on their current and past purchasing behavior irrespective of their attitude or their purchasing pattern. Implementing such a simple, explicit, and fair baseline reward system ensures that all customers are aware of the rewards program. This also ensures that new customers with no previous transaction history with the firm are aware of the rewards program and receive Tier 1 rewards.

- **Collecting customer transaction data.** Tier 1 programs also serve as a way to collect transaction data about the customers. Most loyalty programs use loyalty cards with magnetic strips to record transaction data, and the customers are generally rewarded for using these cards by discount offers and so on. The presence of a Tier 1 rewards program also offers customers the incentive to record their transactions during every purchasing occasion, the data from which can be used to accurately analyze and understand the purchasing behavior.

- **Ensuring scalability of the loyalty programs.** The reward programs should be scalable and attempt to reward customers in proportion to their spending. In other words, the more the customer spends with the firm, the more reward he/she gets.

Based on these objectives, you can see that Tier 1 represents a standard, unidimensional rewards strategy, where customers get instant gratification, because they are rewarded based on their total spending. Tier 1 programs should be administered at the aggregate level to build loyalty across all customers, as shown in Figure 6.2. The terms of earning and redeeming the rewards/points would be the same for all customers and should be clearly stated in the policy documents. Because of this, Tier 1 programs are easy to duplicate by the competition. And, note that the majority of the loyalty programs offered today fall under this category; they mostly reward behavioral loyalty of the customers at the aggregate level.

Tier 2 Rewards

Unlike Tier 1 programs, Tier 2 rewards are forward-looking. They seek to influence the customer attitude and behavior in the future based on the past performance of the customer. Tier 2 rewards are more selective and reward specific customers to cultivate their behavioral loyalty and enhance behavioral and attitudinal loyalty. In Tier 2 programs, firms can decide the following:

- Who should be rewarded?

- What type of reward should be given?

- How much should the reward be worth?

All customers are eligible for Tier 1 rewards, but this pool of customers are further probed on four critical parameters—behavioral analyses, attitudinal analyses, customer profile information, and CLV score—to decide who should receive Tier 2 rewards. The specific objective to be fulfilled by the Tier 2 reward is dictated by the outcomes of the behavioral and the attitudinal analyses. For example, if Luke is a customer who has performed well in the attitudinal analyses and the profitability aspect but is lacking in the purchasing behavior dimension such as cross-buy, the main aim of the Tier 2 rewards would be to encourage Luke to cross-buy among product categories. Also, high-profit customers are rewarded bonus points based on their level of profitability. When instituting Tier 2 rewards, a customer's cumulative status should also be considered. For example, if a customer has a history of profitable purchasing behavior with the firm and returns to the firm after a dormant period, the customer's previous purchase history should be taken into account. This customer should be accommodated in a higher-level rewards program, and it should be made much easier for him to achieve his previous loyalty status.

After this decision to reward has been made, the next question is this: What is the best way to approach Luke with a promotion/offer, in which product category, and what should be the ceiling on the spending on this promotion? In other words, what should be the "type" and "value" of the reward? To answer these questions, the customer profile information and the CLV score of the customer can be used. The customer profile information gives information about which product category Luke is most likely to buy from. (This can be decided based on his age group and on other demographic information.) After the "type" of reward has been decided, the CLV score can be used to decide the total value of the reward. The spending of the promotion should not be greater than the expected future spending of the customer, and care should be taken that such marketing efforts have a positive return on investment for every customer. A forward-looking metric such as CLV can be used to determine this, and thus help in managing both the loyalty and the profitability at the same time. In evaluating a customer's value, the CLV metric takes into account all cost and revenue components of the customer, including the value of the previously awarded Tier 1 rewards. Hence, CLV helps in setting a ceiling for the total dollar amount to be spent on a particular customer.

Characteristics of Tier 2 Rewards

Unlike Tier 1 rewards, Tier 2 rewards are highly differentiated rewards, awarded to selective customers with the goal of sustaining their loyalty. Because Tier 2 rewards are not explicitly divulged to the customers (the program is executed by the firm on a customer-to-customer basis), it is very difficult for the competition to replicate these programs, giving the loyalty program a sustainable competitive advantage. Under this framework, both Tier 1 and Tier 2 rewards are represented in tandem, and they mostly have complementary effects. Tier 2 rewards are designed over and beyond the Tier 1 rewards and are used to further specific goals that are not met with the Tier 1 programs. If used effectively, Tier 1 and Tier 2 programs, implemented concurrently, could yield significant flexibility to any loyalty program.

Evolution of Loyalty Programs

As discussed previously, loyalty programs try to build and sustain profitable loyalty. Also, a framework was introduced that can be used to proactively reward customers *today* for their *future* spending. Advances in database management techniques have made it possible for firms to collect and maintain extensive information about customers. This can be used to design customer-centric loyalty programs, instead of the conventionally used program-centric approach. These steps can be used to reevaluate the various reward mechanisms, options, and schemes to formulate new approaches to create and sustain a profitable customer loyalty program. This new approach to customer loyalty programs is characterized by personalization and customization at the individual customer level. Table 6.1 summarizes the changes in customer loyalty programs that show a discernible evolving dominant logic. The description of the various dimensions are provided here:

- **Operational level.** With the introduction of advanced database management systems, loyalty programs are increasingly implemented at the individual customer level as opposed to the "aggregate" level. Loyalty cards and other methods (frequent-flyer numbers, customer IDs, and so on) are used to collect information and represent loyalty programs at the individual customer level.

- **Program type.** Conventionally, customers are rewarded based on the total amount spent, irrespective of their level of profitability. For example, a customer who buys a discount airline ticket will get the same bonus miles as the customer who buys the ticket at its full price. Whereas, according to the evolving dominant logic, customers will be rewarded based on the profitability aspect, not just on the total amount spent, and based on this approach, the customer who buys the airline ticket at full price will be rewarded at a higher level when compared to those buying at a discounted price.

Table 6.1   Changes in Customer Loyalty Programs

Number	Dimension	Earlier Loyalty Programs: Program-Centric	Evolving Loyalty Programs: Customer-Centric
1	Operational level	Aggregate level	Customer level
2	Program type	Standardized, based on usage or spend	Customized, based on type of usage or type of spend
3	Reward scheme	Standard and uniform, aimed at repeat purchase	Personalized and relevant, aimed at influencing specific behavioral change or attitudinal gratification
4	Reward options	Minimal	Multiple (usually made possible through partners and alliances)
5	Reward mechanisms	Reactive	Reactive + proactive
6	Reward types	Tangible	Tangible + experiential
7	Program objectives	Build market share, increase revenue, build behavioral loyalty through repeat purchase or usage	Link loyalty to profitability, influence behavioral loyalty, and cultivate attitudinal loyalty
8	Metrics used	Recency-Frequency-Monetary value (RFM), Past Customer Value (PCV), Share of Wallet (SOW)	Customer Lifetime Value (CLV)
9	Technology and analytics usage	Minimal	Extensive

Source: V. Kumar and D. Shah, "Building and Sustaining Profitable Customer Loyalty for the 21st Century," *Journal of Retailing* 80(4) 2004: 326.

- **Reward schemes.** Instead of just giving a standard reward to all customers, firms should personalize rewards to influence specific behavioral or attitudinal changes. This could be achieved by rewarding customers based on their customer profile information, their personal interests, and their purchasing behavior.

- **Reward options.** When implementing loyalty programs, customer heterogeneity should be taken into account. Because different customers perceive different value for the same reward, multiple reward options could be offered to accommodate different customer needs. This could be achieved by striking partnerships with other firms and including their products/services in the reward basket. This could enable the firm to offer rewards that are not part of its product profile and satisfy different customer needs at the same time.

- **Reward mechanisms.** Traditionally, loyalty programs were confined to rewarding customers just based on their past and current spending levels. This reactive reward mechanism is similar to the Tier 1 level rewards. In contrast, the evolving loyalty programs attempt to proactively reward customers to influence future purchasing behavior and motivate higher and sustained spending levels.

- **Reward types.** Companies should look beyond just offering tangible rewards and include intangible and experiential rewards for their customers, in addition to the traditional rewards. This is done to influence the attitudinal aspects of customer behavior that might not be covered by the traditional tangible rewards.

- **Program objectives.** Traditionally, loyalty programs sought to increase revenue and build market share. But these efforts might not result in a proportional increase in profitability. Also, the traditional programs were tuned to influence behavioral loyalty alone and were implemented at the aggregate level. In contrast, the evolving loyalty programs have shifted to accommodate the multiple goals of linking loyalty to profitability and cultivating attitudinal loyalty. Also, firms try to influence certain aspects of customer behavior by using the customer behavior data.

- **Metrics used.** As highlighted in previous sections, one of the crucial aspects of the new dominant logic is to have a forward-looking approach and to reward customers proactively to influence their future purchasing behavior. A forward-looking metric such as CLV enables managers to implement such loyalty programs in an efficient manner. The CLV metric, apart from taking into account the profitability of the customer, also helps in allocating marketing expenditure to maximize profit.

- **Technology and analytics usage.** With the advancement in database and information technologies, obtaining and maintaining customer information has become much easier for firms. And technology is poised to play an important role in the future evolution of loyalty programs. With the arrival of cutting-edge technological tools such as radio-frequency ID (RFID) and smart cards, the accuracy and efficiency of obtaining customer-related information is poised to increase tremendously.

Conclusion

Establishing customer loyalty through loyalty programs and other means is very important for firms because it serves as a means to build relationships with their customers. A fresh approach should be taken when designing and implementing loyalty programs. Programs should be designed to maximize both the behavioral and attitudinal loyalty of customers. Customer segmentation can be used as a powerful tool to implement efficient, well-directed marketing efforts. The framework proposed in this chapter can be used to guide the marketing initiatives that seek to maximize both loyalty and profitability simultaneously. Tier 1 rewards are a great tool to establish customer loyalty across all customers, and Tier 2 programs can be used to sustain loyalty among the more profitable customers. When used judiciously, these tools can yield spectacular results, maximizing profit and ensuring sustained growth of the firm.

Endnotes

[1] Stowe Shoemaker and Robert Lewis, "Customer Loyalty: The Future of Hospitality Marketing," *Hospitality Management* 18 1999: 349.

[2] V. Shankar, A. K. Smith, and A. Rangaswamy, "Customer Satisfaction and Loyalty Online and Offline Environments," eBusiness Research Center Working Paper 02-2000, Penn State University, October 2000.

[3] Frederick F. Reichheld, "The One Number You Need to Grow," *Harvard Business Review* 81(12) 2003: 46–54.

4 V. Kumar and Denish Shah, "Building and Sustaining Profitable Customer Loyalty for the 21st Century," *Journal of Retailing* 80(4) 2004: 317–330.

5 W. J. Reinartz and V. Kumar, "The Mismanagement of Customer Loyalty," *Harvard Business Review* 80(7) 2002: 86.

6 *Ibid.*

7 Carl Shapiro and Hal R. Vivian, *Information Rules* (Boston: Harvard Business School Press, 1998).

8 PR Newswire; Business Wire; Marketing Leadership Council Case Book, September 2001.

7

Optimal Allocation of Resources across Marketing and Communication Strategies

---

Relevant Issues

- Is investing on customers who are easy to acquire a sound strategy?

- Is trying to retain all customers a profitable customer management strategy?

- How do we tailor marketing strategies that accommodate the responsiveness of customers toward different marketing channels?

- How do we optimally allocate marketing and communication resources to maximize Customer Lifetime Value?

Often, managers function under a limited marketing budget and have to make decisions as to where, how, and on whom they are going to spend those resources. Given these limitations, contacting all customers is logistically impossible. Therefore, managers must prioritize their customers and contact only high-priority customers with their product promotions and offers. Several measures are used to prioritize the customers, and managers often fall into the trap of using misleading measures to make such decisions. Mostly,

---

managers target customers who are easy to acquire and retain without considering how profitable these customers are. This is a seriously flawed approach because it could lead to firms using their limited marketing budget to chase unprofitable or low-profit customers while neglecting and ignoring high-profit customers. In a recent study involving a catalog retailer, it was observed that when customers were segmented according to their cost of acquisition and retention, the largest segment (32%) of customers, those who were easy to acquire and retain, accounted for only 20% of the total profit.[1] In contrast, the largest share of profit (40%) came from the smallest group of customers (15%), those who were expensive to acquire but cheap to retain.

As such studies reinforce, a prudent marketing strategy will evaluate customers based on their profitability, not on how easy it is to acquire and retain them. The optimal allocation strategy described in this chapter evaluates customers based on their future profitability and recommends appropriate marketing initiatives. Customers are chosen based on their Customer Lifetime Value (CLV) and future profitability. After the decision as to whom to contact has been made, the next question to be answered is this: How responsive are these customers to various channels of contact (email, telephone, direct mail, and so on), and what is the right mix of these channels?

Before answering these questions, consider this scenario: A customer walks into a toy store to buy a gift for his young niece's birthday, and while purchasing he gives his contact information to the sales clerk. In the next few months, the customer will be inundated with toy catalogs and promotions. How relevant or efficient is this marketing move, and what effect will this have on the customer? This is a classic case of "over-contacting," in which firms (retail, catalog-based sellers, and so on) send a flood of mostly unwanted information to existing customers without ever analyzing what the customer wants, and without realizing what effect this behavior has on the customer's future purchasing behavior. Actually, such an approach of sending promotional material unrelentingly and at high frequency has been found to alienate existing customers and force them to terminate their relationship with the firm.[2]

Another problem faced by firms when deciding on a marketing strategy is when to stop chasing customers. As discussed in the preceding chapter, some customers are profitable only in the short term and cease to buy from the firm after a few transactions (butterflies). If the firms keep investing in sending promotional material to these customers, it could severely drain the firm's limited marketing resources. In the example cited previously, if the customer who buys a toy for his niece is a butterfly, the firm needs to determine when to stop sending promotional material.

When the firm determines that a customer is likely to be profitable in the future, and in turn decides to contact that customer, the firm must next decide on the most appropriate mode of communication. Should it contact the customer through email, make a promotional telephone call, or should a sales representative contact the customer? If a mix of communication strategies is used, how does the firm extract the most out of every communication effort made by the firm? What is the sensitivity of each customer to these communication efforts?

These are some common issues faced by firms when implementing marketing initiatives. This question of how to optimally allocate the limited marketing resources and generate the greatest impact or maximum "bang for the buck" spent is addressed in this chapter.

Communication Channels

To simplify the approach of optimally allocating resources, the channels of communication used for marketing purposes can be classified into the following modes:

- **Rich modes.** Including face-to-face meetings, trade event meetings, and telephone calls. These modes can be 50 to 100 times or more expensive than standardized modes. Also, communication via these modes may seem like more personal service.

- **Standardized modes.** Including direct mail and email contacts.

Why do we split them into two modes of communication?

- Cost (both in dollar terms and in human capital resources)
- Personalization (speaking with a person versus impersonal communication)

Each of these two modes of communication has significantly different costs associated with it, and different customers have different levels of responsiveness. These factors will dictate the modes of communication managers choose and the frequency of communication.

Type and Frequency of Communication

Rich modes are associated with high costs, and they have to be used sparingly and when the situation warrants it. Rich modes are preferred when there is a high level of uncertainty in the relationship with the customer. Also, rich modes can be very useful in converting transactional customers to relational customers (as discussed in Chapter 2, "Maximizing Profitability"). Standardized modes are the most cost-efficient channels of individual-level communication with the customers. They can be used to identify customers who are interested in the current promotions initiated by the organization. For transactional customers, standardized modes can be used in conjunction with the rich modes to improve the effectiveness of marketing initiatives. For example, direct mail (standardized) can be used along with telephone sales (rich mode) to improve the return on investment. In the case of relational customers, standardized modes can be used to maintain commitment and trust by regularly communicating the relationship benefits to these customers.

The Risk of Overcommunicating

Even though the rich and standardized modes are very effective in communicating with potential and current customers, managers should be careful not to overdo it. It has been shown that overcommunicating with customers can cause a relationship to be dysfunctional. For example, bombarding customers with catalogs and other promotions will lead customers to ignore any further communication from the company and might even lead to a deterioration of the relationship. Also, with regard to using rich modes of communication, it has been shown[3] that the marginal response to a higher level of communication isn't always higher and in some cases could even be negative.

Each additional marketing communication yields only diminishing returns, and even if the customer's relationship with the firm is not deteriorating, managers can achieve a better return on investment (ROI) on their marketing expenditure by investing more wisely across customers. Based on these observations, it can be said that there is an optimal frequency of communicating using the various channels of communication. Too much or too little communication is not effective. Initially, as the number of marketing interventions made by the company increases, the customer's purchase frequency also increases, and it maximizes at a particular point. And, any further communication or marketing investment on that customer will only result in a reduction in the purchasing frequency. Therefore, companies should find this optimal level of communication for each customer and design their promotions accordingly, to maximize profit.

Inter-Contact Time

The inter-contact time between the suppliers and buyers should be maintained at an optimal level. Contact with customers at regular yet sufficiently spaced intervals will help to maintain relationships. But too much communication could harm relationships. Also, the marginal utility of contacting the customer in a short period is low. If too much time elapses between two communications, customers may forget about the company. If too many efforts are made to contact customers in a short period, the customer may ignore any promotions from the company. Once again, companies should find the optimal inter-contact time and contact customers when necessary. The best approach is to evaluate when customers are most likely to buy based on past purchasing behavior and send communications through the appropriate channel to induce them to purchase.

Bidirectional Communication

Bidirectional communication is an important measure of customer involvement. This shows that the customer is willing to maintain relations with the company and that the customer is comfortable using the various channels of communication. It has been shown[4] that higher bidirectional communication is associated with channel structures that are highly relational. In the business-to-consumer (B2C) setting, customer-initiated contacts are predominantly associated with complaints. This is not the case in a business-to-business (B2B) setting, where customers can initiate contact with the suppliers for various reasons:

- If they have new needs that the supplier might be in a position to provide

- If they need the supplier's assistance to conduct training programs

- If the customer is invited to participate in product development sessions

Predominantly, bidirectional communication strengthens the relationship between the customer and the company, increases customer involvement, and increases the interdependence between the customer and the company. These factors indicate that the higher the level of bidirectional communication, the higher the customer's predicted purchase frequency.

Frequency of Web-Based Contacts

Companies need to pay special attention to web-based contacts because they are initiated by customers and show a high degree of customer involvement. There are various advantages to tracking web-based contacts:

- Web-based contacts are the most cost-efficient mode of communication.

- Web-based contacts provide companies with an idea about the customer's relationship orientation.

It has been shown that[5] organizations motivated to improve their transaction efficiency actively participate in web-based initiatives. Therefore, it is clear that the higher the number of web-based contacts from a customer, the higher the customer's predicted purchase frequency.

The Need for an Optimal Allocation Strategy

As you can understand already from this chapter, a company's contact strategy and the frequency and modes of communication significantly affect the customer's predicted purchase frequency. Traditional marketing methods of just inundating customers with product promotions and catalogs will not only prove a drain on the company's limited marketing resources but will also lead to customer alienation. Different channels of communication have different costs associated with them and have to be used at the optimal frequency and time intervals to maximize a customer's purchase frequency.

Resource-Allocation Strategy and CLV Maximization

In the previous chapters, the use of CLV to select the right customers and to manage loyalty and profitability simultaneously was discussed. A forward-looking metric such as CLV can be used to effectively allocate marketing resources to maximize profit. This framework also provides managers a guideline to evaluate the return on marketing investments; they can identify the optimal channels and frequency of communication for each customer to maximize CLV. A detailed resource-allocation guideline can be generated by following this framework: the number of contacts to be made through each communication channel and the frequency and inter-contact time that should be followed for each customer to maximize his/her CLV. The following factors influence resource-allocation decisions:

- Cost involved in communicating through a particular channel
- Customer's response when contacted through a particular channel

- Frequency of communication

- Customer contact levels across different channels

- Expected profit level from each customer

All these factors are balanced and optimized to generate a comprehensive resource-allocation strategy that can be used to maximize the CLV of a customer.

By linking all resource-allocation decisions to the CLV of the customer, managers can be well prepared for projected transitions and changes in the customer purchasing behavior. For example, a customer's/supplier's transition through the various stages of the life cycle (exploration, evaluation, maturity, and decline) can be accommodated by evaluating their CLV; in turn, this will help to optimize resource allocation.

To illustrate how resource optimization is operationalized using the CLV model presented in Chapter 3, "Customer Selection Metrics," we need to focus on the marketing cost part of the model. The original CLV equation is as follows:

$$CLV_{it} = \sum_{t=1}^{T_i} \frac{GC_{i,t}}{(1+r)^{1/frequency_i}} - \sum_{l=1}^{n} \frac{\sum_m MC_{i,m,l}}{(1+r)^l} \qquad \text{Equation 7.1}$$

The second half of the equation represents the marketing cost to the firm, where $MC_{i,m,l} = c_{i,m,l}$ (unit marketing cost) * $x_{i,m,l}$ (number of contacts). For example, if a firm wants to optimize its marketing contact strategy to maximize profits from each customer, it has to consider how many contact channels (m) it has and how many times it wants to contact each customer in each channel (x_m).

Suppose a firm has two contact channels: email and direct mail. Each customer will likely respond differently to different types and amounts of communication. For example, one customer might be most responsive if contacted three times through email and one time through direct mail. However, another customer might be most responsive if contacted one time via email and five times through direct mail. To determine the optimal contact strategy from this model, you have to follow these steps:

1. Calculate each customer's CLV based on the technique described in Chapter 3.

2. When you understand the relationships (coefficients) that affect the customer's frequency of purchase and gross contribution margin per purchase, you can fix the weights (coefficients) of the CLV objective function and optimize the number of contacts in each channel to maximize each customer's CLV.

The problem with the optimization is that it is complex due to the fact that each of the models is potentially nonlinear in nature. However, there are methods such as genetic algorithms that can determine the optimal marketing contacts per channel per customer.[6]

A practical demonstration of how the resource-allocation strategy can be practiced is provided here. Figure 7.1 shows a schematic representation of the recommended approach.

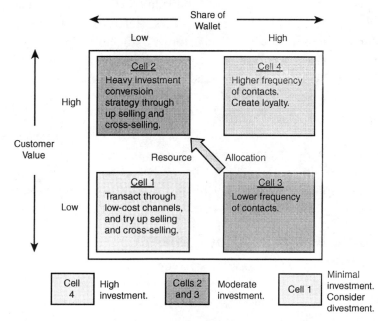

Figure 7.1 Optimal resource-allocation strategy

Here, the customers are segmented based on their Share of Wallet (SOW) and their value to the firm, and appropriate strategies are recommended to manage different types of customers. SOW by itself is not an effective metric to measure and manage customer loyalty and profitability. But by using SOW and CLV to categorize customers, several of these shortcomings can be overcome. For instance, SOW takes into account only the *share* of the customer's wallet, not the *size* of the wallet. Also, it only considers historical spending by the customers in calculating their value to the firm. By combining it with CLV, however, firms can effectively categorize customers based on their loyalty and profitability, and thus an effective resource-allocation strategy can be formulated. Also, by using CLV (which includes the future spending potential of customers), managers can ensure a higher return on their marketing investments.

In the matrix in Figure 7.1, customers in Cell 1 have a low SOW and a low customer value. They are of little value to the firm, and managers should refrain from investing in these customers to avoid loss. Customers in Cell 2 have a high customer value and a low SOW. Firms should adopt a conversion strategy in this case, and should invest in upgrading and cross-selling products to these customers. Customers in Cell 3 have a very high SOW but exhibit low customer value. Firms should shift resources from Cell 3 to Cell 2 with the goal of increasing the SOW of the customers in Cell 2. Customers in Cell 4 have a high SOW and a high customer value. They should be the main targets for customer loyalty programs, and firms should heavily invest in these customers to maintain their loyalty and maximize the profitability.

Optimal Resource Allocation: A Case Study

This optimal resource-allocation strategy was applied to a B2B technology firm, and the results demonstrate the efficacy of this strategy. Traditionally, the customers were categorized based on their SOW. To implement the optimal allocation strategy, a CLV-based framework was used, and customers were further classified based on their CLV. Hence, the customers in the B2B firm were segmented into four sections based on their SOW and CLV (as shown in Figure 7.1). For each segment, detailed recommendations were made as to the optimal use of face-to-face meetings, direct-mail contacts, telesales, and so on. Figure 7.2 summarizes the results of these recommendations; the original level of profitability and marketing spending of each segment is given along with the results generated by switching to an optimal allocation strategy, as recommended in this book.

	Low SOW	High SOW
High CLV	Cost Reduction($): Cell 1 Current spending: $1,008 Optimal spending limit: $2,197 Face-to-Face Meetings: Current frequency: once every 7 months Optimal frequency: once every 5 months Direct Mail/Telesales: Current interval: 6 days Optimal interval: 2 days Profits: Current profit: $109,364 Optimal profit : $178,092	Cost Reduction($): Cell 2 Current spending: $1,385 Optimal spending limit: $2,419 Face-to-Face Meetings: Current frequency: once every 3 months Optimal frequency: once every 1 month Direct Mail/Telesales: Current interval: 6 days Optimal interval: 5 days Profits: Current profit: $534,888 Optimal profit : $905,224
Low CLV	Cost Reduction($): Cell 3 Current spending: $819 Optimal spending limit: $433 Face-to-Face Meetings: Current frequency: once every 5 months Optimal frequency: once every 13 months Direct Mail/Telesales: Current interval: 10 days Optimal interval: 13 days Profits: Current profit: $7,435 Optimal profit: $12,030	Cost Reduction($): Cell 4 Current spending: $1,291 Optimal spending limit: $612 Face-to-Face Meetings: Current frequency: once every 2 months Optimal frequency: once every 10 months Direct Mail/Telesales: Current interval: 8 days Optimal interval: 8 days Profits: Current profit: $10,913 Optimal profit: $28,354

Figure 7.2   Optimal resource-allocation strategy for a B2B technology firm

As you can see from the results, the B2B firm was consistently overspending on the low-CLV customers (Cell 3 and 4 in Figure 7.2). This is a classic example of how firms pursue low-value customers and spend their valuable marketing resources on them. Particularly, the firm was using the expensive face-to-face channel of contact frequently, thus increasing the marketing spending dramatically. (This approach could be justified if they are high-CLV customers.) By adopting a

CLV-based approach, the firm reduced spending by half, while increasing profits by more than 200% for these customers. Specifically, the face-to-face contacts for customers in Cell 3 were reduced to once in 13 months rather than once in 5 months (the original frequency), and a similar measure was adopted for customers in Cell 4.

The firm was consistently underspending on the high-CLV customers (as represented in Cells 1 and 2 in Figure 7.2). This prevented the firm from fully exploiting the profit potential of these high-CLV customers. Based on the firm's new CLV-based approach, it decided to implement a comprehensive strategy that involved almost doubling the marketing spending on these customers by contacting them more frequently (both using face-to-face contacts and direct mail/telesales). These measures unlocked the true potential of these high-value customers and resulted in a tremendous increase in profit from them.

By implementing this CLV-based strategy of reallocating the marketing resources, the firm generated 100% more revenue. Total profit increased by 70% by adopting optimal frequencies for face-to-face meetings and direct mail/telesales in all four cells. As you can see, by carefully monitoring the purchasing frequency of customers, the interpurchase time, and the contribution toward profit, managers can determine the frequency of marketing initiatives to maximize CLV.

Conclusion

This optimal allocation strategy provides a comprehensive CLV-based framework to design an effective marketing strategy. This strategy suggests which customers to acquire and retain based on their predicted CLV. Detailed recommendations are made as to how to use the different channels of communication based on how responsive each customer is to these channels. And an optimal level of communication across the right mix of channels is recommended to achieve maximum profitability. As demonstrated in the case study involving a B2B firm, firms can increase profitability significantly by adopting an optimal resource-allocation strategy (as discussed further in Chapter 12, "Acquiring Profitable Customers").

Endnotes

[1] J. Thomas, W. Reinartz, and V. Kumar, "Getting the Most out of All Your Customers," *Harvard Business Review* (July-August) 2004: 116-123.

[2] Susan Fournier, Susan Dobscha, and David Glen Mick (1997), "Preventing the Premature Death of Relationship Marketing," *Harvard Business Review* 75 (Jan-Feb): 2–8.

[3] *Ibid.*

[4] Jakki Mohr and John R. Nevin, "Communication Strategies in Marketing Channels: A Theoretical Perspective," *Journal of Marketing* 54 (October) 2001: 36–51.

[5] Rajdeep Grewal, James M. Corner, and Raj Mehta, "An Investigation into the Antecedents of Organizational Participation in Business-to-Business Electronic Markets," *Journal of Marketing* 65 (July) 2001: 17–34.

[6] R. Venkatesan and V. Kumar, "A Customer Lifetime Value Framework for Customer Selections and Resource Allocation Strategy," *Journal of Marketing* 68(4) 2004: 106–125.

8

Pitching the Right Product to the Right Customer at the Right Time

---

Relevant Issues

- How does understanding the purchase sequence of products/services of individual customers help firms structure their marketing strategies?

- What is the next product/service that a customer is likely to buy?

- When is the customer more likely to make the next purchase?

Previous chapters in this book have stressed the need for firms to collect and maintain extensive customer buying behavior databases. These databases can be used to track the purchasing behavior of customers—that is, when and what each customer purchases. When this information is available, the next step is to predict the future purchasing behavior of each customer. Predicting customer behavior is a crucial step in designing an effective marketing strategy. These predictions enable managers to not only target the customers who are most likely to make a purchase, but also to pitch the right product. Making the right marketing decision will help managers avoid those customers who are unlikely to follow through and enable them to spend their limited marketing resources on customers who are most likely to purchase something. Also, the predictions help firms avoid alienating customers by inundating them with unwanted or inappropriate promotions and offers. The benefits derived by reducing the mailing and other marketing costs more than compensate for the cost of customizing the promotions sent out, thus ensuring a higher return on investment (ROI) from the marketing budget.

The preceding chapter outlined several strategies that firms can use to optimally allocate resources across various communication channels. After the channel mix and the frequency of communication have been decided upon, the next step is to figure out what message is to be delivered by understanding what the customer is most likely to buy and when.

What Companies Have Been Doing

Companies have been using various strategies to contact customers with their messages and product promotions. One of the most common strategies is mass marketing to all their customers without discrimination. This strategy, apart from draining the company's marketing resources, could also lead to customer alienation. The second strategy followed is to use choice models at the product level; that is, firms find out which product a customer is going to buy next and pitch those products. The disadvantage of this method is that the company could be pitching the right product, but the timing of the message might be completely off track, and therefore have no effect on the customer. The third method used by companies is to use timing models at the product level. In this case, managers know when the customer is going to make a purchase and pitch all the relevant offers at that predicted purchase time. The limitation of this strategy is that customers will receive a lot of special offers to buy products, which might turn them off (and thus again minimize the effect of the marketing message). *The most effective strategy is to predict what product a customer is going to buy and when and approach him with a customized offer or promotion for all the products/services he is likely to buy.*

Various approaches have been suggested to effectively solve this problem. One method that has been used is to build a *timing model* for each product offered by the company and make a prediction as to when the customer is likely to purchase that particular product.[1] By adopting this method, firms can minimize poorly targeted cross-selling initiatives and predict the customer's next purchase choice. Another method to implement a *cross-selling strategy* in a financial services firm was recently suggested.[2] This study used an advanced model to study how customer demand for multiple products evolves over time and how it affects the purchasing patterns and its applications in a financial services firm.[3] However, the method suggested in this chapter is more efficient and flexible in predicting customer behavior and takes into account the context of product offerings, such as the nature of the industry, frequency of purchase, and so on. In this methodology, the timing of a customer's next purchase is predicted first, and given this information, the product most likely to be purchased by the customer is identified. This method allows managers to more accurately predict customer behavior and pitch the right products to the right customers at the right time. The following sections discuss this strategy in detail.

The Question of "What Next?"

All businesses face the dilemma of predicting what their customers will purchase next. Consider the example of a financial services firm that offers a range of services ranging from banking to credit card services to retirement planning and mortgages. If a customer opens a savings and checking account with the firm in the first quarter, can the firm predict the services the customer might need in the following quarters? Will the customer need a mortgage, or should the bank approach him with a credit card offer? Or, does the customer need a retirement plan? Figure 8.1 illustrates this problem. If the firm can predict this, it can customize its message and offer the customer products/services needed and increase its sales. Even though making this prediction seems like a tough call, it is possible to make a reasonable prediction based on the purchasing history of customers who have similar financial profiles and based on other demographic factors. The following sections discuss in detail how to approach this problem.

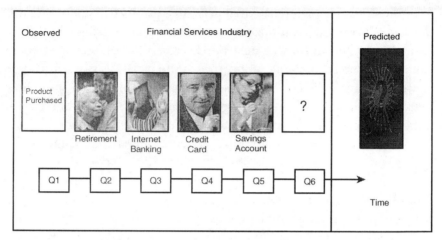

Figure 8.1   Predicting what products/services the customer will buy next

The Accuracy of Current Predictions

Even with extensive information about customer purchasing behavior, companies do a poor job of predicting future customer behavior. A recent study of the purchasing behavior of thousands of customers from two large companies found that predictions about when a customer will buy a particular product were accurate only about 60% of the time (only marginally better than predicting the result of a coin toss).[4] This does not mean that more accurate predictions are not possible. More robust methods are needed to make these predictions, and this chapter identifies those methods and how you can use them to design effective, precisely targeted marketing campaigns that yield great results that help to maximize profit.

Where Companies Falter

To predict customer buying behavior, companies generally follow a two-step approach:

1. Estimate the probability that a customer will choose to purchase a particular product.

2. Estimate the probability that a customer will make a purchase at a particular time.

Many firms stop at the first step, and thereby limit their ability to accurately predict the timing of purchases. However, even those companies that follow the process through might not be successful. In a multi-product firm, it is not easy to accurately predict what product a particular customer is going to buy next. But, from the firm's point of view, this is a valuable piece of information; firms want this information because it can enable them to tailor their message and timing (that is, customize their communication strategy).

Another problem with this traditional approach is that companies assume that the timing of purchase and the product purchased are independent of each other. Often, this is not the case. A customer's decision to buy a particular product influences the timing of the purchase and vice versa. By assuming these two decisions are independent, firms end up with misleading predictions.

Too Small Samples

As mentioned previously, when predicting customer behavior, the timing of the purchase and the product to be purchased must be forecasted. But, firms face a major hurdle, sampling error, for a couple of reasons:

- They rely on a relatively small sample size from which to make their predictions.

- They rely on the same sample of customers to predict the timing of a customer's purchase and the product category to be purchased (often because they have limited information about their customers and have to rely on that information from a small set of customers in their predictions).

To overcome this problem of sampling error, marketing research is turning to a technique called Bayesian estimation. This methodology has been around for more than two decades, but it is just recently becoming a mainstream choice in marketing research due to the constant increases in available computing power and improvements in software applications. Bayesian estimation overcomes this sampling error problem by iteratively calculating the most probable values for the customer behavior data instead of just trying to find a line of "best fit." By doing this, the accuracy of the customer analysis does not suffer by having a small sample size.

An Integrated Approach to Predicting Customer Behavior

In the model presented in this chapter, it is assumed that a customer's decision to buy a particular product is linked to the decision of when to buy it. The purchase sequence is predicted by analyzing the customer's purchasing history and estimating the likelihood of future purchases. This model involves two steps:

1. Estimate the probability that a customer will make a purchase at a particular time.

2. Estimate the probability of a customer purchasing a particular product at the predicted purchase time.

The probabilities in steps 1 and 2 are multiplied to arrive at the final probability. The final probability of a customer purchasing a particular product at a predicted time is then used to devise an ideal contact strategy, as is illustrated in Figure 8.2. To devise an ideal contact strategy, the firm must engage in purchase sequence analysis, as follows:

1. The "right" customer must first be chosen based on his/her Customer Lifetime Value (CLV).

2. After the right customer has been chosen, the firm must predict what product the customer will buy next.

3. Then the firm must predict when the customer is going to buy this product. With this information, the firm can send the promotion through the appropriate channel at the right time (an ideal contact strategy).

In other words, a customer's decisions of what products/services to buy and when can be modeled simultaneously.

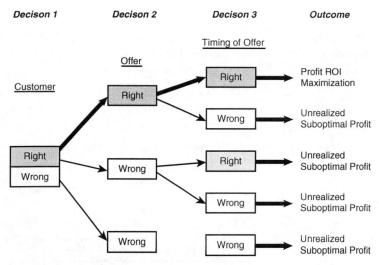

Figure 8.2   Purchase sequence analysis

Estimating the Likelihood of Purchase

To predict the likelihood that a customer will purchase a product during a given period of time, we need to use a likelihood function. The function estimates the likelihood (L_i) that the customer or household (i) will purchase in a given time period. To formulate the likelihood, the first step is to understand the two models at its foundations: a choice model and a timing model. The choice model predicts the probability that a customer will buy a given product. The timing model predicts the probability that a customer will buy a product at a particular time. By estimating the joint probability of the two models simultaneously, the firm can then determine *which* product a customer will buy *when*. The details of the likelihood estimation procedure can be accessed through www.drvkumar.com/mcp.

The Customer Probability Cube

As discussed previously in this chapter, to effectively design marketing initiatives, firms should know what a customer is going to buy and when. To predict this, a customer probability cube is generally used to predict the probabilities of purchase in three dimensions: customers, products, and time. The probability cube shown in Figure 8.3 is for a firm selling four products (P1 through P4), and the probability of the customers (C1 through Cn) buying these products across four quarters (Q1 through Q4) is given. From the numbered cells, you can see that there is a 90% chance that Customer 1 will buy Product 1 in the First Quarter, a 10% chance that he will buy Product 2, a 60% chance of him buying Product 3, and a 20% chance that he will buy Product 4. Firms can use this cube to approach the problem from the product/category side, too. Firms can use the predictions to see which customer is most likely to buy Product 1 in a given quarter and approach that customer with an appropriate message.

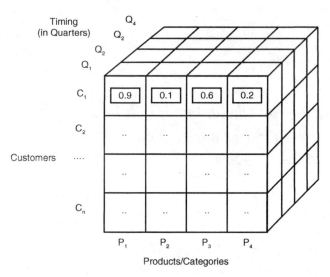

Figure 8.3   The customer probability cube

Source: V. Kumar, R. Venkatesan, and W. J. Reinartz, "Knowing What to Sell, When, and to Whom," *Harvard Business Review*, March 2006: 131–137. Printed with permission from the Harvard Business School Publishing.

Predicting the Next Product/Service: A B2B and B2C Case Study

To prove the merits of this model, we tested it against the marketing initiatives of a large multinational high-tech manufacturer. This firm serves businesses, and its product profile necessitated constant maintenance and frequent upgrades. From the firm's product mix, three different product categories were chosen for this study. Here is a summary of the case study:

- **Current marketing strategy.** Under the status quo marketing strategy, each product category had a dedicated sales force. Salespeople with that force actively pitched products from their respective categories when calling upon customers. Customers were ranked based on the probability of their purchase in that product category, and the timing of contact was left to the discretion of the salespeople. Therefore, a particular customer might be contacted multiple times by salespeople representing different product categories. This approach could lead to an inefficient mechanism whereby customers are contacted irrespective of when they might purchase something.

- **Testing the model.** From among a sample set of 434 business customers, half the customers were assigned to a control group where no changes were made; customers were catered to based on the firm's existing marketing strategy. The other customers were included in the test group and were catered to based on the predictions obtained from the joint-probability model shown previously. Based on this approach, in a given year, customers were contacted only in the quarter in which they were predicted to make a purchase, and by the salespeople from the relevant product category (see Figure 8.4). If a customer was expected to purchase across different product categories, coordinated sales calls were made. In other words, using the model to predict purchasing behavior involves answering the following questions simultaneously:

  - Who is most likely to make a purchase in the next planning cycle?
  - When is a given customer expected to make a purchase?
  - From what product category is the customer likely to purchase?

- **Results of this case study.** Table 8.1 shows the results of this case study. The values represent the increase/decrease in the levels observed during the study. The values in parentheses represent the levels from the preceding year. The model was implemented in four successive quarters, and the results were compared to the results from the respective quarters the preceding year.

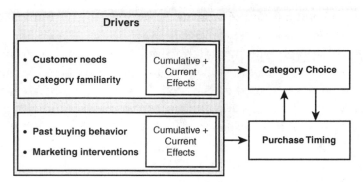

Figure 8.4 Conceptual model to predict customer behavior

Source: V. Kumar, R. Venkatesan, and W. J. Reinartz, "Does Marketing Improve Effectiveness and Efficiency of Sales Campaigns?: Experimental Evidence," 2007, Working Paper, University of Connecticut.

The results shown in Table 8.1 indicate that a significant increase in profit can be realized by predicting the purchasing behavior of customers based on this methodology.

Table 8.1 Results from the B2B Case Study*

	Test Group	Control Group
Revenue ($)	1,463 (12,085)	689 (11,740)
Cost of communication ($)	−1,457 (5,626)	50 (5,052)
Number of contacts before purchase	−3 (10)	1 (12)
Profits ($)	2,735 (6,644)	472 (6,429)
ROI	1.1 (1.1)	0.1 (1.2)

*The reported values have been scaled by an arbitrary constant for confidentiality reasons.
Source: V. Kumar, R. Venkatesan, and W. J. Reinartz, "Does Marketing Improve Effectiveness and Efficiency of Sales Campaigns?: Experimental Evidence," 2007, Working Paper, University of Connecticut.

As you can clearly see from Table 8.1, the joint-probability strategy results in a significant increase in ROI. The results show the following:

- There is a significant increase in the revenue for the test group, whereas no such increase was observed for the control group. This result indicates that the revenue increase was, in fact, due to implementing the joint-probability model.

- There was a significant decrease in the cost of communication for the test group, whereas there was no such reduction observed in the control group. Also, note that there was a significant drop in the number of contacts made by the salespeople for the test group.

- Hence, there is a significant increase in the overall profit and ROI from the customers in the test group. In contrast, no such effect was observed for the customers in the control group.

These results indicate that a significant increase in profit can be realized by predicting the purchasing behavior of customers based on this methodology. Also, the return on the marketing investments improves tremendously. This indicates that this strategy not only allows for effective utilization of marketing resources, but also cuts down on extra marketing expenditure by optimizing the timing of customer contacts; that is, the right customer is contacted at the right time.

How This Model Compares to Traditional Methods

The predictive capabilities of this model were tested in comparison to the traditional methods used to predict customer behavior in a large high-tech firm.[5] When compared to the traditional methods, our model was much more efficient in predicting customer purchasing behavior. These results underscore the effectiveness of our model, in which both the timing of purchase and product purchased are considered jointly. When a customer was predicted via our model to purchase a particular product, he did make a purchase in 85% of the cases. When a comparable prediction was made via the traditional model, the customer made a purchase only 55% of the time. In addition, when our model was used to predict customers who wouldn't make a purchase, 87% of the customers did not make a purchase. As you can see, companies can improve the accuracy of predicting customer behavior by more than 54% by using our model. This shows the effectiveness of the model in predicting customer behavior, a model that can be used to successfully design appropriate marketing strategies.

Increasing the Cross-Sell Ratio: Path to Profitability

One of the main strategies that firms selling multiple products need to adopt is to cross-sell across different product categories. There are several reasons for adopting this strategy. First, when customers are buying from different product categories from the same firm, their propensity to quit the firm is greatly reduced. For example, when a customer is buying telephone, cable, and Internet services from the same company, it becomes a lot more difficult for him to switch firms as compared to a customer who just uses one of the services. Also, the synergy generated by selling products from various categories to the customer strengthens the customer's relationship with the firm and increases profitability.

Firms typically have product portfolios across different product categories. By accurately predicting customer behavior and pitching the right product to the right customer at the right time, firms can increase the cross-sell ratio and at the same time reduce marketing costs. Consider the example of a personal financial services firm that offers various products and services in personal finance, banking, investments, insurance, credit card, and so on. The firm has to predict the behavior of its customers to decide what to offer them in the future. For example, if a customer opens a checking account in the first quarter and applies for a loan in the third quarter, what is the customer most likely to need in the first quarter of the next year? Figure 8.5 shows how firms can approach this problem. Customers are rank ordered based on their likelihood to purchase a particular product, and this is done across all product categories. In Figure 8.5, customers are rank ordered in the credit card, loan, and savings account segments, and they are divided into three segments: very likely to make a purchase, likely, and not likely to make a purchase. Then customers in the top segment (very likely) are considered. As shown in Figure 8.5, Customer C is most likely to make a purchase in the next segment in all three product categories considered here. The firm, instead of sending three separate marketing messages to Customer C, should offer all three products at a discounted rate and induce him/her to purchase them as a bulk package. This action, apart from reducing the marketing costs, reduces the propensity for Customer C to quit the firm in the future (because his relationship with the firm will be much stronger). Similarly, Figure 8.5 shows that Customer B is highly likely to purchase in the credit card and the personal loan segment. Hence, the firm should contact Customer B with a combined offer with discounts that would induce him/her to buy both the products at the same time.

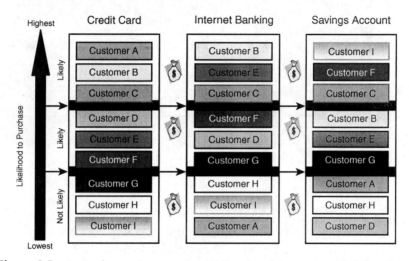

Figure 8.5 Optimal contact strategy in a B2C setting: Customer* rankings based on their likelihood to purchase

Consider a similar example in the B2B setting, where the financial services firm offers services in investment banking, asset-based lending, and global transactions. Figure 8.6 shows the rank ordering of the customers of this firm. Based on their predicted propensity to purchase, ABC Inc is very likely to purchase across all three categories. Therefore, the B2B firm should make a combined pitch that offers a discount for all three products. Similarly, XYZ Corp (per Figure 8.6) is very likely to need investment banking and asset-based lending services, so a combined pitch should be made to XYZ Corp. Such strategies will ensure a reduction in marketing expenditure and increase the lifetime value of the customers.

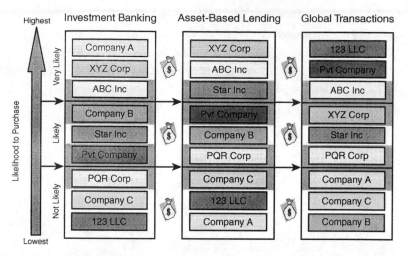

Figure 8.6 Optimal contact strategy in a B2B setting: Customer* rankings based on their likelihood to purchase

The Impact on Profitability

Table 8.2 shows the impact of using our model to design the right marketing initiatives in a high-tech firm and a financial services firm. As you can see, the ROI for the high-tech firm increased significantly, on average about 160%. By implementing our strategy, the high-tech firm's average ROI improved by about 200%. This shows that if the right marketing strategy is used to communicate the right messages to the right customers at the right time, firms can maximize profit. Also note in Table 8.2 the simultaneous reduction in the level of communication: a 31% reduction for the high-tech firm, and a 26% reduction for the financial services firm.

Table 8.2 Improvement in ROI and the Change in the Level of Communication

	Increase in ROI (%)	Change in the Level of Communication (%)
High-tech company	160	−31
Financial services firm	200	−26

Table 8.3 shows the effect of cross-selling on the revenue, profit, and ROI of the high-tech company (B2B) and the financial services firm (B2C). The numbers in the table reflect the difference between the various metrics across the test and the control groups, when they were pitched as individual products or product pairs or other combination of product offerings. Some customers were more likely to buy single products, and individual products were pitched to them. For those who were more likely to buy multiple products, appropriate product combinations were offered. For example, in the case of the high-tech company, some customers come to the company just for their software needs or hardware needs. Others look to the firm to satisfy both software and hardware needs, and for them a combination of products was offered. In the case of the financial services firm, some customers just need loans or insurance or investment services. Others need all three or a combination of products. By following this strategy, accurate predictions were made in this regard, and multiple combinations of products were offered at the same time if appropriate. As you can see from Table 8.3, cross-selling significantly increases all three given measures (revenue, profit, ROI). The increases registered in the return on marketing investment demonstrate the cost savings that firms can realize by adopting this strategy. Also, this table shows how firms can maximize profit by cross-selling and pitching the right product to the right customer at the right time.

Table 8.3   Effects of Cross-Selling

	Buyer Of	Revenue ($)	Profit ($)	ROI
High-tech firm	Product 1	605	1,649	1.5
	Product 2	306	1,897	1.6
	Products 1, 2	198	1,273	1.7
Financial services firm	Product 1	208	591	1.8
	Product 2	247	428	1.7
	Product 3	182	397	1.8
	Products 1, 2, 3	164	402	2.1

Conclusion

Accurately predicting which customer is going to buy what and when could be the motor that drives a company's marketing initiatives. The guiding principle in implementing this strategy is straightforward: Understand customers' needs and give them more of what they want. Choose whom you contact, and customize the promotions according to the individual customer's needs. Avoid inundating customers with irrelevant promotions and offers that might only alienate them and destroy their relationship with the firm.

Endnotes

1. A. Knott, A. Hayes, and S. A. Neslin, "Next-Product-to-Buy Models for Cross-Selling Applications," *Journal of Interactive Marketing* 16(3) 2002: 59–75.

2. S. Li, B. Sun, and R. T. Wilcox, "Cross-Selling Sequentially Ordered Products: An Application to Consumer Banking Services," *Journal of Marketing Research* 42 2005: 233–239.

3. *Ibid.*

4. V. Kumar, R. Venkatesan, and W. J. Reinartz (2006), "Knowing What to Sell, When, and to Whom," *Harvard Business Review,* March 2006: 131–137.

5. *Ibid.*

9

Preventing Attrition of Customers

Relevant Issues

- What is the impact of attrition on the firm's business?
- Who is likely to defect and when?
- When should we intervene?
- How much should we spend on preventing attrition?
- Which products should we offer, and which channel should we use to communicate the intervention offer?

Customer attrition has become a critical concern for many industries, such as telecommunication, retail banking, and insurance. With increased competition, a customer has many more choices of products and services from a number of firms. Coupled with increased choices for consumers, firms are constantly trying to acquire high-value customers from their competitors. As a result, firms find it difficult to retain customers as they easily move from one firm to the other (that is, defect). According to a 2003 report published by Celent,[1] the customer attrition rates in retail banking in the United States and Canada are several times greater than those in the United Kingdom. Even in the United Kingdom, the churn rates have gone up to more than 17% in 2005 compared to less than 10% in 2003.

Customer attrition, also known as customer *churn* or defection, is the loss of customers. The rate of churn is the rate of customer loss in a given period, such as monthly or yearly. Depending on the nature of the business, the customer loss can be considered *lost-for-good* or *always-a-share*. Consider two scenarios. In scenario 1, a customer bought a laptop from Dell Inc. six months ago (his first-ever purchase with Dell, and no purchases since then). Dell finds it difficult to know whether it has lost this customer or whether the customer just hasn't yet required a product that Dell offers. The customer might also buy other products from other laptop marketers, such as Apple, and then come back to Dell for another purchase (perhaps a desktop). This is called an *always-a-share* scenario; a customer shares his/her purchase wallet with more than one firm. Always-a-share scenarios are most likely in noncontractual settings, where a customer can move from one firm to another without breaking contractual obligations.

In another scenario, a wireless phone subscriber has terminated his contract or did not renew the contract. In this case, the firm is almost certain that this customer has defected and that the only way to get him back is to win him back. This is called a *lost-for-good* scenario. Such a scenario occurs most frequently in contractual settings, such as subscription-based businesses, where customers incur a switching cost when they defect. Because the churn event can be easily identified from a firm's data, it is easier to intervene in a contractual setting to prevent customer attrition.

Even in a noncontractual setting, a firm can intervene to prevent customer attrition or a reduction in the revenue contribution from the customer. For example, in a retail setting, firms usually have information about how often customers purchase and the average amount that they spend with the firm. From this data, the firm can model the *inter-purchase time* (IPT) for its customers using appropriate statistical methods. The firm can then use the estimated IPT as a benchmark to predict whether a customer is likely to defect. For instance, if the estimated IPT for a customer is four months, and the customer has not made a purchase for five months, the firm knows from this information the customer is likely to defect. Similarly, the firm can also model the purchase amount for each customer based on past transactions and customer characteristics. If a customer's purchase amount has dropped significantly compared to the estimated purchase amount, this reduction might indicate that the customer has reduced his/her Share of

Wallet (SOW) with the firm. The firm should then develop an intervention strategy for the customer depending on the worth of the customer (as explained later in this chapter).

Impact of Attrition

Customer attrition impacts a firm in several ways. One direct impact is the loss of revenue from the customers who have defected. The extent of revenue loss depends on the level of service commitments the customer had with the service provider. The higher the expected revenue from the customer, the more the impact on the firm. Closely related to this expected revenue loss is the lost opportunity for the firm to recover the acquisition cost incurred on the customer. It is a usual practice in many service industries to offer incentives to new customers. Because of competitive pressures, the cost of the incentives offered, coupled with other acquisition costs, is so high that it sometime takes several months to break even. According to J.D. Power & Associates, the cost of acquiring a new customer in the U.S. wireless service industry is $375 to $475, and providers must retain them for more than four years to break even.[1] This breakeven point is several months beyond the contractual period, which is usually one to two years. If a wireless phone customer quits the service provider after completing a one-year contract, the company will not have recovered a major portion of the acquisition cost. Therefore, any customer lost in the initial period will cost more in terms of irrecoverable acquisition costs.

Further, the firm also loses the opportunity to up-sell/cross-sell to customers who have defected, and this loss can be treated as a loss of potential revenue. In addition to the previously mentioned direct financial loss, there are some "lost" social effects. For instance, had the customer continued with the company, his/her use of the products/services of the firm in public would have influenced others to adopt those products/services. Also, the negative word-of-mouth from the customer who defected might discourage many prospects from buying products/services from the firm.

Whereas the previously discussed costs are associated with the value of lost customers, firms must also invest additional resources to replace those lost customers with new customers. As mentioned previously, acquiring new customers costs much more than the average revenue a customer brings to a firm in the initial period. This drains the firm's resources, which are already impacted by the loss of customers. As you can see, customer attrition impacts both the inflow and outflow of cash adversely.

Because of its significant impact on firms' resources and their performance, if measures are not taken to reduce customer attrition, customer churn can ruin a company. Many firms have realized the importance of controlling the churn and have adopted or are in the process of adopting analytic tools to predict and prevent attrition.

Case Study: Telecommunication Industry

A telecommunication firm offers the following services: local telephone, long-distance telephone, wireless phone, and Internet. Under each of these service categories, the firm offers a variety of options. With wireless phone services, for instance, customers can subscribe (for an additional monthly fee) to a family plan, additional phones, text messaging, and wireless Internet access. Similarly, with Internet services, the firm offers packages with different download speeds, such as 1.5Mbps, 3Mbps, and 15Mbps. Figure 9.1 shows the complete product line and the options available within each line.

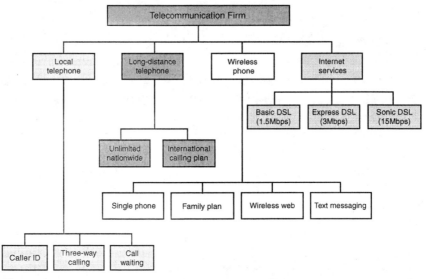

Figure 9.1   Services offered by a telecommunication firm

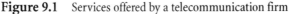

Customer Don has subscribed for local and long-distance telephone services. The firm has observed from the recent bills that Don's number of long-distance calls has dropped significantly. In addition, a local cable operator is running an attractive promotion for three services as a package: telephone, television, and Internet. The firm has started losing some of its customers to the competitor. It is wondering whether it should intervene to prevent customer attrition. However, the critical question that the firm is facing is this: Who is likely to quit and when?

Preventing Attrition

Many firms in the telecommunication industry are facing similar situations every day. As the competition has intensified, they find that their customers are vulnerable and are likely to defect. Because customer churn has a tremendous impact on the firm's performance, it is critical for the firms to develop a successful strategy to prevent attrition. The important questions that need to be answered before developing this strategy include the following:

- How do we identify the customers who are likely to defect?
- When are they likely to defect? Or, can we predict the time of churn for each customer?
- Should we intervene?
- When should we intervene?
- How much should we spend to avoid the attrition of a particular customer?

Answers to these questions will help firms to develop an effective intervention strategy to prevent attrition and to improve the firm's performance. In this chapter, we discuss the answers to each of these questions.

Predicting Churn

Identifying customers who are likely to defect and their expected time of attrition is the first step in developing the intervention strategy. There are two components to predicting the churn. One is to know the customers who are likely to defect. A simple solution for this problem is to identify the characteristics of customers who have defected in the past and identify customers who have matching profiles to this group. However, we also need to know when they are likely to defect. Most of the models to predict churn can answer both these questions by building a propensity-to-quit model. These models give us the probability of a customer quitting at a particular point in time.

There are two approaches in treating customer defection: the *lost-for-good* approach and the *always-a-share* approach. Figures 9.2A and 9.2B show the difference between these approaches.

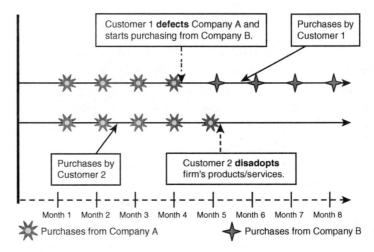

Figure 9.2A   Lost-for-good approach

The lost-for-good approach treats customer defection as permanent. As mentioned previously, this is a scenario we find in subscription-based businesses. When a customer terminates a subscription or service, it is unlikely that the customer will come back to the firm. Either the customer has gone to a competitor or has stopped using that particular service (that is, disadoption of a product category). For instance, a customer of dial-up Internet service might discontinue the dial-up service and start using broadband. Such a customer is unlikely to come back to a service provider that does not offer broadband. In this case, he/she disadopts dial-up service. In Figure 9.2A, Firm A loses Customer 1 to Firm B, whereas Customer 2 did not go to any other firm, but discontinued use of the particular product or service offered by Firm A. In both these cases, what is important for developing an intervention strategy is to predict the time of defection for each customer, even though the scope of intervention in the case of Customer 2 is limited. Even in the case of customer disadoption of a service, a firm can intervene by offering the service the customer wants. For instance, AOL realized that many of its customers were disadopting its dial-up services to contract for broadband services. AOL's strategy became to first retain customers who disadopt dial-up services by offering its broadband services through partnerships it holds with BellSouth, Quest Communications, and AT&T.[2] AOL also offers premium packages such as Privacy Wall, Premium Computer Check Up, and backup dial-up access to customers who have subscribed to other broadband service providers. Such premium packages help AOL to compensate for the loss of profit from its dial-up services.

On the other hand, an always-a-share approach considers customers' switching to competitors as transient. In the earlier example of a customer switching between Dell and Apple, the customer continues to transact with both Dell and Apple. Hence, neither Dell nor Apple completely loses the customer, but they lose/gain a share of the customer's purchase, as shown in Figure 9.2B.

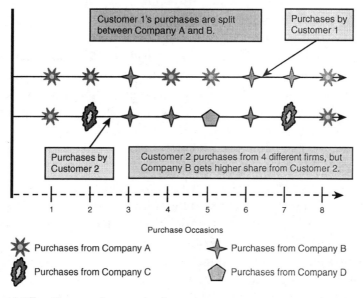

Figure 9.2B Always-a-share approach

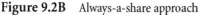

Both Customer 1 and Customer 2 transact with more than one firm. However, their share is split unevenly among different firms. There is no specific time of attrition in such cases. Many consumer goods purchases fall in this category. In this approach, what is modeled is not the time of defection, but customers' transition probabilities associated with each firm or brand. Migration or Markov models are usually used to estimate transition probabilities of customers.

Popular Churn Models

In the lost-for-good approach, the model predicts the probability of a customer defecting. Among many models that can predict the probability of customer defection, two statistical models are commonly used to predict churn in the lost-for-good scenario: logistic regression and hazard models. Even in an always-a-share scenario, firms can effectively use logistic regression to predict the upward or downward migration of customers, as explained later in this chapter.

Logistic Regression

Logistic regression is a form of a regression model in which the dependent variable is binary and assumes only two discrete values (zero or one). In a customer churn model, the dependent variable is whether a customer quits during a particular period. That is, if a customer quits, the value of the dependent variable is one; otherwise, it is zero. The independent variables of the model usually fall into four categories: transaction-based characteristics (or exchange characteristics), customer characteristics, product characteristics, and marketing effort by the firm. Some of the key exchange characteristics used in a churn model are time from the first purchase (duration), time from the last purchase (recency), number of product categories purchased (cross-buy), number of products purchased from each category (focused buying), average IPT or purchase frequency, and average revenue. The customer characteristics usually consist of demographic variables such as income, age, and education. The important product characteristics are the type of products and the current ownership of certain products. The marketing effort that plays a key role in predicting churn includes the number of marketing communications and the contact channels (such as email, telephone, and face to face) used to communicate to the customer.

The firm uses the transactions data and the marketing communication data for a particular duration (for example, for three years) to build the model. This sample data is called the *calibration sample*. The firm also sets aside similar data for a shorter period (for example, one year) to test whether the model estimates obtained using the calibration sample hold good for a different sample. This sample is called the *validation sample*. Both calibration and validation data contain information about whether a customer has quit during this observation period, which gives the values of the dependent variable. This data also has information pertaining to the exchange characteristics, customer characteristics, product characteristics, and marketing communication (that is, all independent variables) corresponding to each value of the dependent variable. The logistic regression model can then be built using the calibration sample to obtain the parameter estimates. In simple terms, logistic regression identifies a set of independent variables that are likely to influence the value of the dependent variable and the weights associated with each independent variable (that is, coefficients that tell us the extent to which each independent variable affects the dependent variable). After the relevant variables and their coefficients have been identified using calibration data, the firm can then predict the value of the dependent variable for all observations in the validation data and compare these values to the actual data. If the model fits the validation data, the firm can predict the values of the dependent variable for future time periods. All the predicted values of the dependent variable in a logistic regression are between zero and one. These predicted values are treated as probability of defection or the propensity of a customer to quit.

Hazard Models

Hazard models used in the analysis of failure time (or time to the occurrence of an event) are built based on the survivor and hazard functions. Even though hazard models were initially developed in the field of biomedical sciences to study the effectiveness of certain treatments on the lifetime of individuals, they are widely used in different fields to study the time of occurrence of particular events. (The events may be failure of machinery or a customer making a purchase, depending on the situations.) Survivor function is the probability of an individual surviving (without the event occurring) until a particular time (t). In the context of product purchase, it is the probability of a customer not making a purchase. (In this case, the event is making a purchase.) Hazard function, on the other hand, specifies the instantaneous rate of failure at time t given that the individual survives until t. In the context of churn, given that a customer has not quit until a particular time period, the probability of him/her defecting from the firm in the immediate time period can be treated as the hazard rate or hazard function. One advantage of a hazard model is that it treats the cases where the event has not occurred as censored observations. For instance, in the sample used for estimating the model, 20 customers have not defected, and the remaining 80 defected during the observation time period. The hazard model treats those 20 observations as censored and includes in the model only the survivor function for these customers because the event has not occurred until now. For the remaining 80 customers, the model includes both the survival and the hazard functions. When a model such as logistic regression is used, 20 customers in the sample are treated as nondefectors and the remaining 80 as defectors. Such a treatment ignores the fact that some of these nondefectors would have defected had the time window been larger.

Although there are a number of different methods for estimating hazard models, one of the most commonly used models is the proportional hazard model. In this model, a baseline hazard rate gives us the shape of the hazard curve. The shape of the hazard curve shows how the probability of defecting for an average customer of the firm increases/decreases or stays constant over time. The model also includes the exchange characteristics, customer characteristics, product characteristics, and marketing communication variables. The effect of these variables is to shift the baseline hazard function up or down. This is like multiplying the baseline hazard by a factor, as can be seen in the following expression for the proportional hazard model:

The probability of a customer defecting in the immediate time period given that he/she has not defected until now (or until time t) = baseline probability × impact factor

Baseline probability can be considered as the probability of a customer who is not influenced by any of the variables defecting in the immediate time period given that he/she has not defected until time t. The effect of all customer-specific variables is captured in the second part of the equation: impact factor. The impact factor shifts the baseline probability upward or downward depending on whether the impact factor is greater than one or less than one (but greater than zero). Thus, the product of baseline hazard rate and the effect of customer-specific variables (that is, the impact factor) for a customer is the hazard rate for that customer. Therefore, when we estimate how each of the variables affects the value of the impact factor and the baseline hazard rate, we can predict the probability of a customer defecting at a particular time period. The details on the estimation of hazard models can be accessed through www.drvkumar.com/mcp.

Both logistic regression and the hazard model can be effectively used to predict the probability of a customer defecting or his/her propensity to quit. However, the way we use each of these models to predict attrition probability differs. If a telecommunication firm wants to predict the propensity to quit for all its customers in the next 12 months (for instance, from January to December) and it wants to use logistic regression, and if the model is built using time-varying variables with a time lag up to 1 month, the firm will first use the model to predict which customers are likely to quit (that is, probability of defection > 0.5) by the end of January. Then, the firm can decide whether it wants to intervene. A similar exercise needs to be done for every month to predict those likely to quit by the end of the month. The main disadvantage in this case is that it is difficult to predict customers' propensity to quit beyond one month (or the time lag allowed in the model). This means the firm has less than one month to intervene. In contrast, when a proportional hazard model is used, the firm can predict when a customer is likely to quit based on the shape of the survival curve and customer-specific variables. This means the firm has more time to intervene.

Logistic regression can also be used effectively to model the upward or downward migration of a customer in an always-a-share scenario. The first step in modeling migration is computing the Customer Lifetime Value (CLV) of every customer and grouping the customers into deciles based on their CLV. Customers in the two deciles can be classified as high value (high CLV), those in the bottom three deciles as low value (low CLV), and the remaining as medium value (CLV neither very high nor very low). This exercise is done for the subsequent year. Comparing the group to which a customer belongs in two consecutive years, we can see whether he/she has migrated upward or downward. For instance, if a customer in the high-value group in the first year has moved to either the medium-value or low-value group in the second year, the migration of that customer is downward. A customer who moves from the medium-value group or low-value group to the high-value group is migrating upward. A logistic regression model can be used to identify the factors influencing the upward/downward migration of customers. The dependent variable in a downward migration model is whether a customer has migrated down to a lower value group. The independent variables are the customer-specific variables, as mentioned previously. Using the estimated coefficients of the model, the firm can predict which customers are likely to migrate downward and when. Then, the firm can decide whether it needs to intervene.

Statistical Issues in Modeling

In the logistic and hazard models previously discussed, the coefficients for each of the covariates (exchange variables, product characteristics, customer characteristics, and marketing communication variables) do not vary for each customer. This means that these models do not account for *heterogeneity* among customers. In other words, the under-lying assumption is that the impact of the covariates on churn is the same for all customers in the data. This might not be true. For instance, a price-sensitive customer might react to an increase in product price more adversely than a customer who is less price sensitive. Therefore, a price-sensitive customer should have a bigger (in magnitude) coeffi-cient for price than a less price-sensitive customer. Similarly, customers might react differently to marketing communication. Therefore, it is necessary to allow for different coefficients for each customer. Researchers have addressed this issue by using advanced estimation techniques such as Bayesian and Random coefficient methods, both of which allow the coefficients to vary across customers.

Intervention Strategy

After the firm has the probability of defection for each customer, it is easy to decide whom to target for intervention, as shown in Figure 9.3

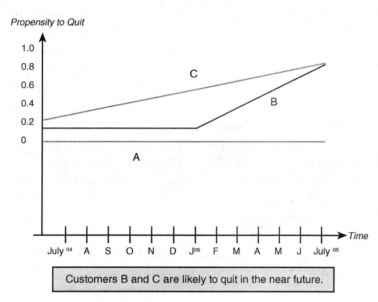

Figure 9.3   Predicting propensity to quit

Figure 9.3 shows the propensity to quit for three customers of the telecommunication firm mentioned in the case study. The propensity to quit of Customer A is 0 for the 12-month forecast period. Customer B's propensity to quit is 0.2 in the first 6 months, but thereafter it increases steadily until it reaches 0.8 in the twelfth month. In contrast, for Customer C, the propensity to quit increases continuously and reaches close to 0.8 at the end of the forecast period. Here, clearly, the firm is not at risk of losing Customer A. However, it is likely to lose Customers B and C if it does not intervene. The time of intervention depends on when their propensity to quit becomes a predetermined value. (Usually it can be taken as at least 0.5.)

Should We Intervene?

When we know *when* a customer is likely to quit, the next important decision is whether we should intervene to prevent attrition of that customer. For instance, should we intervene to prevent attrition of both Customers B and C? The answer to this question depends on whether the customer is worth retaining. This is where CLV plays an important role. As explained in previous chapters, CLV gives us a fair idea of the worth of the customer to the firm, because both the expected revenue contribution from the customer and the cost of serving the customer are taken into account in computation of the CLV. In the context of retention of customers, CLV is the net contribution that a firm can expect from a customer if he is retained. Therefore, any prudent company should spend its resources to retain only those customers who have positive CLVs. If a customer has a negative CLV, the company is spending more to serve the customer than the revenue the customer is generating for the company. For instance, if the cost of maintaining customer records, generating and processing bills, and mailing is $15 a month for a customer who does not use a credit card, the credit card company is spending the resources for this customer without any revenue contribution from the customer (a negative CLV). It does not make sense to retain customers such as these. Therefore, when deciding upon whom the firm should spend resources to retain, the first criteria is that the CLVs of the selected customers should be positive. In the scenario shown in Figure 9.3, if Customer B's CLV is negative, the firm should not be spending its resources to retain that customer.

Whereas the decision might be fairly straightforward in the case of a customer with a negative CLV, it might not be so clear in the case of profitable customers or customers who have positive CLVs. A profitable company might have a large number of customers who have positive CLVs but are likely to defect. In addition, there might be a huge variation in the actual value of their CLVs. Some of them might be high-CLV customers, the others might have low CLVs. Therefore, it doesn't make sense to spend the same amount to retain all customers. The key decision in this case is not whether to retain but when to intervene and how much to spend on each customer. We will first address the question of when to intervene.

Intervention Timing

Suppose both Customers B and C in Figure 9.3 are customers with positive CLVs, and therefore the telecommunication firm decides to spend resources to retain both of them. The time of intervention, however, might not be the same for both, as illustrated in Figure 9.4.

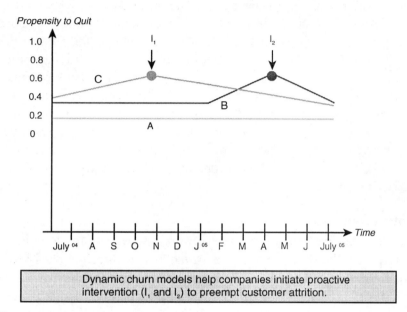

Dynamic churn models help companies initiate proactive intervention (I_1 and I_2) to preempt customer attrition.

Figure 9.4 Proactive intervention strategy

In Figure 9.4, the propensity to quit for Customer C reaches 0.5 in October 04. At that time, Customer B does not show signs of attrition. Therefore, the proactive intervention in October 04 should be targeted to Customer C, not Customer B. This intervention is shown as I_1 in Figure 9.4. An effective proactive intervention will help to regain the customer's confidence and trust in the firm and can reduce the customer's propensity to quit. The intervention strategy I_1 therefore reduces Customer C's propensity to quit, as shown in Figure 9.4. Meanwhile, Customer B's propensity to quit increases and reaches 0.5 in April 05 and becomes the likely target for intervention. The time of intervention should be decided in a similar way for all profitable customers who show a tendency to defect.

In the preceding example, the firm intervenes when the propensity to quit becomes greater than 0.5. This need not be the case for all other firms. Depending on the industry, the response time (or the time needed for decision making) of customers may be longer. Also, in some cases, the propensity to quit may increase at a very high rate. In both these cases, it might be necessary to intervene even before the propensity to quit reaches 0.5 to give more time for customers to respond to an offer. Another challenge in deciding the time of intervention is changing propensities. Some industries are so competitive and volatile that the competitive promotions change frequently. As a result, customers are bombarded with attractive offers from competing firms that make them vulnerable. Therefore, it is critical for firms to constantly update the propensities to quit for their customer base to capture changing propensities, which is the basis for an effective proactive intervention strategy. In other words, the churn models should be dynamic, and the periodicity of updating churn probabilities should be based on industry characteristics.

Intervention Cost

Another key element of the intervention strategy is the amount of resources to be spent on each customer. This is directly linked to the worth of the customers or their lifetime value. Suppose the firm has an intervention strategy in which the cost of intervention (that is, the cost to the firm) is $100 per customer. It does not make business sense to offer this promotion to a customer whose CLV is $50. The firm should instead intervene with an offer that costs less than $50 to the firm. Ideally, firms should design a number of different intervention strategies with varying costs so as to cater to all customers. For instance, the telecommunication firm mentioned in the case study can offer caller ID for three months for free to a low-CLV customer (for example, a customer with only the basic local phone service). On the other hand, the firm can offer a free upgrade to Sonic DSL service for a customer with wireless phone and basic Internet services (or other moderate CLV customers). The simple rule of thumb in deciding the amount to be spent on intervention is that the cost of intervention should not exceed the CLV.

Products to Offer

An intervention strategy is not complete without specifying what products are to be offered. When a firm deals with a number of product/service categories within which there are different options, the important decision the firm has to make is whether the intervention offer should be for additional features in the already subscribed-to service or for additional services. In the case of the telecommunication firm, one of the intervention offers for a customer with basic local telephone services may be adding caller ID at a discounted price. Another offer could be free long-distance calling for three months. Although the first offer is for adding a feature to the existing service, the second offer is for adding a new service. Firms need to decide which of the two options are best for a particular customer, considering customer needs, his/her worth to the company, and the competitive scenario. In another example, a movie rental firm such as Blockbuster can either offer an option of more movies at a time or the convenience of downloading movies directly to a PC/laptop. This is adding a new feature to the subscribed-to service: movie rental. A publishing company such as Time Inc. offering online access for a limited time to *Fortune* to a subscriber of *Time* magazine who shows signs of attrition is an example of offering an additional product/service.

Intervention Channels

When a firm finalizes the cost of intervention and the products to be offered to a customer, it has to decide which contact channel to use to communicate the offer to the customer. Often, this key decision determines how a customer will respond to an intervention offer. The available contact channels often include email, website, telephone, and face to face. The choice of the contact channel depends on the worth of the customer and his/her past response to marketing communications through various channels. Even though email might be cheaper in terms of cost of communication, customers' response rate to email communication may be poorer compared to other channels. If a customer is a high-CLV customer, it is not a good idea to communicate the offer through a channel for which the response rate is low. Instead, the firm should use the telephone or the face-to-face channels. For instance, if a telecommunication firm were likely to lose the business of a large public university, which is one of its largest B2B customers for telephone and broadband services, the best channel for communication is face-to-face contact. At the same time, if the firm is to intervene to prevent attrition of a residential user, it might use email or telephone channels.

Results of Intervention

The telecommunication firm mentioned in the case study adopted the steps mentioned previously to prevent customer attrition. In a pilot study, the firm first computed the propensity to quit for all its customers using three years of transaction and marketing communication data. Then, it created two groups of matched customer pairs who were similar in terms of their propensity to quit and their exchange characteristics, such as their revenue contribution to the firm and duration. In other words, the customers in both groups had the same probability of quitting. The average revenue per customer in both groups was $600 per year. Figure 9.5 shows the design of the study.

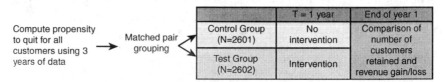

Figure 9.5   Study design (telecommunications firm)

As you can see in Figure 9.5, the study was for a period of one year; at the end of the study period, the performances of both groups were compared. Table 9.1 lists the results of the study.

Table 9.1   Empirical Results (Telecommunications Firm)

	No Intervention	Intervention
Number of customers sampled at the beginning of the study	2,601	2,602
Time period of study	1 year	1 year
Number of customers at the end of the study	1,768	2,412
Number of customers lost	833	190
Number of customers saved	—	643
Revenue gain	—	$385,800
Retention cost	—	$ 40,000
Incremental profit	—	**345,800**

At the beginning of the study, one group had 2,601 customers, and the other had 2,602, as shown in Table 9.1. The first group (2,601 customers) was used as a control group to see the impact of intervention on the other group. For the first group, there was no intervention. For all customers in the second group, however, the firm predicted a propensity to quit and identified those customers who were likely to quit. Based on the CLV of each customer, the firm designed customer-specific intervention strategies for all vulnerable customers. The total cost of intervention (cost to the firm and not the actual value to the customer, which is much higher) was $40,000 for the second group. The number of customers at the end of study period and the revenue contribution from customers during the study were compared to see whether the intervention had any significant impact. The number of customers in the control group at the end of study period was 1,768, indicating a loss of 833 customers in 1 year. The group for which the firm intervened retained 2,412 customers, which means that the number of customers lost was only 190 (compared to 833 in the control group). Considering the fact that both groups were behaviorally the same, the intervention could have saved 643 (833 – 190) customers. By multiplying the number of customers by the average revenue contribution per customer, we get a total revenue gain of $385,800 for the group with which the firm intervened. Therefore, even after taking into account the cost of intervention, the firm had a net revenue gain of $345,800 by preventing attrition, and the return on investment was close to 860% (a revenue contribution that was 8.6 times the investment).

Conclusion

No business can afford to ignore the impact that customer churn can have on the profitability and even the survival of the business. The key to retaining customers is to identify early the customers who are likely to quit and intervene with them to prevent attrition. The churn models discussed in this chapter help to identify the customers who are likely to quit. With that information, firms can take affirmative steps to develop an intervention strategy based on CLV to effectively intervene to retain valuable customers, as shown in the case study.

Endnotes

[1] www.celent.net/PressReleases/20030102/CustomerAttrition.htm

10

Managing Multichannel Shoppers

Relevant Issues

- Should multichannel shopping be encouraged?

- Are multichannel shoppers more profitable?

- How can firms profitably manage customers for multichannel adoption?

In March 2007, Wal-Mart introduced a new program called Site-to-Store, which is an online service that allows customers to choose from a wider variety of products that will be shipped to their local store for free pickup.[1] The goal of this program is to add convenience for the customer, who can now choose from a wider assortment of products (tens of thousands of products in more than 100 categories) without paying any shipping costs. All the customer has to do is order the products online and pick up the products at his or her local Wal-Mart store. Wal-Mart hopes that this program will convince regular shoppers to consider purchasing new products from Wal-Mart that are not usually available in the store, and still come to the local store to purchase items they purchase during regular shopping trips. So, does this program have a chance to mutually benefit Wal-Mart and its customers?

Several recent marketing studies have found that more than 60% of customers not only want to use multiple channels for making purchases,[2] but also more than one-third of customers who regularly buy products already use at least three or more channels to make purchases.[3] Also, because of the arrival of complex distribution systems for various industries and sectors and the growth of web-based sales, firms are spreading themselves across various channels to appeal to diverse customer segments. Each distribution channel services a different set of customers and provides varying levels of services. This can lead to a reduction in the overall service cost, resulting in an increase in profitability for the firm.

However, many firms worry that increasing the number of channels will only spread the same revenue across multiple channels—that is, each new channel will cannibalize sales from other channels. But, is the reduction in service cost by moving lower-profit customers to lower-cost channels the only benefit of increasing the number of distribution channels? The clear answer to this question is no. Increasing the number of channels also leads to many other positive outcomes for businesses, including giving customers more searching and purchasing options and giving firms synergistic effects on customer profitability across channels; that is, customers who buy across more channels buy more products in total from the firm. Therefore, this chapter shows why it is profitable for firms to start operating business across multiple channels (even if some channels offer only search information and do not allow purchases) and discusses the difference between single- and multichannel shoppers and how firms can strategically manage customers across multiple channels. This relationship between multichannel shoppers and profits is examined by using several marketing case studies from firms in both the business-to-business (B2B) and business-to-consumer (B2C) industries.

Search First, Then Purchase

Today, most firms have ventured into at least a few different channels to serve customers. In many cases, these channels not only offer customers a chance to make purchases via multiple channels, but they also offer customers the chance to search for product information in one or more channels and purchase in a completely different channel. A recent marketing study by DoubleClick showed that almost half the customers who bought from a particular retailer did research on the Internet before going into the brick-and-mortar store to make a purchase.[4] This means that even if a firm is unable to manage the Internet as a product distribution channel, posting products and product descriptions on the Internet can potentially serve the purpose of locking a customer in on a specific retail store. For example, a customer is interested in buying a new pair of athletic shoes but is unsure about which brand and model to purchase. That customer might choose to go online to a store's website to check out the store's athletic shoe selection and get descriptions about each of the shoe styles the store has to offer. If the customer can find the shoe he wants at the price he wants, he still may not choose to buy the product online. Instead, this customer might want to go into the store directly and try on different sizes of the shoe before deciding to buy it. This is a common example where a customer uses one channel, the Internet in this case, to search for product information and then uses a different channel to make the purchase.

So, how does the research shopper (a customer who searches in one channel and purchases in another) give us insight as to the potential of multichannel shoppers to provide the firm a significant increase in overall profit? Even in the case of research shoppers, the findings from these studies suggest that firms benefit from introducing multiple channels to their customers. These cross-channel synergies offer the firm a better chance to lock customers into their brick-and-mortar retail store, where it is much easier to convert a shopper into a customer. For example, firms should not necessarily worry that setting up a website with information allows customers to search on their website and buy from someone else. Although the Internet doesn't always entice customers to purchase online and from a particular firm (after all, customers can quickly check out many different websites), when firms effectively provide customers with enough clear product information in their preferred searching channel (for example, Internet), customers are more likely to actually buy the products in their preferred purchasing channel (for example, a brick-and-mortar retail store). Firms that sell products that require some level of customer involvement (for instance, trying on apparel or shoes) or whose products are complex (perhaps the product needs to be visually inspected or tested) may find that shoppers visit their brick-and-mortar sites armed with more information and ready to purchase. However, to understand a little more about customers who are likely to shop in multiple channels, we need to understand which customers are typical multichannel shoppers and, in turn, determine whether multichannel shoppers tend to be more profitable than single-channel shoppers.

Who Are Multichannel Shoppers?

To answer this question, it is necessary to understand the following:

- **Customer characteristics.** For example, how many categories a customer purchases in

- **Supplier-specific factors.** For example, how often a customer receives marketing communications.

- **Customer demographic information.** For example, income levels

This information helps us to generally identify the differences between multichannel and single-channel shoppers. In turn, we can determine whether these multichannel shoppers are more profitable and more frequent customers than single-channel shoppers.

We can empirically evaluate the association of customer-specific and supplier-specific characteristics and demographic information with multichannel shopping using an ordered logistic regression. This statistical model captures the differences in the effect of each of the preceding drivers on the probability of a customer buying from a single channel or multiple channels. For details on the model specification, please access www.drvkumar.com/mcp.

After we obtain the weights for each of the drivers by estimating the model, we can see how each driver influences a customer's decision to shop in a single channel or multiple channels.

To understand how these drivers and outcomes relate to the behavior and characteristics of multichannel shoppers, we consider a recent marketing study done with a B2B firm that identifies the drivers and customer-based metrics (for example, customer value and Share of Wallet [SOW]) of multichannel shopping (see Figure 10.1).[5]

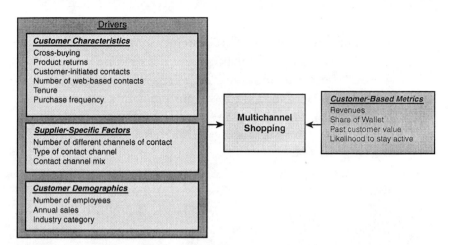

Figure 10.1 Typical drivers of multichannel shopping behavior

Source: V. Kumar and Rajkumar Venkatesan, "Who are Multichannel Shoppers and How Do They Perform?: Correlates of Multichannel Shopping Behavior," *Journal of Interactive Marketing* 19(2) 2005: 44–62. Printed with permission from the American Marketing Association.

Figure 10.1 lists different factors that are likely drivers of multichannel shopping behavior, including customer characteristics, supplier-specific factors, and customer demographic information. It also compares the results of some customer-based metrics of single-channel and multichannel shoppers. An understanding of how these drivers will enable firms to better identify who the multichannel shoppers are will give managers insight into how to properly manage multichannel versus single-channel shoppers.

Customer Characteristics

- **Cross-buying.** As noted in previous chapters of this book, cross-buying occurs when customers buy products in different categories. It is widely believed by marketers that customers often choose different channels to buy different product categories. For example, a local bank may offer various products such as a savings account, checking account, and home mortgage. Customers may choose to manage and use their checking and savings accounts through an online interface but apply for and manage their home mortgage through a direct salesperson.

Customers do this because different products from this bank have different attributes. This customer may choose to manage the savings account online because it is a straightforward, simple-to-use product. However, because the mortgage is so complex and customized to each customer, this customer may feel more comfortable if there is a direct salesperson to talk to about the details of the mortgage. Therefore, it is more likely that customers who buy across multiple product categories (those who rate highly on cross-buying) are also customers who are buying across multiple distribution channels or are candidates to venture into new channels of product distribution that a firm might introduce.

- **Product returns.** Customers who return products are not necessarily bad customers. In fact, a company that can offer a satisfactory return process can actually use this as another "touch" point with the customer and continue to strengthen the firm-customer relationship. To this extent, it makes sense that as customers begin to return some of the products (up to a point) that they purchase that they are becoming more familiar with the retail store's different product offerings and distribution channels. Often, firms can use product returns as a way to migrate customers into different channels. For example, if a customer purchases a product online and wants to exchange it, he might be able to return the product to a local brick-and-mortar store. If the customer had only previously made purchases online, this introduces the customer to a new distribution channel (the brick-and-mortar store) and potentially encourages him to consider products in the store he was less likely to buy online. However, this does not mean that a firm should necessarily encourage customers to return more products; after all, no firm wants to have customers returning most of the products they buy. But, a customer who is given the opportunity to return or exchange unsuitable products (usually this turns out to be around 5% to 15% of the total number of purchases) will be more likely to venture into new distribution channels to make purchases because he will feel less threatened about buying products. In other words, knowing that they can easily return or exchange any unsuitable products makes customers feel a lot safer about buying products in the first place.

- **Customer-initiated contacts.** Customer-initiated contacts occur when customers contact the firm with regard to any aspect of using or purchasing a product. Many marketing field studies have shown that customers who initiate contact with firms exhibit higher levels of customers' loyalty, involvement, and dependence on each of the other product distribution channels. For example, if a customer takes the time to send an email or call a firm on the phone (and that customer receives satisfactory support), the customer has shown the willingness to take an initiative to contact the firm. Often, these customers are looking for the firm to assist them because they want to continue their relationships with the firm. It is the customers who choose not to contact the firm who feel less of a connection with the firm and are more likely to begin buying from other firms. Therefore, if a customer initiates the connection with the firm, he is signaling the desire to have a relationship with the firm and is more likely and willing to buy across multiple distribution channels.

- **Frequency of web-based contacts.** Web-based contacts are similar to other customer-initiated contacts. However, when customers use the web to initiate contact with companies, it also shows that these customers have a stronger grasp of technology, in general. These more tech-savvy customers show that they trust the Internet as a way to securely communicate with a firm. Not only does this mean that they are more likely to buy through an online channel, it also means that they believe that the firm is properly handling their relationship. So, customers who communicate with you through email are not only signaling a desire to have a relationship, but are also telling you that they trust your firm (because the communication is coming through what is normally considered the least secure and most impersonal communication channel). Therefore, these customers are usually more likely and willing to shop in multiple channels because they have a higher level of trust with the firm.

- **Customer tenure.** Customer tenure refers to the duration during which a customer has been purchasing products from a company. Customers who have longer tenure are usually considered more behaviorally loyal. In addition, customers who regularly purchase over time are customers who are likely to be more familiar with a firm's product offerings and purchase channels. These "loyal" customers have already established that they desire to purchase mainly from one firm. So, if the firm can introduce them to a new channel that offers different services and conveniences, these customers are more likely to venture into that new channel than a customer who is less behaviorally loyal. For example, a customer who has been making regular trips to Stop & Shop for the past ten years might be interested in automating part of their weekly shopping list by considering Peapod as a grocery-delivery option. Because this customer already has shown that he or she trusts Stop & Shop for the weekly grocery trip, helping him/her to automate part of the list might seem like an attractive prospect.

- **Purchase frequency.** In this case, frequency refers to how often a customer purchases from a firm. Customers who buy frequently are likely to desire efficiency in their transactions and therefore become quite familiar with the firm's offerings and distribution channels. Because of this, customers who purchase frequently are also likely to shop through multiple channels. Just as in the previous example with customer tenure, customers who buy frequently are also likely and willing to venture into new channels that might offer them a higher level of convenience. These customers may be interested in simplifying part of their purchasing behavior and are more likely to consider other channels as purchase options.

Supplier Factors

- **Number of channels used for contact.** Retailers can usually choose from many different contact channels when contacting customers. These can include direct mail, email, telemarketing, sales personnel, and retail stores. These marketing pieces not only give customers information about the products that they can purchase, but they can also guide customers to purchase through difference channels. For example, Sephora sent out an email to its customers allowing them to shop the online catalog, download a printable copy of the catalog, request a catalog be sent to them, order online, order by phone, and even find store locations (see Figure 10.2).

Figure 10.2 Sephora multichannel email

This email from Sephora exposes customers to all its products through multiple distribution channels, enabling customers to do some research. It also gives them access to information about places where they can buy the product. So, when firms can communicate to customers through different channels and about different channels, the customer is more likely to be a multichannel shopper.

- **Type of contact channel.** Just as the number of channels used for contact makes a difference in the customer's willingness to multichannel shop, the type of channel through which the communication is received by the customer also impacts the likelihood of multichannel shopping. For example, when a consumer is contacted through highly personal contact channels (for example, face-to-face interaction), he has a higher likelihood to buy across multiple channels. This is because firms that contact a customer through a highly personal channel can customize the message and reduce the customer's perceived risk about purchasing from the company. Consider, for example, a customer who has been purchasing in your brick-and-mortar retail store. Based on this customer's purchasing behavior, you know that he is a likely candidate to buy through the Internet during the next sales event. If you send a customized message to this customer giving him an incentive to buy online, it is more likely that he will respond to the message and buy in the new channel.

- **Contact-mix interactions.** The number and type of channel contacts can help to predict whether a customer is a multi-channel shopper or a single-channel shopper. However, when there are different interactions between the number and type of contacts, synergistic effects can happen with relation to multichannel shopping (perhaps because marketing message received from different channels may reinforce that message in the customer's mind). This reinforced message is not only likely to cause a customer to make purchases in multiple channels, but it is also likely to lead the customer to buy incrementally more from the firm given the appropriate channels and the appropriate message in that channel for that customer. Just as in the last example, if you know that based on a customer's previous transactions he is likely to buy in a new channel (for example, the Internet), and if you can contact him in multiple channels with the same message, the customer will be more likely to respond. For example, if you send a direct mail to the customer that gives him the incentive to buy in the new channel and then follow up with either an email or a phone call, this customer is more likely to remember this message and is more likely to act upon it and buy in the new channel.

Customer Demographics

Customer demographics are used mainly to try to help profile the different customers who buy in multiple channels. For example, in the case of the B2B firm used in the marketing study described in this section, annual sales, firm size, and firms that resided in particular industries were positively related to multichannel shopping. This information would vary based on the products being offered and the firms who were likely to purchase these products. This means that it would vary in each situation. Customer demographics included in any analysis of customers helps managers understand not only the profile of their own customers who are likely to purchase in multiple channels but also the profile of prospects that are most likely to buy in multiple channels. Armed with this knowledge, this firm can identify new prospects that are more likely to be multichannel shoppers based on their profile information alone and achieve a higher success rate of acquisition of multichannel shoppers. This can prove helpful when a firm has limited resources and has to make key decisions about which customer is most likely going to be profitable in the future.

Are Multichannel Shoppers More Profitable?

Much of the previous section focused on the relationship between a set of drivers and their relationship to customers who are multichannel shoppers. Now that firms can identify multichannel shoppers, are multichannel shoppers really more likely to buy in the future, do they spend more money, and are they more profitable than single-channel customers? To the right side of multichannel shoppers in Figure 10.1 is a list of customer-based metrics commonly measured by firms. These include how much a customer spends (revenue), the percentage of money a customer spends on that firm's products versus a competitor's products (SOW), the customer's past profitability (Past Customer Value [PCV]), the likelihood that a customer will buy in the future (likelihood of staying active), and the Customer Lifetime Value (CLV). These customer-based metrics were compared for customers who shop in one, two, three, and four channels for a specific firm. Table 10.1 lists the results of this analysis.

Table 10.1 Comparison of Customer-Based Metrics

	Shopped in Single Channel	Shopped in Two Channels	Shopped in Three or More Channels
Revenue	$4,262	$5,736	$16,100
SOW	20%	35%	60%
PCV	$6,681	$10,874	$25,625
Likelihood of staying active	11%	15%	54%
CLV	$7,672	$10,325	$28,980

Source: V. Kumar and Rajkumar Venkatesan, "Who Are Multichannel Shoppers and How Do They Perform?: Correlates of Multichannel Shopping Behavior," *Journal of Interactive Marketing* 19(2) 2005: 44–62.

Table 10.1 explicitly shows that as a customer shops across more channels (from one channel to four channels), he spends more revenue with your firm, spends a higher proportion on your firm (rather than with a competitor), has a higher past profitability (which is correlated with future profitability), and has a higher likelihood of buying in the future. Therefore, if a firm wants to identify candidates to encourage to shop in multiple channels, that firm needs to see which customers show the right signs of being potential multichannel shoppers based on the drivers in the previous section and try to leverage those drivers to encourage multichannel shopping behavior. However, although this shows how multichannel shoppers can be identified by their drivers, it does not necessarily identify actionable strategies for firms to identify which channel a customer is best suited to adopt next.

Determining the Next Channel a Customer Adopts

Based on the previous results, we know that multichannel customers tend to be more profitable than single-channel shoppers. However, when firms want to encourage customers to shop in multiple channels, it is important to identify which channel a customer is likely to adopt next and when he will adopt that channel. This knowledge helps firms to send the right marketing message at the right time to that customer. By doing so, a firm can optimize its marketing spend, increase its return on marketing investment, and in turn encourage the right customers to adopt the right channels at the right time. Therefore, in this section of the chapter, the drivers of channel adoption are identified for a set of customers in a B2C firm that mainly sells apparel in discount stores, full-price stores, and through the Internet. Although these drivers differ slightly because they are in a B2C setting, they are quite similar to the drivers of the B2B firm (see Figure 10.3).

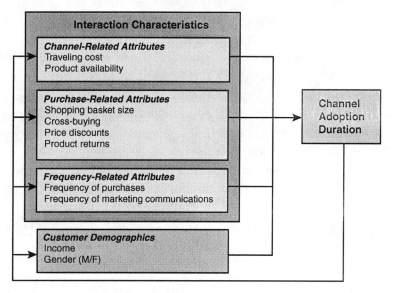

Figure 10.3   Typical drivers of channel adoption

Source: Adapted from Rajkumar Venkatesan, V. Kumar, and Nalini Ravishanker, "Multichannel Shopping: Causes and Consequences," *Journal of Marketing* 71 2007: 114–132.

Channel-Related Attributes

To calculate the time frame until the next channel is adopted, you have to consider that each channel has different attributes, which include the time between when the product is ordered and when the product is received (product availability) and the accessibility and convenience of obtaining the product (travel cost). These channel attributes are key factors of when a customer is likely to venture into a new channel:

- **Travel cost.** In this study, the travel cost is the distance between the customer and the retail store. In the case of an actual retail store, the travel cost (in time and effort) involves the customer actually traveling to the store to make a purchase. In the case of an online store, this travel cost is negligible, especially if the customer has access to the Internet at his home or office. Because of these varying travel costs across channels and the incentive for customers to always reduce their total travel costs, a customer who travels a lot to make purchases is more likely to venture into a channel that requires less travel cost than a customer who travels very little to make purchases. In a nutshell, this means that it is more likely for a customer who travels to the retail store to shop to enter into a new channel of purchasing (for example, the Internet) than it is for a customer who already shops in a channel with a very small travel cost. For example, if a customer lives an hour away from a key shopping destination (for example, a shopping mall), the customer will make fewer trips because the cost to travel there is so high in both time and effort. This does not mean that the customer will never travel to shop; but if a firm could enable this customer to purchase between shopping trips in a setting that requires fewer traveling costs (for example, online or catalog), this customer will be more willing and ready to adopt the new channel more quickly.

■ **Product availability.** The immediate availability of a product refers to the time frame between which a customer chooses to purchase a product and when he can actually use the product. When some customers make purchases, they want to have the product in their hands immediately. In addition, some customers want to have a richer experience with the product (that is, the ability to interact with the product). For example, a customer who buys a pair of shoes through a retail store can go in and try the shoes on before purchase (interaction) and then receive the product immediately after the decision to purchase has been made. On the other hand, a customer who makes a purchase through a mail-order catalog has to wait for the product to arrive after the order has been placed. That customer can interact with the product only when it arrives in the mail. Because of this, customers who are not able to have their product immediately available are more likely to adopt a new channel sooner that can offer them immediate product availability.

Purchase-Related Attributes

- **Shopping basket size.** In this case, the size of a customer's shopping basket refers to the number of items a customer purchases in a single shopping trip. Different-size baskets are often related to different patterns of shopping behavior. For example, a customer who always has a small basket size (fill-in trips) often has an immediate or unplanned shopping trip for which only a couple items are needed to fill the basket. This customer is usually more willing to pay higher prices for the products because the need and immediacy of the shopping trip is so urgent. For example, a convenience store often charges higher prices than a larger grocery store, but customers who only need to buy one or two items find the convenience worth the price premium. On the other hand, a customer who tends to have a large basket size is more likely to plan the shopping trip and make consistent visits to a particular store. This customer is usually satisfied with the particular store because he is behaviorally loyal (making consistent trips over time) and buying a large basket each time. However, the customer who buys only a moderate amount each time usually is the customer who is the most sensitive to the price of the products. This customer tends to purchase items that are on sale or display. This implies that these customers are more deal prone and have a transactional rather than a relational focus with the firm. That is, if another firm offers him a better deal, there he will likely switch. For these reasons, the general size of a customer's shopping basket can give firms different signals about channel adoption. Customers with very large or very small basket sizes are more likely to adopt new channels sooner because they are looking more for convenience and the automation of regular large shopping trips than are deal-prone customers with an intermediate basket size.

- **Cross-buying.** Similar to the previous section on the typical correlates of multichannel shoppers, cross-buying refers to the number of product categories from which a customer purchases. Because a customer who buys across more channels is more likely to be a multichannel shopper, it is also the case that a customer who buys across multiple channels tends to adopt new channels sooner. The reasoning for this is similar because customers who buy across more product categories are more familiar with the firm's offerings and distribution channels and in turn may find that different channels offer different benefits for different product categories.

- **Price discounts.** The level of price discounts refers directly to the depth of the price discounts that a store puts on its products. Firms that place higher discounts on products are more likely to encourage customers to adopt new channels sooner. This is especially the case when customers are offered discounts in channels that they have yet to adopt. When customers venture into a new channel with this price discount incentive, they are not only more likely to adopt the channel sooner, but they are also encouraged to buy more across multiple channels. Consider the case of a customer who has been buying regularly from Best Buy, for instance. If Best Buy sends that customer an offer to purchase through the online store with a 15% discount if he buys within the next two weeks, the customer is more likely to adopt the new channel than if he receives a similar message that does not offer a discount.

- **Product returns.** Product returns are not necessarily bad; they can help build the relationship between the firm and the customer when handled in a satisfactory manner. To this extent (similar to the previous study), the number and timing of product returns by a customer can signal the willingness of a customer to adopt a new channel. For example, if a customer buys a product through the online store, the firm can tell the customer that the product can be returned (if it's not satisfactory) to the local brick-and-mortar store. This policy gives the customer a chance to work with a salesperson face to face (in case of a return) and may introduce the customer to the brick-and-mortar store as a potential new channel for purchases. Customers who are comfortable returning unsatisfactory products tend to be more willing than customers who do not return products to adopt a new channel of purchase (especially when the purchase and product return occur across different channels).

Frequency-Related Attributes

- **Frequency of purchase.** Just as in the previous study, customers who purchase more frequently are more familiar with what the firm has to offer and what its distribution channels are. To the extent that the purchase occasions are satisfactory for the customer, the customer begins to feel less threatened when buying from that company and is more willing to adopt new purchasing channels. Therefore, the higher the purchase frequency, the shorter the duration until the customer adopts the next channel.

- **Frequency of marketing communications.** The marketing communications that a firm has with a customer plays a significant role in the channels that a customer adopts. Referring back to Figure 10.2 (Sephora email), a firm that can help guide the customer to new channels can get customers to venture into new channels sooner by just making them aware of the channels and giving them incentives to purchase in those new channels. However, a firm needs to be careful not to saturate the customer with too many marketing communications. A customer who receives too many marketing communications will begin to tune out the firm and ignore the purchasing incentives. Therefore, a firm needs to send a moderate number of marketing communications with the "right" messages to get the most out of the marketing communications. For this reason, marketing communications are related in a U-shaped manner to the time until a customer adopts a new channel.

Customer Demographics

Just as in the previous section, customer demographics are again included in the study to help firms identify the types of customers who

---

are most likely to adopt a new channel sooner. In this study, gender and income were used to help classify customers to identify multichannel shopping prospects. The results of this study showed that male customers with lower incomes were more likely to adopt a new channel sooner than female customers with higher incomes. Although this result may vary for different industries and firms, by using customer demographic information in the framework of this study, the focal firm can better identify prospects who are more likely to adopt new channels sooner and in turn acquire prospects who are more likely to adopt new channels faster.

The duration to adopt a channel by a customer can be modeled using a modified proportional hazard model. For each customer, the duration to adopt the second channel and the third channel, respectively, may be influenced by a common factor that is specific to that customer. We need to take into account the effect of such a customer-specific factor, which is called *shared frailty*. Incorporating the impact of shared frailty and those of the drivers of channel adoption, we can express the modified proportional hazard model as follows:

$$
\begin{array}{c}
\text{The probability of a customer} \\
\text{adopting } j^{\text{th}} \text{ channel in the} \\
\text{immediate time period given that} \\
\text{he/she has not adopted the} \\
\text{channel until now}
\end{array}
=
\begin{array}{c}
\text{Baseline probability} \times \\
\text{impact factor} \times \\
\text{shared frailty.}
\end{array}
$$

The details of the model specified can be accessed through www.drvkumar.com/mcp.

The coefficients (or weight for each driver) of the model are estimated using maximum likelihood estimation, which selects the coefficients such that the duration of adoption predicted by the model matches best with the observed durations of adoption of second and third channels. Because the shared frailty terms are customer specific, the model accounts for customer heterogeneity.

Channel-Adoption Duration

Knowing the timing and adoption patterns of each customer is a key piece of information that enables managers to target certain customers at certain times for multichannel marketing. In fact, the average time it took for a customer with this firm to adopt a second channel was around 15 months, and then an additional 10 months to adopt the third channel. However, the results of this marketing study with the B2C apparel company showed that it did matter which channel was adopted first, when considering which channel is most likely to be adopted next and when that channel will be adopted. For example, when adopting a second channel, customers who first adopted the full-price store took 27% longer than the customers who first adopted the discount store and 6% longer than the customers who first adopted the web channel. So, managers should not necessarily assume that it will take each customer the same amount of time to adopt the second and then the third channel.

So, how close was this study able to get in accurately predicting the actual time until the next channel adoption? The mean absolute deviation between the predicted time to adopt and the actual adoption time for each customer is about five months for the second channel adoption and about four months for the third channel adoption. These results show that managers can accurately assess the time and channel that each customer is most likely to adopt next. Therefore, managers *can* target selected customers with the right multichannel marketing message at the right time to encourage timely new channel adoption.

Implementation

The model to predict the channel-adoption duration was applied to a sample of customers from this B2C retail firm consisting of single-channel and two-channel shoppers. A marketing campaign was developed to target the single-channel shoppers, encouraging them to adopt the second channel. Similarly, the two-channel shoppers were targeted to adopt the third channel. The sample size chosen for this specific implementation was 3,800. From this base, a test group and a control group were formed of approximately equal size.

The campaign offered a discount certificate to encourage the customers to purchase from another channel. This incentive ranged from $5 to $25 depending on the CLV of the customer. The higher-CLV customer was given a higher level of incentive. Based on the campaign, of the 1,902 customers in the test group who were targeted, 77% of them adopted the additional channel. In the control group, of the 1,898 customers, only 12% adopted the additional channel during the campaign period of 6 months. The shopping behavior of the customers in the test group was monitored for a period of 12 months. The net gain in revenue due to the addition of one more channel was on average about 80%. In other words, if the customers were spending on average $400 in one channel, they were now spending about $720 when another channel was added to their shopping portfolio. The average marketing campaign cost, including the discount, was about $40. The increase in revenue was about $320. Therefore, the return on investment was about 8 times (or 800%). As you can see, contacting the right customers at the right time to encourage adopting another channel results in higher profitability.

Are Multichannel Customers More Profitable?

The results of the two field studies in this chapter explicitly show that managers can grow customer profitability by encouraging them to shop in multiple channels. By creating this multichannel experience for customers, managers derive several benefits, especially with regard to customer relationship management (CRM) initiatives: customer retention and customer growth. One of the main reasons managers see multichannel shoppers as more profitable is because a customer can get so much more out of multiple channels. For example, the attributes of channels provide different incentives to purchase from a firm. A customer who only seldom makes trips to a specific retail outlet might begin to purchase more if encouraged to enter the online or mail-order catalog channels. Even if customers enter these other channels, they can still make regular trips to the retail store (and make add-on purchases in the online environment that they would not usually make).

In addition, by providing customers with multiple channels to purchase and research, firms have the chance to create some channel lock-in and channel synergies that are not available with only one channel. An online channel, even if direct online purchasing is not available, may encourage some customers to visit the store to make a purchase. In some cases, enabling a customer to buy online and pick up in the store can even give more channel synergies. This scenario combines online research (convenience) and retail store pickup (immediate product availability).

Finally, customers who purchase in multiple channels tend to have a deeper relationship with the firm and are more loyal to the firm, because the customer is exposed to more of the products/services a firm provides and can get more utility out of doing business with the firm. Therefore, the strength of the relationship increases, and in turn the customer will rely more on that firm for his or her purchasing needs, thereby increasing the customer's spending and profitability with the firm.

Does Order of Channel Adoption Matter?

As the latter study showed, the order in which a custumer adopts a new channel and when depends on the attributes of the channels in which the customer currently shops and the attributes of the channels that the customer has yet to adopt. If a manager can understand the relationship between customers and specific channels, the firm can better target customers for multichannel (existing and potential) marketing campaigns.

For example, perhaps a firm currently has a brick-and-mortar store and a mail-order catalog and is considering introducing a new Internet channel. The firm must ask whom it should target to buy in this new channel. To answer this question, the firm needs to understand which of its customers are most likely to adopt a new channel with attributes similar to that of the web channel (low travel cost and low immediate product availability) and how this channel can potentially fit in with the existing channels offered (for example, buy online and pick up in the store). Targeting the right customers with the right incentives can provide a big payoff for the firm.

Managing Multichannel Resources

How does a firm manage its resources when it comes to multichannel shopping? A firm that wants to implement a campaign to encourage customers to adopt new channels should consider running a field experiment on a sample of its own customers before reaching out to the entire customer base. By doing so, a firm can first determine which of its own customers are multichannel shoppers and which customers are most likely to adopt this new channel. Then, the sample customers' responses to the field study can be used to assess the return on marketing investment of a potential campaign to all the customers and whether the customer-firm interactions changed after the customer adopted the new channel. Based on a successful field study, the firm will better understand multichannel shoppers and be able to identify not only its own customers who are most likely to adopt new channels, but also new prospects who are likely to be multichannel shoppers.

Conclusion

Increasing the number of channels leads to positive outcomes for businesses—including giving customers more search and purchase options and giving firms synergistic effects on customer profitability. Therefore, it is profitable for firms to operate businesses across multiple channels. The framework discussed in this chapter provides managers with several demographic variables that profile customers who are likely to shop across multiple channels. Higher profitability results from contacting the right customers at the right time—and encouraging the customers to adopt another channel. Finally, managers can investigate the benefit of designing reward programs to offer incentives to customers for purchasing across multiple product categories and channels.

Endnotes

1 www.walmartfacts.com/FactSheets/352007_Site_to_Store_Program.pdf

2 B. Boa, "Welcome to the World of Multichannel Retailing," *Flora* magazine, March 2003 (details from a KPMG and Indiana University study).

3 J.C. Williams Group and Bizrate.com, "MultiChannel Retail Report 2001" (conducted for shop.org).

4 DoubleClick, "MultiChannel Shopping Study—Holiday 2003," at www.doubleclick.com/us/knowledge_central/research/email_solutions/.

5 V. Kumar and Rajkumar Venkatesan, "Who Are Multichannel Shoppers and How Do They Perform?: Correlates of Multichannel Shopping Behavior," *Journal of Interactive Marketing* 19(2) 2005: 44–62.

11

Linking Investments in Branding to Customer Profitability

Relevant Issues

- Should we invest in building brand equity or customer equity?

- How does building Individual Brand Value (IBV) maximize customer profitability?

A typical dilemma faced by any corporate board is whether to invest in building brands or to invest in building the customer base. Which of these routes ensure maximum profitability? The obvious answer is probably to invest in both. However, it is difficult to estimate how investing in brand building contributes toward attaining higher profitability.

Consider the example of two leading electronics manufacturers, Samsung and Nokia. The change in brand value and the net income for Samsung and Nokia (2001 through 2005) is shown in Figures 11.1 and 11.2, respectively. Figure 11.1 shows that Samsung's brand value has been steadily increasing over that period, and the net income for this period has been following an upward trend. This correlation shows an association between a firm's brand value and the firm's net income.

Figure 11.2 shows that Nokia's brand value has been following a declining trend between 2001 and 2005, and the net income is almost stagnant over the same period. This correlation shows that declining brand value can affect a firm's overall performance. Even though these trends clearly demonstrate the importance of building brand value and how doing so will affect the bottom line, firms do not have a clear set of guidelines as to how to structure their marketing and brand investment strategies to boost their brand value. Typically, what they have is the aggregate-level brand value perception. To design and execute effective brand management strategies, firms need to understand exactly how each of their actions will affect the customer's Individual Brand Value (IBV). In this chapter, we forward a framework that firms can use to effectively link an IBV to the Customer Lifetime Value (CLV). These strategies help firms better understand this link and redesign their strategies to suit the needs of the individual customer.

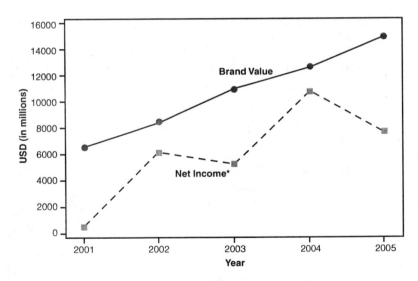

The net income has been scaled by a factor of 1,000 to make it comparable.

Figure 11.1   The change in brand value and net income for Samsung (2001–2005)

Source: The data for this figure was obtained from http://bwnt.businessweek.com/ brand and Annual Reports from www.samsung.com.

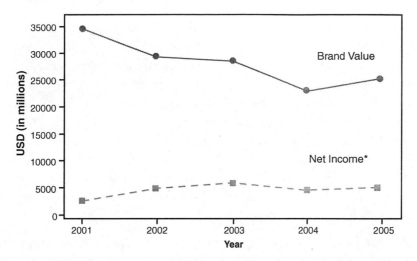

* The original values of net income in euros (million) have been converted to U.S. dollars (million).

Figure 11.2   The change in brand value and net income for Nokia (2001–2005)

Source: The data for this figure was obtained from http://bwnt.businessweek.com/ brand and Annual Reports from www.nokia.com.

Brand equity and customer equity have traditionally been viewed as two separate marketing assets. However, building a brand through traditional approaches does not necessarily achieve growth in the CLV. Traditionally, the effect of brand was measured through immediate change in sales, after implementing a marketing initiative. This cannot be a good measure for evaluating the brand because brand building also seeks to influence customer behavior in the long term. Brand value has an effect both on the "behavioral" (demonstrated by short-term purchase behavior) and "attitudinal" (long-term behavior) loyalty of the customer, and any brand evaluation measure should incorporate both these factors to obtain a comprehensive picture. Customers with greater attitudinal loyalty have a greater likelihood of future purchase and are more likely to recommend the brand to others. Hence, when evaluating a brand, it is not only the financial value generated by the brand that should be considered, but also how the customers perceive the brand.

Aggregate versus Individual Brand Value

To address the question "how does brand add value to a firm?" we need to understand how a given brand is perceived by its customers and how customers react to the brand. Traditionally, this customer-brand relationship has been explored only at the aggregate (or collective) level. It was believed that by shaping a strong brand idea in the marketplace, all the customers would react in a similar manner. In reality, the value of a brand is individual based, and different customers have a varied perception of a brand. Therefore, if a firm focuses solely on managing the brand value at the aggregate level, it severely limits the firm's ability to reach each of its customers effectively.

Various factors affect a customer's brand perception; therefore, firms shouldn't restrict themselves to sending a uniform brand message to all the customers. Also, firms should understand that not all customers are equally profitable. Therefore, firms should specifically attempt to target such profitable customers and send specialized brand messages.

Framework for Linking Brand Value to CLV

A key to address these issues is to establish a link between an IBV and CLV to manage individual customer brand value. CLV is particularly well suited to address this issue because when calculating the CLV of a customer, firms must consider both the short-term and long-term "attitudinal" and "behavioral" loyalty of a customer. Linking CLV to IBV can help to maximize the lifetime value of customers. Therefore, this chapter explores the link between IBV and CLV and explores the relationship between IBV and CLV. First, a conceptual framework is introduced, as illustrated in Figure 11.3, which can be used to link IBV to CLV. This framework enables a firm to optimize a customer's lifetime value, thereby allowing simultaneous growth in brand equity and customer equity.

According to this framework, linking the IBV to the CLV is a dynamic process, in which each aspect of the individual's brand value such as brand knowledge, brand attitude, brand behavior intention, and brand behavior contributes toward the individual's lifetime value with the firm, as shown in Figure 11.3. A customer's brand knowledge plays an important role in this process. Brand awareness and brand image are the two aspects that make up a customer's brand knowledge. A customer's brand knowledge contributes toward building his/her brand attitude, which consists of the customer's trust in the brand and brand effect. By influencing the brand attitude of a customer, the firm can influence the brand behavior intentions of the customer, and in turn affect the brand behavior. The brand behavior is driven by building brand loyalty, which in turn influences brand advocacy and premium price behavior of the customer. By following this framework, the firm can effectively manage the brand value associated with each customer, and thus influence the overall lifetime value of the customers. The following sections discuss each of these components of IBV in detail and explore their link to the overall CLV.

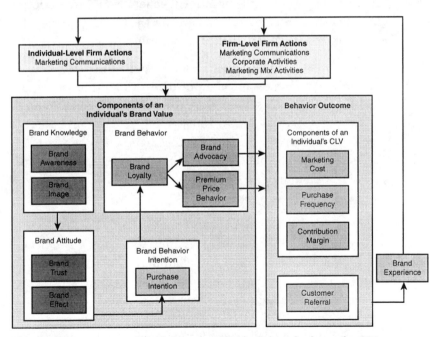

Figure 11.3 Framework for linking an individual's brand value to the CLV

Source: V. Kumar, M. Luo, and V. R. Rao (2007), "Linking an Individual's Brand Value to the CLV: An Integrated Framework," Working Paper, University of Connecticut.

Brand Knowledge

The true value of a brand lies in how customers perceive the brand, not in the brand itself. Hence, a positive brand knowledge held by the customers will positively impact the brand value. Brand awareness and brand image constitute the two components of brand knowledge:

- **Brand awareness.** Awareness of a particular brand has multiple effects on the customer's purchasing behavior. Brand awareness guides new customers into purchasing a particular product, even if the customer is new to the product category. This will continue even after the customer has made the first purchase. Thus, increased awareness of the brand increases the purchase probability. Hence, repeated efforts should be made to make the brand a part of the customer's consciousness. Also, such repeated exposure to the brand will generate a positive outlook in the customer. Therefore, the greater the brand awareness for a customer, the greater his/her brand value.

  Coca-Cola is a good example of a firm that enjoys extraordinary brand awareness throughout the world. At the moment, Coke's products are sold in more than 200 countries around the world, and Coke has almost 100% brand recognition in the Western world.[1] In the words of Asa Chandler, Coke's first proprietor, "We are firmly convinced that wherever there are people and soda fountains, Coca-Cola will…win its way quickly into the front rank of popularity."[2]

- **Brand image.** Brand awareness represents only the first level of brand knowledge. Brand image is affected by how customers perceive a particular brand and what they associate it with. Hence, brand image is not only influenced by how a firm markets its brand, but also by all other brand-related activities undertaken by the firm. Also, note that a customer's brand image changes with time, as the customer becomes more familiar with the products/brand. So, as the customer's expertise and knowledge about the product and brand increases, the customer becomes more aware of how effectively the brand could satisfy his/her needs. Brand image assumes an important role in building brand knowledge, and it can lead to a negative brand value if the customer has an unpleasant brand image associated with it. Therefore, the greater the brand image for a customer, the greater his/her brand value. Samsung has, over the years, created a hip image among its customers with its cutting-edge technology and world-class design from a low-end brand image. Recently, it organized a competition to invite members of its brand community to come up with designs for its upcoming MP3 gadgets. This, apart from involving the members of the brand community, reinforces Samsung's brand image of being hip and cutting-edge.[3]

Brand Attitude

Brand attitude is the attitude each customer forms about the brand, and it is mainly formed by brand trust and brand effect:

- **Brand trust.** Brand trust refers to a customer's willingness to trust the brand to satisfy his/her needs. Brand trust assumes particular significance when customers cannot objectively evaluate the quality of a product. Brand trust is developed over time, as the customer acquires positive brand knowledge through experience and through information from external sources. As the customer becomes more familiar with the brand, brand trust moves into the next level of brand intimacy. Brand intimacy is important to cultivate attitudinal loyalty with the customers. Therefore, the greater the brand trust for a customer, the greater his/her brand value. BP's practice of moving into solar and hydrogen energy has established its brand image as environmental friendly. However, its accidental oil spills from the trans-Alaskan pipeline could easily break consumers' trust and cast doubts on the company's real philosophy on environment issues.[4] It is essential for a firm to be consistent in practices to build brand trust.

- **Brand effect.** Brand effect is a customer's positive emotional response toward a brand. Whereas brand trust generates a positive rational response toward a brand, brand effect tries to generate a positive emotion toward the usage of the brand.

Brand effect can be demonstrated in different levels of the relationship between the firm and the customer. Brand effect is created by positive associations and past experience and indicates a deeper relationship between the brand and the customer. One standout example of brand effect is the strong negative reaction incited among customers when Coke Classic was changed to New Coke.

The greater the brand effect for a customer, the greater his/her brand value. Several years ago, British Airways developed a beautiful advertising campaign with the slogan "It's the way we make you feel that makes British Airways the world's favorite airline." Many people might take such a message to heart: It is the journey rather than the destination that counts. It serves as a perfect example of selling the product to the heart of consumers.[5]

Brand Behavior Intention

Brand behavior intentions constitute the brand advocacy of customers, the brand loyalty, whether customers are willing to make a purchase at a premium price, and the actual brand purchase behavior. This reflects the actual effect of the marketing actions on the brand behavior of the customers:

- **Purchase intention.** Brand behavior intention shows how much a customer values a brand and is demonstrated by the brand purchase intentions. The purchase intention of a customer gains importance when there are multiple competitors in the market and gives the focal brand an edge in various purchasing situations. Therefore, the greater the brand purchase intention of a customer, the greater his/her brand value. Wal-Mart increases the purchase intentions among its customers by offering low prices and through its marketing slogan "everyday low prices," which has attracted shoppers around the world. In 2003, 138 million shoppers visited Wal-Mart stores every week. In 2002, 82% of all American households made at least one purchase at Wal-Mart.[6] These numbers show how successful Wal-Mart has been in creating purchase intention among customers.

Brand Behavior

- **Brand loyalty.** A customer has brand loyalty when he/she makes repeated purchases of a preferred brand and shows both attitudinal and behavioral loyalty to the brand. Fluctuations in the market and competitors offerings will have little effect on a customer's brand loyalty. The higher the brand loyalty toward a brand for a customer, the higher his/her brand value. Apple Computers (now Apple) is known to have a customer base with strong loyalty to the Apple or Mac brand. Its customers go beyond brand loyalty and exhibit a religious-like zeal toward Apple and its products.[7] Building and maintaining such devotion toward the brand has been crucial for the recent success of Apple's products.

- **Brand advocacy.** Brand advocacy refers to the customer establishing a relationship (through joining a brand community and encouraging other customers to do so) with other customers who use the brand. Harley Davidson is a good example of a brand with a strong brand advocacy forwarded by a community of customers who are very loyal to the brand. The company-sponsored Harley Owners Group has 886,000 members, who regularly organize rides, training courses, social events, and charity fund-raisers. About a quarter of a million of them went to Milwaukee on Labor Day to celebrate the brand's centennial in 2003.[8] Such brand communities share information, promote a subculture, and provide assistance to other customers. Therefore, the greater the brand advocacy for a customer, the greater his/her brand value.

- **Brand price premium behavior.** Brand price premium behavior refers to the customer's willingness to pay a premium price to buy a preferred brand over other products. This behavior reflects the customer's brand loyalty and a willingness to pay extra to maintain the quality. This also proves that the customer will be less willing to switch to a competitor's brand.

Therefore, the greater the brand price premium behavior of a customer, the greater his/her brand value. For example, customers from all over the world spend about $1,000 or more for a Louis Vuitton handbag in the new Murakami line.[9] Because Louis Vuitton has built such an exclusive brand image over the years—through exclusive brand-building events, stringent quality control, and other measures—its customers are willing to pay a great price premium for its products.

Predicted Behavior Outcomes

Customers with greater brand value, it has been found, are more likely to engage in activities that result in an increase of CLV when compared to customers with low brand value. The various factors that constitute the individual's brand value, such as brand knowledge, attitude, and behavior intentions, affect the behavior of customers, and they are linked to the CLV through the following customer behavior outcomes:

- **Lifetime duration.** Various factors, such as the purchase frequency, profitable lifetime duration, and contribution margin in every purchase occasion, are used to measure the lifetime value of a customer. The word-of-mouth behavior of customers also factors into the calculation of the CLV. The various factors that affect IBV, such as brand knowledge, attitude, and behavior intentions, affect the CLV. Therefore, the greater a customer's individual brand value, the greater his/her lifetime value.

- **Purchase frequency.** Purchase frequency is a measure of the intensity of the customer's relationship with the brand. The more frequently the customer purchases a brand, the greater utility the customer perceives in the brand. Purchase frequency can also be increased by positive brand knowledge. The better the customer can recall the brand and its attributes, the more he/she is likely to purchase from the brand. A customer familiar with the brand also seeks out additional product information, and this creates opportunities for the firm to sell more. A customer with a higher level of brand advocacy is more likely to resist offers and promotions from competitors, and therefore is more likely to come back to the focal brand for more purchases (and thus increase the purchase frequency).

- **Contribution margin.** A customer who pays a premium price for a brand drives up the contribution margin. Another method of increasing the contribution margin is brand extension. By building on the core image of the parent brand, firms can introduce new products/services. This is aided by the customer's knowledge of the brand and awareness. Because this involves a lower cost of introduction, an increase in contribution margin results. Therefore, the greater the brand value of a customer, the greater his/her contribution margin.

- **Customer referrals.** Customers tend to recommend a brand to others when they are more aware of it. Customer satisfaction and trust also play a great role in generating positive word-of-mouth. Brand satisfaction and brand advocacy are factors that directly and positively influence customer word-of-mouth behavior. Because one of the main functions of brand advocacy is to propagate information about the brand through building relationships with other customers and through brand communities, it directly contributes to a positive word-of-mouth behavior.

How to Link the IBV to CLV

The various components of the IBV and the CLV were discussed in the previous section. The next step is to link these components by using the existing data and the modeling techniques. First, information regarding the various components of the IBV can be obtained from survey data, and customer transaction data can be used to obtain the information required to calculate the various components of CLV. After this information has been gathered, the next step is to use sophisticated estimation techniques to estimate how these components affect each other. The components of IBV are obtained using a ten-point scale from a sample of customers. For the same customers, CLV is computed at that time. The following equations map out the interaction between these components.

How the various components of IBV are linked:

Brand Attitude = function of (Brand Knowledge)	Equation 11.1
Brand Behavior Intention = function of (Brand Attitude)	Equation 11.2
Brand Behavior = function of (Brand Behavior Intention)	Equation 11.3

How IBV and CLV are linked:

CLV = function of (Brand Behavior)	Equation 11.4

These equations show the dynamic process of transferring an individual's brand knowledge (brand awareness and brand image) to his or her brand attitude (brand trust and brand effect), brand purchase intention, and brand behavior (brand loyalty, premium price behavior and brand advocacy), and then ultimately to his or her lifetime value to a firm.

The equations could be simultaneously estimated using Seemingly Unrelated Regressions (SURs). To improve the regression estimates, SUR utilizes the correlations among the errors in equation 1 through 4. When the coefficients from the system of equations are obtained, genetic algorithm can be used to achieve the optimal level of IBV so that a customer's lifetime value is maximized under the budgetary constraint.

To obtain the optimal level of CLV, brand behavior such as brand advocacy and premium price behavior need to be optimized, too. Therefore, appropriate brand message should be sent to increase a customer's level of brand awareness and favorability of brand image. Such favorable brand knowledge would shape a customer's positive attitude in terms of brand trust and brand effect. Brand purchase intention will be affected and revealed through behavioral brand loyalty (manifested as higher purchase frequency). Finally, a truly loyal customer would not only advocate a brand but also be willing to pay a premium price for the quality of the product.

Therefore, it is essential to monitor the components of an individual's IBV. Most important of all, it is necessary to understand the process of building brand knowledge that eventually leads to brand behavior, which induces favorable behavior outcomes such as longer duration, higher purchase frequency, higher contribution margin, and customer referral. A customer's lifetime value is calculated based on the behavior outcomes, as mentioned earlier. In summary, the components of IBV will be simultaneously optimized so that CLV is maximized.

By following these steps, managers can devise an overall strategy to deal with each of the components of IBV and CLV and to maximize the brand value of the customer so that CLV is ultimately improved.

The Role of Communication in Linking IBV to CLV

Communication plays an important role in linking IBV to CLV. This communication includes both planned and unplanned marketing initiatives. These include word-of-mouth, product messages, corporate activities, marketing-mix activities, and marketing communications. Business practices, overall philosophies, mission statements, and so on can be communicated through corporate events. These activities have an important role to play in building a brand. The product performance, price, choice of distribution channel, and so forth form the core of the product message. But the satisfaction derived by the individual customer by using the brand moderates the relationship between the brand communication and the IBV. The new information gathered by the individual through using a brand will lead to the formation of a complex form of brand knowledge. Customer satisfaction (or dissatisfaction) goes a long way in deciding a customer's brand knowledge.

Implications of Linking IBV to CLV

To successfully implement this strategy and achieve positive growth in both IBV and CLV, the following seven steps are suggested:

1. Calculate the CLV of customers at the individual level (as described in Chapter 3, "Customer Selection Metrics").

2. Rank order the customers based on their CLV.

3. Segment the customers into ten deciles, from the highest to the lowest CLV scores.

4. Take a small percentage (say 10%) of customers from each decile and obtain information about the components of their brand value.

5. Using this information, link the components of the IBV to the CLV and obtain an importance or weight for each component of the brand value.

   Consider this example where the focal firm is measuring the brand value of one if its important customers, Bob.[10] Bob's IBV and its various components are shown in Figure 11.4. You can see from the figure that Bob has an acceptable level of brand awareness and brand image, and he trusts the brand, but he has no attachment to it. However, Bob has lower brand behavior intentions (because he scores low on premium price intention, brand loyalty, and brand advocacy).

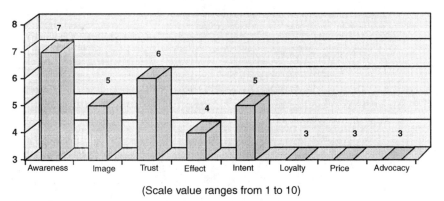

(Scale value ranges from 1 to 10)

Figure 11.4   Bob's measured individual brand value

6. After the individual attributes of Bob's brand value have been measured, the firm can take measures to optimize the value of the various factors of his brand value to maximize his CLV.

   Implementation of this strategy will be subject to the budget constraints of the marketing resources allocated to Bob based on his CLV score. Such optimized values of the components of Bob's brand value are shown in Figure 11.5.

7. After the components of brand value have been optimized, the firm can translate these optimized values to concrete brand management strategies.

For instance, it is shown in Figure 11.5 that Bob's brand value increases tremendously with his brand effect and loyalty. Therefore, the focal firm can send personalized marketing messages to enhance Bob's emotional connection with the brand. If the firm finds out that there are other high-CLV customers who share Bob's view of the brand, the firm can enhance its brand effect by initiating a suitable advertisement campaign.

The firm sent out an invitation for Bob to join the loyalty program to build his brand loyalty. After implementing the new brand management strategies, the focal firm found that Bob's CLV curve (as illustrated in Figure 11.6) improved greatly, and such an increase was driven directly by increasing Bob's brand value. By the firm implementing these brand value strategies, Bob's CLV score increased from about $12,000 to about $18,000, and the cost of implementing these customized strategies to Bob was about $600. The ROI on implementing these strategies for Bob is 10, or 1,000%. This demonstrates the effectiveness of these strategies and how implementing these will directly lead to profit maximization.

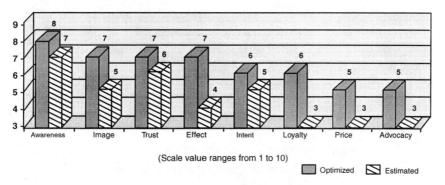

Figure 11.5 Bob's estimated and optimized IBV

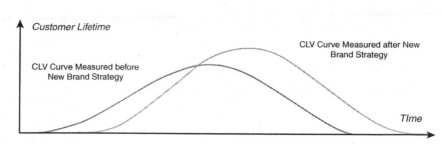

Figure 11.6 Bob's CLV curve measured at different times

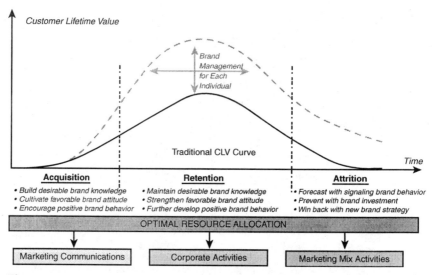

Figure 11.7 Customer life cycle brand management: An integrated framework

The goal of a successful individual brand management strategy is to maximize a customer's lifetime value, driven by a brand in all three stages of the customer life cycle: acquisition, retention, and attrition, as shown in Figure 11.7.

When approaching a potential customer, the firm's goal should be to build the brand knowledge of the customer, cultivate desirable brand attitude, and encourage positive brand behavior intentions. When the customer moves into the intention stage, a firm should try to maintain or update the existing brand knowledge of the customer by sending personalized brand messages. The customer's brand attitude and brand behavior intentions can be further developed by inviting the customer to participate in brand communities and loyalty programs. More crucially, firms should predict when a customer is reaching the attrition stage by closely observing the downward trend in the components associated with the IBV. The firms should take measures to prevent the customer from leaving, and in the case of customers who have left, efforts should be made to win back those customers.

As shown in Figure 11.7, there are three main paths for reaching a customer: marketing communications, corporate activities, and marketing-mix activities. In adopting a successful brand management strategy, the firm should optimally allocate its marketing resources across these three paths to attain maximum value.

How to Acquire Customers with Potentially High CLV

To acquire customers with potentially high CLV, firms can first prioritize their existing customers based on IBV. Then, by analyzing the profile of customers with high brand value, firms can target potential customers with similar profiles. When a new customer purchases from the firm, his potential brand value can be predicted by comparing it to an existing customer with a similar profile, as outlined in Figure 11.8.

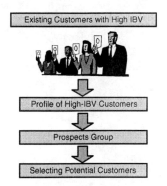

Figure 11.8 Acquiring customers with potentially high CLV

Conclusion

By understanding the link between IBV and CLV, firms can efficiently allocate their resources to generate maximum value. Several factors affect the IBV, such as brand knowledge, brand attitude, and brand behavior intentions. By linking these factors to the final customer behavior outcomes, firms can thus link the IBV of their customers and their CLV. A clear understanding of the various factors that affect IBV and its link to CLV enables firms to take appropriate corrective measures to simultaneously build both the customer's IBV and CLV.

Endnotes

[1] www.brandchannel.com/features_effect.asp?fa_id=40

[2] *Ibid.*

[3] www.venturerepublic.com/resources/Samsung_Building_brand_equity_through_brand_community.asp

[4] www.businessweek.com/innovate/NussbaumOnDesign/archives/2006/08/bps_green_brand.html

[5] David Dunne, "Branding the Experience," *Marketing* 38 2004: 11.

[6] www.businessweek.com/magazine/content/03_40/b3852001_mz001.htm

[7] http://news.bbc.co.uk/2/hi/business/4170591.stm

[8] www.businessweek.com/magazine/content/04_31/b3894094.htm

[9] www.businessweek.com/magazine/content/04_12/b3875002.htm

[10] V. Kumar, M. Luo, and V. R. Rao, "Linking an Individual's Brand Value to the CLV: An Integrated Framework," Working Paper, University of Connecticut.

12

Acquiring Profitable Customers

Relevant Issues

- Is it prudent to use acquisition and retention rates as a measure of overall marketing efficiency?

- Will a firm's profits be maximized by optimizing customer acquisition and customer retention expenditures, separately?

Each year companies are spending more and more on advertising to try to acquire new customers. In March 2007, Nielsen reported that spending on advertisements in 2006 rose by around 4.6% from 2005, to a total of $139.07 billion.[1] With the increased ability of firms to collect and analyze data that includes each customer's purchase behavior and demographic information, firms can now better customize marketing campaigns to individual customers and increase the overall effectiveness of those marketing campaigns. However, evidence shows that many firms are still struggling to justify their direct marketing expenses, partly because they are not properly allocating the right amount of resources between customer acquisition and retention.

A field study was conducted with three companies—a B2B firm, a pharmaceutical firm, and a catalog retailer—to determine optimal levels of spending on direct marketing to maximize profitability. Table 12.1 shows the results.

Table 12.1 Optimizing Direct Marketing Expenditures

Company	How Much More/Less Should Be Spent on Direct Marketing to Reach Optimal Levels?	How Much Profit Would Increase If Spending on Direct Marketing Were at the Optimal Level?
B2B	–68%	42%
Pharmaceutical	31%	36%
Catalog retailer	–31%	29%

Source: J. Thomas, W. Reinartz, and V. Kumar, "Getting the Most Out of All Your Customers," *Harvard Business Review*, July-August 2004: 116–123.

The results of this study show in all three cases what each firm was spending from the optimal amount on direct marketing to maximize profitability (68%, 31%, and 31% off of optimal). The firms did not have to decrease their spending on direct marketing to maximize profitability. The pharmaceutical firm, to achieve maximum profitability, had to increase its spending on direct marketing by 31%. In addition, the impact of the changes in optimal spending on direct marketing shows that by not spending close to the optimal amount on direct marketing, these firms were falling short of maximizing their profitability (by 42%, 36%, and 29%). Why is it that these firms are so far from maximizing their profitability even with the increased customer information?

Too often when marketers make decisions about allocating resources for direct marketing, the customers targeted by these campaigns are those who are inexpensive (easier) to acquire and inexpensive (easier) to retain. This mindset overemphasizes the short-term gain of cheaply acquiring and retaining customers, instead of going after customers who are going to be most profitable in the long run. In addition, managers are too quick to try to maximize each stage of the acquisition and retention process, thereby failing to look at the bigger picture of balancing acquisition and retention together. This, in turn, means that they are managing the whole customer relationship instead of just focusing on one aspect. In the next section, we take a closer look at how a firm's efforts to manage the acquisition and retention process tend to go wrong and what the firm can do to overcome these issues.

Pitfalls to Balancing Acquisition and Retention

1. Law of Diminishing Returns

All too often, firms look to a single metric within a process to determine the overall success of acquisition and retention. In many cases for acquisition and retention, this metric is the acquisition rate and retention rate. The acquisition rate refers to the percentage of people targeted by a marketing campaign who actually become customers. The retention rate is the percentage of people who are retained as customers at any given time. Managers use these two metrics mainly because they are simple and easy to understand and track, mostly because companies are interested in the outcome of these metrics: higher market share. In some cases, a higher acquisition and retention rate (and in turn market share) are reliable predictors of business performance. For example, a local cable operator is likely able to use acquisition and retention rates as a predictor of firm performance for basic cable. As the local cable operator acquires and retains more customers for the basic cable service, it can directly relate each newly acquired customer and each additional month a customer is retained to a higher market share and higher profitability. This is because the product being offered (basic cable) costs the same for each customer and is contractual in nature. In many cases, however, firms do not have a contractual relationship with all their customers. Even if a contractual relationship exists, the many different types and numbers of products offered make the benefit of adding one additional customer vary greatly. So, let's reconsider the situation with a cable company. Many cable companies offer more than just basic cable, such as digital cable, telephone service, and Internet service (with each product offering different levels of service at different price points). There is no clarity as to whether one additional customer adds the same profit as the next customer. As a result, when the cable company has to decide how to evaluate the success of a marketing campaign, should it look at maximizing the acquisition rate, retention rate, or profitability?

The answer to this question seems straightforward: The cable operator would want to maximize profitability. This is not always clear because it goes against the current mindset that achieving the highest acquisition rate possible is ideal. What every firm needs to understand is that as acquisition rates and retention rates increase, firms' profits do not always increase. After a certain point, the cost of acquiring an additional customer outweighs the future stream of profit that acquired customer will bring to the firm. How does a firm find a balance between acquisition rate, retention rate, and overall customer profitability? To get a fairly straightforward answer to this question, we look to a marketing study by Robert Blattberg and John Deighton.[2] The goal of their study was to examine a potential solution to the problem of balancing acquisition rates and retention rates with customer value. In this study, they asked a manager how much was spent in the past year to acquire customers and how many of those customers were actually converted from being prospects to actually making a purchase. The manager was asked how much was spent in the previous year to retain each customer and what was the percentage of customers still with the company. Based on the responses to these questions, the authors were able to derive the optimal level of spending on acquisition and retention for that particular firm (see Figure 12.1).

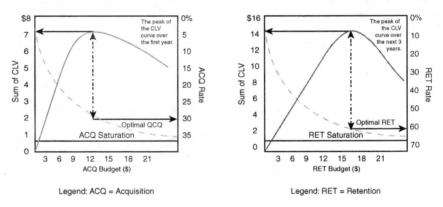

Figure 12.1 Acquisition and retention rates versus CLV

These results show that in the cases of both acquisition and retention, there is an optimal point at which the firm can maximize its profitability by having the right acquisition rate (around 25%) and retention rate (around 50%). These numbers will vary from firm to firm. The purpose of the study is clear. There is a diminishing return in profitability as each additional customer is acquired and retained, and at some point in time continuing to increase the acquisition or retention rate only leads to a diminishing level of overall profitability. This is because it becomes harder (more expensive) to acquire or retain the "next customer." Firms should only make decisions to acquire or retain the next customer if the cost of doing so is less than the value the customer brings back to the firm, either through his own future purchases (Customer Lifetime Value [CLV]) or by helping the firm gain new customers through word-of-mouth and referrals (see Chapter 13, "Managing Customer Referral Behavior"). Many firms have already started to realize this and have taken steps to reward managers who are profitable and not the ones who only maximize metrics such as acquisition and retention rates. This can lead directly into the next pitfall of balancing acquisition and retention: focusing too much on short-term profit.

2. Short-Term versus Long-Term Outlook

Because firms are beginning to realize that customer profitability is the desired outcome (and not necessarily acquisition or retention rates alone), managers are looking to get the most out of each customer. This means that they do not consider the long-term profitability of the customer, only what they can get out of the next transaction. Usually, this problem surfaces when managers begin to group their customers into one of four buckets: those customers who are easy or hard to acquire and those who are easy or hard to retain. Then, to maximize short-term profitability, managers look to the customers who are easy to acquire and easy to retain to get the most customers at the lowest overall cost. This would not be a problem if each bucket of customers were equally as profitable. This approach of targeting the easiest customers to acquire and easiest customers to retain makes the false assumption that acquisition costs and retention costs are the major driver in customer profitability. The results show otherwise.

A recent marketing study with a catalog retailer was undertaken to analyze the relationship between acquisition costs, retention costs, and customer profitability.[3] In this study, a cohort of customers was tracked over a three-year time period. This cohort was split into one of four buckets based on how expensive it was to acquire and retain the customers. Then, based on the transaction behavior of these customers, this study determined how much each of the four groups of customers contributed to the overall profitability of the cohort of customers. Figure 12.2 shows the results of this study.

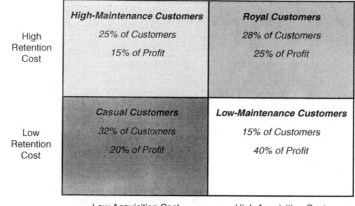

	Low Acquisition Cost	High Acquisition Cost
High Retention Cost	**High-Maintenance Customers** 25% of Customers 15% of Profit	**Royal Customers** 28% of Customers 25% of Profit
Low Retention Cost	**Casual Customers** 32% of Customers 20% of Profit	**Low-Maintenance Customers** 15% of Customers 40% of Profit

Figure 12.2 Do acquisition and retention costs drive profits?

Source: Adapted from Thomas J., W. Reinartz, and V. Kumar, "Getting the Most Out of All Your Customers," *Harvard Business Review*, July-August 2004: 116–123. Printed with permission from the Harvard Business School Publishing.

As expected, the largest segment of the group comes from the customers who are easiest to acquire and easiest to retain (Casual Customers). However, this group only contributed 20% of the overall profitability of the entire group. The customers who were hard to acquire but fairly easy to retain (Low-Maintenance Customers) were actually contributing the most to the profitability of this cohort (40%) and only made up 15% of the total number of customers. In fact, even the group of customers who are hard to acquire and hard to retain (Royal Customers) contributed more in profit (25%) than the Casual Customers and was made up of fewer customers than the Casual Customers (28%). These results are not unique to catalog firms. Many firms are seeing the same breakdown of how acquisition and retention costs drive profits.

It is not ideal for managers to solely focus on short-term profits by acquiring and retaining the customers who are easy to acquire and easy to retain. The additional costs of acquiring and retaining customers who are more costly to acquire and more costly to retain seem justified from a long-term view of customer profitability. Now that managers have the tools to identify profitable customers, as discussed in the earlier chapters in this book, managers can dive into each of these cells and pick out the profitable customers. Managers can target these customers for marketing campaigns with the added benefit of knowing how much they will need to spend to acquire or retain the customers.

3. Treating Acquisition and Retention Strategies as Independent

Many companies have tried to address the first two pitfalls mentioned but are trying to do so with acquisition and retention departments that are independent of one another. This inevitably leads to the acquisition department trying to acquire the most customers possible, which inevitably leads to attracting some customers who are not profitable in the long term. If the retention department works on retaining all the customers acquired by the acquisition department, they will be trying to maximize the retention budget on many customers who are not very profitable in the long term. What's worse is that none of the customers who are highly profitable but hard to acquire (Royal Customers and Low-Maintenance Customers) will be targeted by the acquisition department because of their high acquisition costs.

This behavior is more common than we might realize. Many firms still practice this strategy today. For example, many credit card companies spend a lot of money on acquiring every possible customer who is out there. These companies send a lot of direct mail, set up booths at airports and college campuses, and call many potential customers via the telephone. The acquisition departments of these credit card companies are looking to acquire as many customers as possible without thinking about how many of these customers will actually be retained and profitable. Then, after all these new customers have been acquired, the retention departments of these credit card companies spend significant resources trying to retain all these customers, in many cases spending a lot of resources on customers who will never be profitable.

What can be learned from this example? It is a good idea for firms to integrate their acquisition and retention departments. This integration allows the departments to take a long-term view of customer profitability. Then, they won't spend too much time acquiring only those customers who are easy to acquire and then trying to retain all those customers. This long-term view allows managers to identify the most profitable customers and spend the right amount of resources acquiring and retaining them. This example also shows that linking the acquisition and retention strategies will produce a more profitable result. In some cases, firms are already taking this approach. However, in almost every case, firms that try to predict the best customers to acquire are relying on the wrong information.

4. Relying Too Much on Current Customers

Firms that try to predict the potential profitability of prospects often fall into the final pitfall of acquisition and retention. Many of these firms try to use information from current customers to predict the profitability of prospects. The problem that arises is referred to by statisticians as *selection bias*. Selection bias occurs when the customers used in a modeling exercise to predict the behavior of another set of customers aren't a representative sample. In this case, it means that the current customers are used to predict the potential behavior of the prospects. The inferences made from these predictions can be very misleading, causing managers to incorrectly allocate resources to a set of prospects and thus lead to a suboptimal level of profitability. However, this pitfall of acquiring and retaining customers can be solved. In the following section, we present a framework called Allocating Resources for Profit (ARPRO) that enables managers to properly balance resources between acquisition and retention to maximize profitability.

Solution to Balancing Acquisition and Retention: ARPRO

When a company is able to avoid the previously discussed four pitfalls, three key questions need to be answered to achieve an optimal allocation of resources to maximize profit between the acquisition and retention of customers. These questions concern how a firm should allocate resources across different modes of contact (face-to-face, telephone, email, and so on), because different contact modes offer different levels of interpersonal interaction, whether it is more critical to focus on acquisition or retention expenditures when considering customer profitability, and whether acquisition and retention rates are maximized at the same point as customer profitability. The three questions are as follows:

- Given the budget constraint, how does the profit-maximizing strategy allocate resources between the contact modes that vary in their degree of interpersonal interaction and costs?
- Which is more critical for profitability, acquisition or retention expenditures?
- Does the contact strategy that maximizes customer profitability also maximize acquisition and retention rates?

To answer these questions, firms need to adopt a framework that can reveal the true relationships between acquisition, retention, and profit. This can be done using a model we call ARPRO, Allocating Resources for Profit. This model involves complex regression analysis, with long-term profitability as a function of several key factors, and with factors that are weighted and corrected for sample selection bias.[4] However, it is important to understand how the framework can be operationalized for a specific firm and how the implementation can impact the bottom line of the firm. Figure 12.3 illustrates this framework.

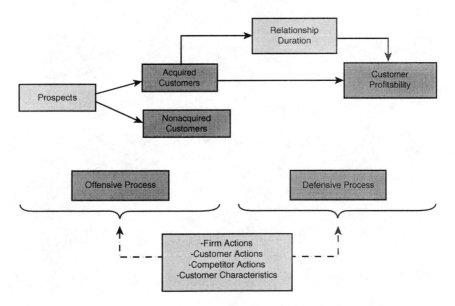

Figure 12.3   Linking acquisition, retention, and profitability: A framework

Source: Adapted from Werner Reinartz, Jacquelyn S. Thomas, and V. Kumar, "Balancing Acquisition and Retention Resources to Maximize Customer Profitability," *Journal of Marketing* 69(1) 2005: 63–79. Printed with permission from the American Marketing Association.

The objective of Figure 12.3 is to identify the relationship between prospects, acquired customers, relationship duration (retention), and customer profitability, by analyzing how firm actions, customer actions, competitor actions, and customer characteristics play a role in driving customer profitability. This is done by first considering "offensive" strategies to go out and acquire customers, and then following this up with "defensive" strategies to try to retain these customers from switching to competitors. Because of the ability of this framework to link together all these processes within a firm, it allows managers to identify different trade-offs between how much and how to invest in the acquisition of customers and in turn how much and how to invest in the retention of customers to maximize profitability. To determine the values of these trade-offs, it is important to understand what the drivers of acquisition, retention (duration), and profitability are and how they can be leveraged to achieve maximum profitability (see Figure 12.4).

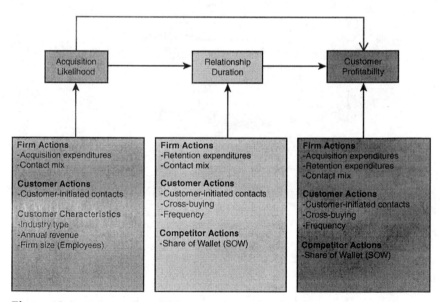

Figure 12.4 Drivers of acquisition, retention, and profitability

Source: Adapted from Werner Reinartz, Jacquelyn S. Thomas, and V. Kumar, "Balancing Acquisition and Retention Resources to Maximize Customer Profitability," *Journal of Marketing* 69(1): 63–79. Printed with permission from the American Marketing Association.

The drivers listed in Figure 12.4 come from a recent marketing study with a B2B high-tech manufacturer.[5] The customer firms in the data included firms that sell to both B2B and B2C firms. For each of the three parts of this model (acquisition likelihood, relationship duration, and customer profitability), the drivers were seen as significant predictors of the outcome. However, it should also be noted that these drivers are somewhat generalizable, because similar drivers were found to be important in predicting each of the three pieces of this model for a pharmaceutical company, too.[6]

For each part of this framework, the model identifies drivers that can help predict the acquisition likelihood, relationship duration, and customer profitability and are broadly defined into four main categories: firm actions, customer actions, competitor actions, and customer characteristics.

In this case, firm actions refer to the different controls that a firm has when marketing to customers. This can include various expenditures on each customer to acquire or retain the customer or any changes to the general marketing-mix variables to each customer (for instance, promotions). Because these are the drivers that the firm has direct control of, managers can focus on how small changes in these drivers affect each aspect of acquisition, retention, and profitability.

Customer actions can be broadly defined as any actions that a customer takes to begin or continue a relationship with the firm. These can include inquiries about products or even product support requests for currently used products. Although a firm has less control over these drivers, when a customer initiates contact with a firm, it can be a strong signal about that customer's future behavior or future desire to build a strong relationship.

Customer characteristics represent either the firmographics (that is, demographics of firms; for example, firm size and number of employees) or demographics of a customer. Although these customer characteristics rarely change, especially in the short term, knowing these characteristics of your customers can help in the profiling of prospects or the profiling of current customers. This in turn allows managers to identify customers for specific marketing campaigns, and it may even help when no information is available to allow you to differentiate between two different customers. For example, if you have two prospects and you have no transactional information about these prospects (only demographic information is available), how do you choose which customer is more likely to respond to the marketing contact? If one of the customers is older than the other, and you know that an older age plays a key role in acquisition likelihood, you would choose to market to the older customer to get a better chance of product adoption.

Finally, competitor actions refer to the amount of access competitors have with a given customer. If you can have a strong relationship with your customer and get your customer to purchase exclusively from you, it is much harder for competitors to convince that customer to switch to a different firm. In the B2B case, this is often operationalized by a driver called Share of Wallet (SOW), which refers to the percentage of a customer's budget for a particular product category that is used to purchase from you, with the remaining percentage used to purchase from a competitor. If the SOW for a customer is high, the customer purchases almost exclusively from a focal firm and likely has a low probability of switching to a competitor. However, customers with a low SOW are already purchasing from competitors and could potentially be swayed to purchase more (or exclusively) from a competitor, because their switching costs are likely to be much lower than the customer with a high SOW.

When you can identify all the drivers for each of the three parts of the ARPRO model, you can determine the relative impact each of the drivers has on profitability by running these three models as a simultaneous regression model. This simultaneous model will resemble the setup shown in Figure 12.5. More details on the model estimation process can be accessed at www.drvkumar.com/mcp.

$$\left\{ \begin{array}{l} \text{Profitability} = f \text{ (Firm Actions}_{\text{profit}}, \text{ Customer Actions}_{\text{profit}}, \text{ Competitor Actions}_{\text{profit}}) \text{ (Model 1)} \\ \text{Duration} = f \text{ (Firm Actions}_{\text{duration}}, \text{ Customer Actions}_{\text{duration}}, \text{ Competitor Actions}_{\text{duration}}) \text{ (Model 2)} \\ \text{Acquisition} = f \text{ (Firm Actions}_{\text{acquisition}}, \text{ Customer Actions}_{\text{acquisition}}, \text{ Demographics}_{\text{acquisition}}) \text{ (Model 3)} \end{array} \right.$$

Figure 12.5 ARPRO regression model

When a manager gets the weights for each of these drivers for each of the models of the framework, determining the amount to spend on acquisition and retention for each customer can be done simultaneously to maximize profitability. You can just plug in the values with the weights, and it will determine the optimal acquisition and retention spending for each customer to maximize profit. How can a firm answer those three key questions, and what is the potential downside of not taking the ARPRO strategy?

The Profit-Maximizing ARPRO Strategy

The ultimate goal of the ARPRO framework is to develop a strategy that will maximize overall profitability in the long term. In the case of acquisition and retention, making suboptimal decisions can severely affect overall profitability. For example, based on the drivers and weights of the drivers computed for the pharmaceutical firm in a recent marketing study, the optimal average acquisition spending across customers should be $10, and the optimal average retention spending across customers should be $60 (see Table 12.2).

Table 12.2   Average Customer Profitability

		Retention Spending				
		$40	$50	$60	$70	$80
	$1	$1,423	$1,543	$1,583	$1,543	$1,423
Acquisition	$5	$1,437	$1,557	$1,597	$1,557	$1,437
Spending	$10	$1,443	$1,563	$1,603	$1,563	$1,443
	$15	$1,437	$1,557	$1,597	$1,557	$1,437
	$20	$1,418	$1,538	$1,578	$1,538	$1,418

Source: J. Thomas, W. Reinartz, and V. Kumar, "Getting the Most Out of All Your Customers," *Harvard Business Review*, July-August 2004: 116–123. Printed with permission from the Harvard Business School Publishing.

This optimal spending on acquisition and retention gives the highest overall customer profitability for the firm. Although the difference between the levels of profitability seems small—around a 1.2% decrease in profitability for about a 10% savings in costs—the loss in profit grows fast when the number of customers in the sample grows.

For example, if a firm cuts its marketing cost by 10%, and the savings in cost is around $250,000, the reduction in profit is around 1.2%. This means that if the base of customers is around 60,000, the resulting loss in long-term profits would be around $1.2 million. This clearly shows that when firms choose suboptimal amounts to spend on acquisition and retention, the impact on profit can be drastic.

In addition, acquisition and retention spending should not be done in isolation. For example, if the same firm only tried to maximize relationship duration (retention) by itself, the optimal spending level would be at $70 per customer (see Table 12.3). However, the previous example showed that the optimal spending was actually $70 on both acquisition and retention: $10 on acquisition, and $60 on retention per customer. By optimizing the relationship duration by spending $70 instead of splitting the $70 on acquisition ($10) and retention ($60), the profitability would decrease from $1,603 to about $1,543 (a drop of 3.7%). See Table 12.2 for values.

Table 12.3 Average Customer Relationship Duration

Retention spending (per customer)	$40	$50	$60	$70	$80
Estimated relationship duration (days)	122	135	142	143	138

Source: J. Thomas, W. Reinartz, and V. Kumar, "Getting the Most Out of All Your Customers," *Harvard Business Review*, July-August 2004: 116–123. Printed with permission from the Harvard Business School Publishing.

This shows that spending too much on marketing is detrimental, but it also shows that spending too little on marketing can be just as or more detrimental to profits than spending too much. This question of spending on acquisition and retention creates a problem as to whether it is more important to spend on acquisition or spend on retention.

Which Is More Critical: Acquisition or Retention Spending?

The differences in the impact of acquisition and retention spending on profitability make it difficult to decide how much to invest in each customer. This critical question arises often in marketing when budgets are constrained and decisions have to be made about whether to cut acquisition spending or retention spending. For example, if the firm in this study had to cut its marketing budget by 5%, one simple way to do this is to cut 5% from the acquisition budget and 5% from the retention budget. However, the firm could also choose to cut only the acquisition budget and not touch the retention budget. This would cause the acquisition spending to drop by 33% from the previous example based on spending $10 per customer before and $6.5 per customer after. Deviating from the optimal spend will cause a decrease in profitability, but is it better to cut 5% in each or 25% in acquisition spending?

In this case, the results showed that every $1 underinvested in acquisition and retention spending led to profitability being reduced by $1.25. If the entire cut were in acquisition, for every $1 decrease in spending the resulting decrease in long-term profitability would be $3.03. This obviously shows that if these two strategies had to be considered (equal decrease in acquisition and retention versus decrease only in acquisition), the equal decrease in spending for acquisition and retention would result in a higher long-term customer profit. However, these results might change based on many different factors, making it necessary for each firm to analyze how deviations in spending affect overall profitability.

Maximum Profits, Acquisition Likelihood, and Relationship Duration

What does all this mean for acquisition spending, retention spending, and overall profitability? It means that it is not only necessary to consider acquisition spending and retention spending at the same time, but also that profitability is based on how the two interact. Therefore, it is not necessarily important to consider exactly how much to spend on acquisition or retention alone, but instead on how you balance your acquisition and retention spending together to maximize profitability.

In addition, although results were presented at the "average" customer level, in many cases it is necessary to be more granular in your approach. Many firms now have access to customer data at the individual level and can determine the exact allocation of resources to each customer. Although the average spending for the pharmaceutical firm in this study was $10 for acquisition and $60 for retention, it is necessary to find customers in each of the four cells from Figure 12.2 (easy/hard to acquire/retain). This is because profitable customers come from each of the four cells, and it might be worth going after a customer who is very hard to acquire and very hard to retain if the pay-off is there in the long term. Managers should be able to allocate the right resources to the right customers by correctly linking acquisition and retention spending to each customer. They can achieve this by using the ARPRO model and determining the right drivers that lead to maximum profitability.

Conclusion

The top priority of marketing managers should be the ability to know when, what and how much resources to allocate in the communications channels so that we don't overspend or underspend on customers. This will help the firm to invest on the most profitable customers at the most appropriate time—and in the most effective way. However, many companies continue to spend resources on a large number of unprofitable customers. This is because they either invest in customers who are easy to acquire or retain but are not necessarily profitable, thereby leading to wastage of limited resources. Allocating resources optimally to maximize profit between the acquisition and retention of customers is achieved through the introduction of the ARPRO framework. Case studies discussed in this chapter provide evidence that optimal allocation of marketing resources helps companies increase their revenue, balance acquisition and retention strategies, and manage customers profitably.

Endnotes

[1] Katy Bachman, "Nielsen: Ad Spend Rises 4.6% in '06," March 19, 2007, at www.mediaweek.com/mw/news/recent_display.jsp?vnu_content_id=1003560033.

[2] Robert C. Blattberg and John Deighton, "Manage Marketing by the Customer Equity Test," *Harvard Business Review* 74(4) 1996: 136–144.

[3] Jacquelyn S. Thomas, Werner Reinartz, and V. Kumar, "Getting the Most Out of All Your Customers," *Harvard Business Review* 82(7,8) 2004: 116–223.

4 The method for the complex regressions can be found in the following research
   paper:
   Werner Reinartz, Jacquelyn S. Thomas, and V. Kumar, "Balancing Acquisition and
   Retention Resources to Maximize Customer Profitability," *Journal of Marketing*
   69(1) 2005: 63–79.

5 *Ibid.*

6 J. Thomas, W. Reinartz, and V. Kumar, "Getting the Most Out of All Your
   Customers," *Harvard Business Review,* July-August 2004: 116–123.

13

Managing Customer Referral Behavior

Relevant Issues

- How do we account for attitudinal behavior of customers when designing strategies?
- How do we measure the indirect contribution (referrals or word-of-mouth) made by customers toward the firm's profit?

Many firms now use viral marketing programs to harness the power of word-of-mouth and referrals to acquire new customers. For example, Sprint PCS is currently running a referral campaign: If you are a current customer and you refer a new customer to sign up, you get a $25 Visa debit card.[1]

In addition, certain companies are harnessing the power of referral behavior to help spread the word about their current or new products. For example, given the success of their word-of-mouth program, P&G's Tremor, which is targeted at teens and currently has a membership of more than 250,000 teens, P&G has recently launched another word-of-mouth marketing program called Vocalpoint. Vocalpoint has the goal of enlisting women across the country who have children under the age of 18 to serve as advocates for their products. These women receive messages from P&G that are custom designed in such a way that they encourage members to share them with other women they interact with on a daily basis. They are also sent coupons and free samples to hand out to their friends. According to Steve Knox, CEO of Vocalpoint, "We know that the most powerful form of marketing is an advocacy message from a trusted friend." So far, P&G has enlisted more than 500,000 women in the program, and it's still growing. P&G has spent a great deal of time and effort in understanding how word-of-mouth influences individuals and what message content needs to be to drive action.

Many of these same firms are using customer selection metrics such as Customer Lifetime Value (CLV) to identify their "best" customers and then allocating resources to target these customers with the highest CLV for these referral campaigns. In the process, these firms frequently alienate low- and medium-CLV customers because of the lower-level service provided and the differentiated treatment. An important question we need to answer is whether these low- and medium-CLV customers may in fact be of value to a firm because of their word-of-mouth and referrals, and if so, what their value to the firm is.

Although the CLV metric has been shown to outperform all other behavioral metrics, such as RFM (Recency, Frequency, and Monetary value) or SOW (Share of Wallet), in predicting a customer's future value to the firm, it does have one main limitation as a complete measure of a customer's value. Even though all customer relationship management (CRM) programs collect data on transactions and demographics, they fail to directly measure customer attitudes (for example, satisfaction). But, leaving satisfaction out of the CLV calculation is not necessarily a problem because it is already manifested as part of the buying process. However, it is clear that customers can not only contribute value to the firm through their own transactions (direct profits), but they also have an impact on the transactions of other customers through word-of-mouth and referrals (indirect profits) by helping the firm to acquire new customers at lower costs. So, how can managers determine the value of a customer's ability to spread word-of-mouth and make referrals?

Customer Referral Value (CRV)

This chapter introduces the concept of Customer Referral Value (CRV), which is defined as a customer's expected future referral value with the firm. This metric enables managers to measure and manage each customer based on his ability to generate indirect profit to the firm. This indirect impact on the firm's profit comes through savings in acquisition costs and through the addition of new customers by way of customer referral. Then, this leads to the following question: How does a firm measure a customer's ability to make referrals?

Some recent marketing studies have suggested that a link exists between a customer's willingness to make a referral and the growth in a firm's profit.[2] However, it might be short-sighted to think that there is a high correlation between customers' stated intentions to recommend products or services and their actual behaviors. A field study was conducted on customers from firms in two separate industries: a financial services firm (n = 6,700) and a telecommunications firm (n = 9,900). This field study was conducted to better understand what mechanisms were driving growths of new customers from referrals for each firm. In other words, four more questions need to be asked to first determine whether the customers who are willing to recommend new customers actually follow through with it and bring new and profitable customers into the firm:

- If a customer intends to refer a product to a friend or a colleague (prospect), how frequently does that customer actually follow through and speak to the prospects?

- Are the prospects willing to listen if the customer talks to them about the product or the company?

- Do the prospects actually become customers, even if they are willing to listen?

- Even if they become customers, do the prospects spend enough to be profitable for the firm?

Working with managers from a telecommunications firm and a financial services firm, we asked these questions to a set of their customers and tracked their behavior and the behavior of the prospects over time to see whether their stated intention to recommend actually occurred and led to the acquisition of new and profitable customers. The results of this survey clearly show that there is a gap between their stated intent to recommend and following through in making recommendations, as well as in whether a prospect who became a customer is being profitable. Table 13.1 shows the results of this study.

Table 13.1   Intentions versus Actual Referral Behavior

Item	Financial Services (n = 6,700)	Telecommunications (n = 9,900)
% Stated intention to recommend	68	81
% Actually referring	33	30
% Prospects becoming customers	14	12
% Prospects who are profitable customers	11	8

These findings show that there is a definite gap between a customer's willingness to refer and his actual referral behavior. In addition, it clearly shows that using a measure for "willingness to recommend" falls short when it comes to actionable strategies to manage customers. For example, in the case of the financial services firm, only 68% (n = 4,556) of customers intended to make referrals. However, only 33% (n = 2,211) actually did make the referrals. In addition, the results show the difference in the number of referrals to prospects (33% [n = 2,211] for financial services) and how many of those prospects actually bought products and services (14% [n = 938] for financial services). We can also see how many of the referred customers were actually profitable (11% [n = 737] for financial services). Therefore, it is not sufficient to know whether a set of customers is willing to refer your products or services; it is also necessary to understand how the flow of information moves from each customer to potential prospects. Therefore, each customer's CRV was measured using a general equation (see Equation 13.1), where each part of the equation was estimated using a four-step process: determining whether the customer would have bought the product or service anyway, predicting the future value of each referred customer, predicting the future number of referrals, and finally predicting the future timing of the referrals.

$$CRV_i = \sum_{t=1}^{T} \sum_{y=1}^{n1} \frac{(A_{ty} - a_{ty} - M_{ty} + ACQ1_{ty})}{(1+r)^t} + \sum_{t=1}^{T} \sum_{y=n1}^{n2} \frac{(ACQ2_{ty})}{(1+r)^t}$$

Equation 13.1

where,

T = number of periods that will be predicted into the future (for example, years)
A_{ty} = gross margin contributed by customer y who otherwise would not have bought the product
a_{ty} = cost of the referral for customer y
1 to n1 = number of customers who would not join without the referral
n2 – n1 = number of customers who would have joined anyway
M_{ty} = marketing costs needed to retain the referred customers
$ACQ1_{ty}$ = savings in acquisition cost from customers who would not join without the referral
$ACQ2_{ty}$ = savings in acquisition cost from customers who would have joined anyway

A CRV is measured by summing up the values in all the time periods during which individuals come to the firm via referrals by the original referring customer. The value contributed by referrals for each customer can include both direct and indirect referrals, which means that we add the value of the referrals that the customer makes (direct) and the value of the referrals that the referred customers make (indirect). It is important to capture both the direct and the indirect referral values under each customer's value to the firm for two reasons. First, it is important because when customers buy only because of the referral, and if the direct referral does not occur, it is also unlikely that the indirect referral would follow. Thus, credit, at least in part, for the indirect referral could also belong to the original referrer and be a part of his value to the firm. This would also help the managers search for customers who will not only make direct referrals, but also those who will refer customers who are likely to refer new customers (indirect) because the cascading value of the direct-to-indirect referrals can be very significant.

In addition, various aspects of a referral need to be considered in this process. First, the timing of the referral is important to determine the proper discounting of predicted value in the future to today's dollar terms. In addition, we must consider the number of referrals that will be made each year and how each of these referrals will contribute to the gross margin of the firm. If a firm rewards referral behavior, we must subtract that cost from any value attached to the referring customer for the referral. Finally, if a new customer emerges from the referral process, the company saves money in the acquisition cost. These savings apply to two different groups: those customers who would have joined anyway at some time, and those who would only join with a referral. It is important to take into account the entire transaction for the latter category of customers because the company would not have realized this sale otherwise. However, the only aspect of the referral counted in the case of a customer who would have joined anyway is the savings in acquisition cost. A CRV to the firm can be calculated when all these components are combined. To estimate the value of each of these components, we use the following four-step process.

1. Determine whether customers would have bought anyway.

   To determine whether the referred customer would have purchased without the referral, a simple question was asked when he became a customer: "How likely is it that you would have subscribed to this service without a referral in the next 12 months?" This was operationalized as a binary (0/1) outcome that separated the customers into the two different groups: the customers who would have bought anyway, and the customers who bought only because of the referral. After these customers were separated into the two groups, we estimated the future value and timing of the referrals from the customers who would not have bought without the referral.

2. Predict the future value of each referred customer.

   To compute the value of all the customers who would not have joined without the referral, we captured their transaction data and the company's marketing communication data for a short period of time after the referral was made and they became a customer, which included amount, category, channel, and demographic information from each referred customer, to estimate the increase in the value each of these new customers will have on the firm's profit in the future. The drivers that we selected to predict the future stream of profit that the referred customers will give to the firm (Contribution Margin – marketing costs, or $A_{ty} - M_{ty}$) were based on past marketing studies that were able to predict the drivers for relationship duration, customer profitability, and marketing costs for retaining newly acquired customers.[3]

   To operationalize this into our CRV model, we used the following approach. First, based on the first three years of data for each customer, we predicted the average referral contribution margin for each customer in each period (see Figure 13.1). This was done for each customer by looking at each of his referrals and computing the average profits that each referral brought to the firm in every time period in the first three years. We then used those values to predict the future profit for each referral per period in the holdout year. Next, we predicted the average cost of retaining each customer's referrals by looking at the past marketing costs for each period and projecting that average marketing cost into the future.

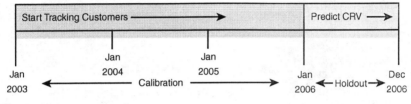

Figure 13.1 Timeline data

3. Predict the number of referrals.

   We used a similar method to predict the future number of referrals that each customer was likely to have. This number is based on using the average number of referrals in the first three years for each customer and projecting that number into the holdout year. We found that the average number of past referrals was also a good predictor of the actual number of referrals that a customer made. When we computed the average number of referrals based on the past referral behavior, we rounded it off to the nearest integer.

4. Predict the timing of customer referrals.

   The timing of the referrals in this case was based on the timing of past referrals by customers from each of the firms in the two industries. For example, because the financial services firm collected data semi-annually, we were able to split the prediction of the timing of referral into the first half of the year and the second half of the year. If the customer averaged six total referrals per year, and all the referrals came in the first half of the year, in the CRV prediction all the referrals would be credited to the first half of the year. However, if another customer referred all six customers in the second half of the year, the CRV prediction would have all the referrals credited to the second half of the year. Splitting up the timing of referrals into two time periods (first half of the year and second half of the year) is important because it can have a dramatic impact on the value of each customer's CRV. A customer who refers customers earlier rather than later not only accelerates the time when the firm receives the profit from the referred customer, but it also allows more time for the new customer to make his or her own referrals.

Calculating CRV: A Typical Customer

To value customers and see how they truly impact the bottom line of the company, we provide another example based on work we have done with a company from the telecommunications industry. For this example, we show how to use the information about this customer's referral behavior to compute his referral value (CRV). We first needed to obtain data from the telecommunications industry concerning both the transactions and referral behavior for a typical customer from Decile 6 from Table 13.3. Table 13.2 shows this information.

Table 13.2   Behavior of a Typical Telecommunications Customer (Quarterly Data)

Statistics (per 6-Month Period)	Typical Customer
Average contribution margin	$70
Number of referrals per period	3
Number of indirect referrals made by referred customers	3
Cost of referral	$20
Acquisition cost savings	$10
Marketing costs	$3
Number of referrals who would have joined anyway	1 out of 3
Yearly discount rate	15%

As Table 13.2 illustrates, this customer will most likely refer three customers for the next three periods, of which one would have joined anyway, and each of those customers will refer three customers in subsequent periods. Therefore, we need to calculate the net present value of the profit that each direct referral will bring to the company over the next three periods. In this case, we take a conservative approach and only value those customers who were directly referred by the original customer and made a purchase. However, in cases where it seems appropriate, a manager could add the additional value of the indirect referrals to the value of the original referrer's CRV, where an indirect referral is a customer who was referred by a customer who was, in turn, referred by the original customer. To estimate the referral behavior value of this customer, we will first show how to calculate the CRV for this typical customer for one period, and then we will display the overall CRV for that customer over three periods.

First, we need to separate our calculation into two parts:

- The value of the customers who would not have joined without the referral

- The value of the customers who would have joined anyway at a later time

Because the first set of customers would not have joined without the referral, we need to consider what they contribute in terms of profit, how much we saved by not spending money ineffectively in an attempt to acquire them, how much it cost us to give a referral incentive, and finally how much it cost us to retain these customers. Going back to Table 13.2, we can find the descriptive data of our typical customer in the financial services firm. We find that this customer is likely to contribute $70 in profit for this period, which we call A_t or the "contribution margin" of customer t. Next, we also need to add the acquisition cost savings to this referral's value. The acquisition cost savings for this customer is $10, which we call $ACQ1_t$ or the acquisition cost savings of customer t. Then, we need to consider the costs incurred when this customer was referred. These costs include the $20 we spent on giving the referral incentive, which we label a_1, and the marketing costs we had to spend to retain this customer in this period ($3), which we label M_t. These values will help us calculate the CRV for those customers who would not have joined anyway. We also need to consider the situation where a customer was going to start buying products or services but had not begun the process. In this case, we only need to consider the value of the savings in acquisition cost because the benefit of the referral was mainly to save the firm's resources from acquiring this customer. Therefore, the value of the customer who would have joined anyway is $10, which we label $ACQ2_t$, or the savings in the acquisition cost for the customer who would have joined anyway. Using these values, this referral behavior value for the first period is calculated as follows:

Period 1:

$$CRV_1 = 2\left(\frac{A_1 - a_1 - M_1 + ACQ1_1}{\text{discount rate}}\right) + 2\left(\frac{ACQ2_1}{\text{discount rate}}\right) \qquad \text{Equation 13.2}$$

$$CRV_1 = 2\left(\frac{\$66 - \$8 - \$18 + \$5}{(1.15)^{0.5}}\right) + 2\left(\frac{\$5}{(1.15)^{0.5}}\right) \approx \$102$$

Now, as we move forward to future periods, the calculations for the referral value of a customer begin to grow rapidly because new customers are referred in the second period and their purchases need to be added to the purchases from the customers who were referred in period 1. The main reason for this is because not only is the original customer referring prospects in each period (in this case, three), but also because the customers from the last period are continuing to purchase in the second period. Therefore, to compute the value for referral behavior across all the periods together, we need to use a general algorithm that allows us to account for the different referral numbers and timings of referrals for each customer. We have had success in using our general CRV equation. This can be implemented by calculating the present value of the CLV of all customers who would have joined only with a referral and adding the present value of all the acquisition cost savings for customers who would have joined anyway later without a referral. This general formula allows you to separate those customers who would not have joined without the referral from those customers who would have joined even without a referral.

As the results show, the impact grows as time progresses. The main reason for this is the growth of the customer base due to referrals in each period. In period 1, there were only three new customers, whereas in period 2 there were five customers in the value of the CRV (three new customers and two customers from period 1 who bought only because of the referral). In period 3, there were seven customers in the value of the CRV (three new customers and two customers each from periods 1 and 2 who bought only because of the referral).

In addition, because this is a conservative estimate of the value of customer referrals (that is, only the direct referrals are used in the CRV), it does not tell the whole story in terms of the number of new customers who have been acquired by the firm and the total value all these new customers are worth to the firm. If we want to see how many new customers came on board over these three periods that stem from the original customer and the value of these new customers, we need to look at both the direct and the indirect referrals. If each of the customers who were referred during a specific period also made some referrals in subsequent periods, we would see an exponential growth in the total number of new customers who were acquired in the first three periods and the total CRV for those customers. Therefore, if we go back to Table 13.2, we see that a typical customer who was referred to make a purchase will make three additional referrals in the subsequent periods. This means that starting in period 2, the three customers who were referred in period 1 will each refer 3 new customers, making a total of 16 customers (the original customer, the 3 customers referred in the first period, the 9 referrals made by these 3 customers, and 3 more new referrals made by the original customer in period 2). In period 3, if each of the referred customers from period 1 and 2 makes an additional referral, the total number of customers will be 55.

Are CLV and CRV Related?

After the CRV of each customer has computed, it is important to understand the relationship between CLV and CRV. Now that we have a measurement for both CLV (from Chapter 3, "Customer Selection Metrics") and CRV, we know the value provided by the actual purchases made by the customer (CLV) and the influence that customer has on other potential customers (CRV). With this information, managers can begin to make decisions about how to treat and market to customers based on the various combinations of whether the customer is low or high on CLV or CRV (high CLV and high CRV; low CLV and low CRV; and so on).

As noted previously, many firms are using CLV as a method for selecting customers for word-of-mouth and referral campaigns. If the customers who rated highly on CLV were the same customers who rated highly on CRV, managers would not need to use both metrics when managing customers. However, because only transactional and demographic data (not attitudinal data) has played an important role in predicting CLV, customers who score highly on CLV are probably not the same as those who are successful at referring new customers. In fact, a recent marketing study suggested that the most powerful word-of-mouth comes from customers who are less behaviorally loyal to the firm.[4] To investigate this further, using the transaction and referral behavior data from a telecommunications firm (n = 9,900), we measured each customer's CLV and CRV and made predictions for CLV and CRV to see whether the two were related (see Table 13.3).[5]

Table 13.3   Customer Deciles of CLV and CRV for a Telecommunications Firm

Deciles (Ranked by CLV)	CLV ($) (1 Year)	CRV ($) (1 Year)
1	**1,933**	40
2	**1,067**	52
3	**633**	90
4	360	750
5	313	**930**
6	230	**1,020**
7	190	**870**
8	160	96
9	137	65
10	120	46

As illustrated in Table 13.3, after ranking the customers by CLV (high to low) into ten deciles, the top 30% of customers based on CLV (deciles 1, 2, and 3) have no overlap with the top 30% of customers based on CRV (deciles 5, 6, and 7). This means that managers who focus on customers based on CLV alone and provide them the best service are missing the high-CRV customers and therefore ignoring these profitable customers. Even worse, they are perhaps alienating these potentially profitable customers, because they do not score highly on CLV, even though they do score highly on CRV. This can potentially lead those customers who are alienated to slow down customer growth by stopping their referral behavior or, even worse, spreading negative word-of-mouth. Therefore, because customers who score highly on the CLV measure are not the same customers who score highly on the CRV measure, firms should measure both CLV and CRV to implement marketing campaigns that focus on customers based on both dimensions. This will allow firms to both increase the profitability of each customer and, in turn, increase the number of new customers buying products and services. To show the impact of measuring and managing these two metrics simultaneously, we conducted a field study with a financial services firm to see how effective a firm could be when measuring and managing CLV and CRV simultaneously.

Typical Marketplace Phenomenon

So, how does a firm implement the CLV and CRV metric? Many companies already have some or all the data needed to measure both CLV and CRV. To start the process, this behavioral or transactional data needs to be integrated with the referral database. If your company does not have the data at hand, you can begin to collect information from new customers by asking them questions such as these: Were you referred, and if so, by whom? Or, to what degree did the referral from Mr. X/Mrs. Y impact your decision?

For example, some companies like Bank of America have introduced a very value-oriented referral incentive program that gives both the referral and the referring customer $25. Bank of America provides $25 for a customer referral, $10 for a student referral, and $50 for a business referral. These incentives seem to be in proportion to the typical value brought in by each member in the respective referral groups. An example of the campaign is shown in Figure 13.2. Similarly, EarthLink company in the technology communication industry has a referral incentive program.[6] In the Airline industry, United Airlines has a referral program where it gives 5,000 miles for each referral, as shown in Figure 13.3.

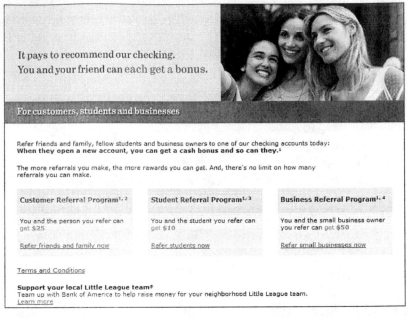

It pays to recommend our checking.
You and your friend can each get a bonus.

For customers, students and businesses

Refer friends and family, fellow students and business owners to one of our checking accounts today:
When they open a new account, you can get a cash bonus and so can they.[1]

The more referrals you make, the more rewards you can get. And, there's no limit on how many referrals you can make.

Customer Referral Program[1,2]	**Student Referral Program[1,3]**	**Business Referral Program[1,4]**
You and the person you refer can get $25	You and the student you refer can get $10	You and the small business owner you refer can get $50
Refer friends and family now	Refer students now	Refer small businesses now

Terms and Conditions

Support your local Little League team[5]
Team up with Bank of America to help raise money for your neighborhood Little League team.
Learn more

Figure 13.2 Sample referral program from Bank of America

UNITED
Mileage Plus

Introduce someone to the benefits of Mileage Plus, get up to 5,000 miles for yourself

To register for this offer, fill out your information below. Then press "Continue" and start referring friends, family members or business associates. You'll be on your way to up to 5,000 bonus miles and you'll be closer to earning award travel.

Please do not enter mobile phone email address.

Your first name: _____ *
Your last name: _____ *
Your email address: _____ *
Re-enter your email address: _____ *
Your Mileage Plus number: _____ *

Continue

Figure 13.3 Sample referral program from United Airlines

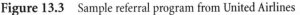

To see how this type of program can actually work for a firm, we will demonstrate an example of the usefulness of measuring the CLV and CRV metric. The telecommunications firm we worked with conducted a field study to identify the independent impact measuring and maximizing CLV and CRV has on a firm's profits. Using two different samples of 9,900 customers (a test sample and a control sample), we first measured each sample's CLV and CRV based on the equations we provided in this book. The customers in both samples were then divided into four cells of a 2×2 matrix based on high/low CLV and high/low CRV. The cutoff points used to determine the low and high CLV and the low and high CRV were determined based on the median value for both the CLV and CRV measures. The results of this are summarized in one table because matched pairs of customers were used for both groups; that is, each group contained 9,900 customers, with almost the same distribution of CLV and CRV scores (see Table 13.4).[7]

Table 13.4   CLV and CRV for a Telecommunications Firm (n = 9,900)

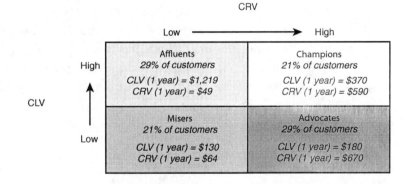

The results of this measurement of CLV and CRV show that there are distinct sets of customers found in the four different cells based on the large differences in the values for CLV and CRV across the cells. More important, a significant difference exists between the customers who are high on the CLV measure and those who are high on the CRV measure. First, we define the labels we have given each cell:

- **Affluents.** These customers purchase a lot of products and services for themselves, but they do not refer many new customers to buy products and services, which is why these customers have a high CLV and a low CRV.

- **Misers.** These customers do not purchase much or refer many new customers. They might never purchase too much because they are brand switchers, they have a small SOW, or they might be waiting to find out from others whether the product is worth purchasing.

- **Advocates.** These customers are less likely to be heavily involved in purchasing products for their own use, but they are active in searching and disseminating information to other customers to encourage them to buy products. For this reason, these customers are low on CLV but high on CRV.

- **Champions.** These customers are more likely to be highly involved with purchasing the product and disseminating information about the product, giving them both high CLV and CRV.

Looking across the high-CLV row, the cell with the highest CLV (upper-left box) is found to have a lower CRV (Affluents) than the adjacent high-CLV cell (Champions). The value of CRV in the Champions cell is more than ten times greater than the Affluents cell. Looking down the second column, which has the high-CRV customers, note that the lower-right box has the highest CRV (Advocates), but it also has a lower CLV (about half the CLV) when compared to the other high-CRV cell (the Champions). Then, there is also the lower-left corner cell that contains those customers who are low on both the CLV and CRV metric (Misers).

These numbers provide strong empirical evidence that customers who score highly on the CLV measure (direct profits) are not necessarily the same customers who score highly on CRV (indirect profits). Therefore, the customers in each of the cells should be evaluated differently with respect to their total value to the company and then approached with different types of marketing offers to get the greatest overall value from them. To show the value of treating them differently, the telecommunications firm initiated three different campaigns over the course of one year to try to get customers to migrate from low CLV/CRV to high CLV/CRV. Each campaign was carried out on the test sample of customers and carried out in each quarter for a one-year period. The control sample did not receive any of these targeted marketing communications. The campaign objectives and results (and details about the campaigns themselves) are explained in the following sections.

Campaign Objectives

Each of the three campaigns was designed with a different goal in mind. The first campaign was set up to target the customers who are Misers (see Figure 13.4). These customers are the lowest-CLV and -CRV customers in the sample. However, this does not mean that these customers do not have the potential to either be strong advocates or high-CLV customers. What may be missing is an opportunity to build a relationship. Therefore, the campaign to target the Misers not only offered incentives for them to buy more products for their own use, which would increase their CLV, but the campaign also offered them incentives to refer new customers, which would increase CRV. By motivating these customers to either buy more products for themselves or refer new customers, the goal of the company is to migrate them toward one of the other three cells (Affluents, Advocates, or Champions), depending on whether the campaign increased their CLV, their CRV, or both their CLV and CRV.

The second campaign was set up to target the customers who are Affluents (see Figure 13.5). These customers are the highest-CLV customers, but their CRV is low because they do not refer (or are not successful in referring) new customers. Therefore, the goal of this campaign was to encourage these customers to refer new customers using referral incentives, while making sure they kept their CLV at the highest level. The result of generating new referrals from these customers will cause them to migrate toward the Champions cell because their CRV will be increasing. Notice, too, that if this campaign is successful, the average CLV of the Champions cell will increase over time, as the Affluents bring their high CLV with them.

The third campaign was set up to target the customers who are Advocates (see Figure 13.6). These customers are already the highest on the CRV metric, but although they are successful in referring customers, they do not spend a significant amount on purchasing products and services for themselves. The goal of this campaign is to encourage these customers to spend more while at the same time keep-ing their CRV at the highest level. Moving customers from the Advocates cell toward the Champions cell will generate a greater amount of direct profit from these customers.

These customers were targeted with bundled offers for one or more products, such as savings accounts, checking accounts, and investment accounts, through a personalized communication sent via direct mail and followed up with another direct-mail piece within a two-week period. A phone call was also made to those customers to answer any questions regarding the additional services and the value of obtaining the additional services. In addition, the value of making referrals for new customers was highlighted for these customers by telling them that a $20 incentive would be given to them and the referred customers following a referral.

Figure 13.4 Campaign 1: Targeting the Misers

These customers were targeted with emphasis on the referral incentive for both them and the referred customers. These customers were also sent a direct-mail communication, followed by another direct-mail communication within two weeks. The main goal of the direct-mail communication was to emphasize a $20 incentive each for both the referring customer and the referred customer for signing up for products/services.

Figure 13.5 Campaign 2: Targeting the Affluents

These customers received a personal communication in the form of a direct mail that included offers for bundling one or more products such as savings accounts, checking accounts, and investment accounts. To follow up and make it more likely that the offer was received by the customer, the financial services firm sent an additional piece of direct mail within two weeks and called a sample of these customers via the telephone to answer any questions regarding the additional services and the value of subscribing to multiple products/services.

Figure 13.6 Campaign 3: Targeting the Advocates

Campaign Results

At the end of the one-year period, it was clear that each of the three campaigns had a significant impact on the customers in each of the three targeted cells. To determine whether the campaign was successful at moving customers toward a higher CLV or CRV cell in the 2×2 matrix from Table 13.4, the migration patterns of the customers along with their change in CLV and CRV were followed for each of the three cells (Misers, Affluents, and Advocates) one year after the campaign began. To determine whether a customer migrated toward a better cell in the matrix, the CLV and CRV were measured after the end of the campaign for each of the customers in the sample set. The numbers showing the migration of these customers can be found in each of the following three figures.

Figure 13.7 shows how customers who were originally in the low-CLV and low-CRV cell moved toward each of the other three better cells (higher CLV [Affluents], higher CRV [Advocates], or both higher CLV and CRV [Champions]).

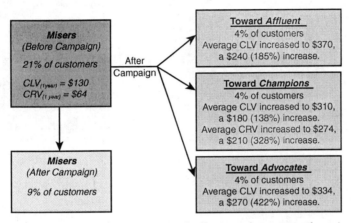

Figure 13.7   Migration from Misers toward Affluents, Advocates, or Champions

Source: Adapted from V. Kumar, J. Andrew Petersen, Robert P. Leone, "How Valuable Is Word of Mouth," forthcoming, *Harvard Business Review*.

Before the campaign started, 21% of the customers in the sample fell into the low-CLV and low-CRV cell based on the median split criteria. After running the campaign, 12% of the customers moved toward more profitable cells, with 4% going to each of the other three cells. Not only did these customers move up to a more desirable cell, the gains made on average were fairly substantial. For example, a customer who moved toward Champions from Misers after the campaign had on average a CLV that was $180 higher and a CRV that was $210 higher. This means that these customers increased their CLV scores by more than 100% (from $130 to $310) and CRV scores by more than 300% (from $64 to $274). Therefore, of the original sample of customers from this cell

(2,079 or 21%), 396 of them moved toward Champions and produced increases of CLV of $71,280 and CRV of $83,160. Although these numbers might not seem like large gains for multimillion-dollar companies, if we were to project these gains to a sample size of 990,000 customers rather than 9,900, the gains in CLV and CRV from these 4% of total customers (396 out of 9,900) would generate gains in CLV of around $7 million and gains of CRV of around $8 million.

Figure 13.8 shows how customers from Affluents (high CLV) were affected by the second campaign directed at moving them toward Champions by increasing their CRV while maintaining their very high CLV.

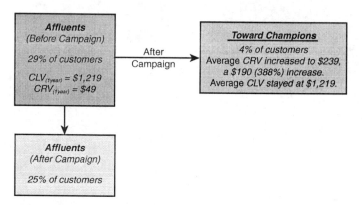

Figure 13.8 Migration from Advocates toward Champions

In this case, of the 29% of customers who were Affluents before the campaign was started, 4% of the customers moved toward Champions (high CLV and high CRV), and these 4% of customers increased their CRV on average by $190, which is 388% higher than it was initially ($49). Once again, the impact of this migration of customers is large when you see that 4% of your customers increase their CRV by that much. This means that not only is the telecommunications firm increasing its revenue from all its customers, but the customer base is growing, too. This allows the firm to greatly expand its customer base and find new revenue sources outside of just trying to cross-sell and up-sell to its current customers.

Figure 13.9 shows how Advocates (high CRV) were affected by the third campaign directed at increasing their CLV.

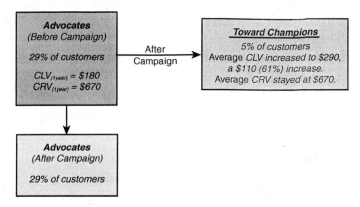

Figure 13.9 Advocates
(Before Campaign)

29% of customers

$CLV_{(1year)} = \$180$
$CRV_{(1year)} = \$670$

After
Campaign

Toward Champions
5% of customers
Average CLV increased to $290,
a $110 (61%) increase.
Average CRV stayed at $670.

Advocates
(After Campaign)

29% of customers

Figure 13.9   Migration from Advocates toward Champions

Source: Adapted from V. Kumar, J. Andrew Petersen, Robert P. Leone, "How Valuable Is Word of Mouth" forthcoming, *Harvard Business Review.*

This cell also started with 29% of the customers, but after this campaign, 5% of the customers increased their CLV and moved toward Champions, and each of the 5% of customers who moved averaged an increase in their CLV of approximately $110. Although this increase in CLV increased by 61% over the original CLV for each customer, the impact is still significant because of its long-term effects. In this case, the telecommunications firm has been able to take customers who it would have initially ignored if they were looking only at CLV because of their low CLV and moved them toward the most desirable cell in the 2×2 matrix (those with high CLV and CRV).

With these results, we can see that each of these campaigns was successful in not only migrating customers toward better cells—with 4% moving toward Affluents, 4% moving toward Advocates, and 13% moving toward Champions, the most desirable cell—but all of these customers who moved to these cells also have significantly higher CLV, CRV, or both CLV and CRV. However, the success of migrating customers from one cell toward another is not the only measure of a good campaign. In addition, we need to factor in the cost of running the campaign and compare it to the amount of profit generated to determine this campaign's ROI. The cost of the three campaigns, which included direct mail, email, and selected telephone calls for the 7,821 customers (these are from the three cells targeted in the campaign: Affluents, Misers, and Advocates) in the sample, was approximately $31,500, making the campaign cost around $4 per customer. The over-all profit obtained either from increasing each customer's CLV or CRV from each of the three campaigns was $486,090. Therefore, the overall ROI of the campaign was around 15.5. Table 13.5 shows a summary of the results.[8] We also want to note that a similar set of campaigns was run with a financial services firm, with an ROI of 13.6.

Table 13.5 Campaign ROI (Telecommunications Firm)

	Profit (CLV and CRV)	Cost	ROI
Campaign totals	$486,090	$31,500	15.5

What does this indicate for the telecommunications firm for a much larger sample of customers from their customer database? In Table 13.6, we not only show[9] what the gains would be if these campaigns were projected across 1 million and 10 million customers for the telecommunications firm (their customer base has more than 40 mil-lion customers), but also if the period of measuring CLV were moved from 1 year to 3 years.

Table 13.6 Gains in CLV and CRV for a Telecommunications Firm

	1 Million Customers		10 Million Customers	
Projected	*CLV (millions)*	*CRV (millions)*	*CLV (millions)*	*CRV (millions)*
1 year	$22.3	$26.8	$223	$268
3 years	$66.9	$80.4	$669	$804

As evident in Table 13.5, the ROI from running these three customized campaigns has generated significant gains in profit. Note that because these campaigns were customized to a specific firm in the telecommuni-cations industry, these might not fit ideally to every situation, although similar gains were observed for the financial services firm (obviously, from another industry). However, it is clear that there are a lot of oppor-tunities for firms who traditionally have used only CLV as a metric to increase their revenue and profitability by selecting customers for marketing campaigns based on both their CLV and their CRV.

Managerial Implications

Is there a trade-off when maximizing one versus the other? In this chapter, we argue that each of these measurement tools should be managed separately because the campaigns used were customized based on the objective (maximize CLV or CRV). In some cases, however, resources limit managers to selecting one or only a few campaigns. How do you, as a manager, know which campaign to choose? It is potentially unclear whether it is better to maximize CLV or CRV without the knowledge of the impact that either will have on future profit. But, knowing the objective of the campaign, the stage of the product in its life cycle, the potential number of prospects in the pool, and the nature of competition in the market could give some insights on the program that will drive revenue and profit.

For example, in a situation where the goal of a campaign is to get users to buy more in a specific category or buy across more categories, a campaign should emphasize maximizing CLV within the customer base. This is likely to happen in competitive markets where it is tough to acquire new customers or in niche markets where the prospect pool is very limited. However, in cases where the current customers are already spending the majority of their budget with the company, programs to increase cross-selling or up-selling are not as appropriate. In these cases, it is likely better for managers to try to acquire more customers by using their current customers to reach out to new prospects through referral incentive programs. Managers should be careful not to assume that high-CLV customers are the best customers to target. As this case study has shown, current customers who are low-CLV customers can have the highest impact on new customers.

In addition, after running a set of campaigns similar to those in this paper and using the results of the campaigns, a manager will have the ability to select much smaller segments of customers in each of the three cells (Misers, Affluents, and Advocates) who have the highest likelihood of increasing their CLV, CRV, or both CLV and CRV. This can be determined by identifying the differences in characteristics of the customers who increased their CLV/CRV from those who stayed unchanged after the campaign. Managers can then target additional customers in new campaigns who also have the characteristics of those customers who were most responsive to the previous campaigns. Thus, whichever marketing campaign is chosen to increase the overall revenue and profit obtained from customers, we have shown the importance of measuring the value of your customer's own transactions and the value of their impact on the transactions of other customers, and not one or the other in isolation. This is an important point because many sources provide ways to measure only a customer's behavioral CLV or only a customer's attitude (for example, intention to refer or overall satisfaction). As a manager, you should look to measure the customer's future value to the firm through both his or her own transactions (CLV) and the impact that he or she will have on other customers (CRV) because

- Not all behaviorally loyal customers provide referrals.

- Not all customers who provide referrals are behaviorally loyal.

- Targeting only higher-CLV customers for increasing the number of referrals is not an optimal strategy.

The key to success is to encourage customers to build social networks and to trigger them, along with customers who already have strong social networks, to talk to individuals in their network by using marketing programs that reward word-of-mouth and referrals. Thus, without considering referral behavior when deciding how to allocate differential resources to customers, a company might actually ignore customers or give bad service to customers who would offer great returns through direct (CLV) or indirect (CRV) profits, causing degrading customer relationships and poor service experiences. Because managers have been ignoring these customers who score highly on CRV, some have become "turned off," which causes them to feel alienated from the firm and worse, spread negative word-of-mouth about the company. The consequence could mean monetary penalties if these customers don't purchase any more or stop referring new customers. In addition, they might even begin to spread negative word-of-mouth, causing potential prospects to not only *not* join via referral, but also to have a negative attitude toward the company, causing the acquisition costs of those prospects to increase. If these customers were to be Champions for the firm, the result of their defections could result in turning many current or potential customers against the firm.

In addition, firms do have opportunities to introduce new products by utilizing the referral base of customers. Just like movies that have sneak previews to generate a "buzz," one can also generate a buzz for one's new products by making sure the right customers—those with the large social networks and strong influence on potential customers—have the information and even materials to pass along. (For example, P&G is testing a program that encourages mothers to forward email information and coupons for the new product to other mothers in their social network.) Even if prospects do not purchase the new product, others may reach out to them for their knowledge and opinions to make decisions, so the fact they are equipped with up-to-date knowledge would be a benefit. This even allows firms that are new at entering the market to take leadership in the marketplace with not just an innovative product, but also innovative marketing to harness the power of referrals.

Building a strong social network can be a long-term competitive advantage for both the customers and the firm by causing a series of positive externalities. It becomes harder for the competitors to lure away customers who are tightly locked in to their social network, while at the same time this benefits consumers because a strong social network allows ease of information sharing about products and services and the use of common products and services across a set of customers. We have observed evidence subsequent to this study that not only is the customer base growing for the two firms we studied, but the number of referrals per customers is also increasing as these social networks strengthen. Customers know (or are learning) where they can receive information, such as reviews and recommendations, from trusted sources and also who to turn to when issues arise. This growing cycle adds to the theories on trust and reinforcement behavior in a new way because giving referrals to groups of customers and building trust among these customers leads to much stronger social networks of customers. Finally, whereas the positive benefits of building a strong social network lead to these advantages, the negative impact of word-of-mouth from customers who are "turned off" on the products and services of a firm can be much steeper. Therefore, a firm should view its customers as skilled resources and work with them to build strong social networks through which both the firm and the customer can benefit.

Conclusion

This chapter introduces the concept of CRV, which is defined as a customer's expected future profits obtained through his referrals. Managers need to use both CLV and CRV metrics when managing customers. Customers who rate highly on CLV are not the same customers who rate highly on CRV. Thus, a customer brings in value through CLV or CRV—or both. However, customers should be evaluated differently—with respect to their total value to the company—and then they should be approached with different types of marketing offers catering to maximizing CLV and/or CRV. This allows firms to increase the profitability of each customer and, in turn, increase the number of new customers buying products and services.

Endnotes

[1] www.sprintpcs.com/pages/refRewards.html

[2] Frederick F. Reichheld, "The one number you need to grow," *Harvard Business Review*, 2003.

[3] Werner Reinartz, Jacquelyn S. Thomas, V. Kumar, "Balancing Acquisition and Retention Resources to Maximize Customer Profitability," *Journal of Marketing* 69(1) 2005: 63-79.

[4] David Godes and Dina Mayzlin, "Firm-Created Word-of-Mouth Communication: A Field-Based Quasi-Experiment," Working Paper, Yale School of Management, 2004.

[5] V. Kumar, J. Andrew Petersen, Robert P. Leone, "How Valuable Is Word of Mouth" forthcoming, *Harvard Business Review*.

[6] http://www.earthlink.net/membercenter/referrals/

[7] V. Kumar, J. Andrew Petersen, Robert P. Leone, "How Valuable Is Word of Mouth" forthcoming, *Harvard Business Review*.

[8] *Ibid.*

[9] *Ibid.*

14

Organizational and Implementation Challenges

Relevant Issues

- How can a firm change from the product-centric approach to the customer-centric approach?

- What does adopting a customer-centric approach involve?

- How can a firm address the implementation challenges while adopting a CLV framework?

IBM is one leading multinational firm that markets hardware, software, and services to business-to-business (B2B) customers. Recently, IBM tested the effectiveness of adopting a Customer Lifetime Value (CLV)-based framework to maximize overall profitability. For many years, IBM has been using various customer selection metrics to select profitable customers and to develop customer-level marketing strategy. Until recently, Customer Spending Score (CSS) was used as one of the key customer selection metrics to score each customer and to sort customers into deciles based on this score.1 Customers from the top one or two deciles were selected for future targeting. Although the CSS metric was effective, it focused primarily on revenue from customers and largely ignored the variable cost of catering to a customer. Hence, it was necessary to identify a new scoring metric that takes into account the marketing cost in addition to the expected revenue.

CLV, which considers both marketing cost and expected revenue, was proposed as an alternative to the CSS scoring metric. The CLV metric was adopted to find solutions to three major questions faced by IBM:

- Which customers to select for targeting

- How much resources to allocate to those customers

- How the selected customers could be nurtured to increase future profitability

As part of the implementation of the CLV framework, the customers were first divided into two groups: the Not Touched Group and the Touched Group. The customers who were contacted through salespersons, direct mail, telesales, email, and so on in year 2004 were categorized as the Touched Group. Customers who were not contacted by 2004 were categorized as the Not Touched Group. The CLVs of each customer were then computed, and the customers within each group were sorted to deciles. Based on the CLV of customers in each decile, it was recommended that marketing resources from low-CLV customers in the bottommost decile of the Touched Group be reallocated to the high-CLV customers in the top three deciles of the Not Touched Group. The probability of purchase of different products/services from IBM in the next year was predicted for customers in the top three deciles of the Not Touched Group, and they were selected for targeting.

As a result of an improved targeting strategy, the revenue of the Not Touched Group increased ten times compared to revenue in the previous year. The effectiveness of the model was reflected in the superior performance of the sales revenue metric. The improved profitability was made possible by the successful implementation of CLV strategies.[2] However, implementation of the CLV-based framework posed certain organizational challenges to IBM. One challenge was synchronizing goals and activities of different departments. Before the implementation of the CLV framework, each department had group-specific communication goals, which could make customers feel that they were interacting with different companies. For example, the hardware group might communicate information about their products to a set of customers. Similarly, the software group might reach out to the same customers to sell the same products. However, for successful implementation of a CLV-based framework, a firm has to adopt a customer-centric view—that is, use a single source to market to the customers the product/service they need.

Next, we discuss other organizational and implementation challenges that a company faces when migrating to a CLV-based framework.

Organizational Issues

The key organizational challenges to the implementation of a CLV-based framework can be broadly categorized into two dimensions: business dimension and people dimension.

Business Dimension

The business dimension has to deal with defining and articulating the business case for change and the desired outcome of change. One of the major challenges in business dimension is changing a firm's focus from product-centric to customer-centric marketing. The basic philosophy of the product-centric approach is to sell products to whoever is willing to buy. In this approach, the organization focuses on universal customers, their needs and problems, and tries to provide solutions for those problems. Thus, a product-centric firm focuses on the product portfolio and concentrates on increasing the product line for its customers. As a result, a product-centric organization tends to ignore specific needs of customers, which can lead to dissatisfaction and defection of customers.

On the other hand, the basic philosophy of a customer-centric approach is to serve specific customers and thereby provide customized services to customers. Customer-centric firms concentrate their strategy on customers rather than products. Several new firms have moved away from the product-centric approach and have gained huge profits by adopting a customer-centric approach. Whereas record labels such as EMI, BMG, and Sony did not focus on individual customers, Apple iTunes has rejuvenated the music industry through an emphasis on the individual customer-centric approach. Similarly, casinos such as MGM Grand and Ceasar's Palace focus on attracting as many customers as possible, whereas Harrah's success results from its ability to identify and pursue serious gamers.

Changing from a product-centric to a customer-centric approach also necessitates changes in the organizational structure. The organizational structure for a product-centric firm requires product managers and product sales team managers, whereas the customer-centric firm has customer relationship managers. Firms need to realign their organization structure to successfully adopt the customer-centric approach. Wells Fargo, a leading financial institution, has realigned its organization structure by creating a two-tiered sales structure. Within this structure, a relationship manager manages the relations with customers and is externally focused. A product manager, who is internally focused and provides input for the product development, helps the relationship manager to sell the products more effectively.

Table 14.1 identifies the differences between a product-centric approach and a customer-centric approach.

Table 14.1   Comparing Product-Centric and Customer-Centric Approaches

Strategic Questions	Product-Centric Approach	Customer-Centric Approach
What is the underlying philosophy?	Sell products; sell to whoever will buy.	Serve customers; all decisions based on customer-level opportunities.
What is the business approach?	Transaction oriented.	Relationship oriented.
How should the product be positioned?	Highlight product features and advantages.	Highlight product's benefits in terms of meeting individual customer needs.
How is the organization structured?	Product-based profit centers, managers, sales team.	Customer-based segment centers, segment sales team, customer relationship managers.
What is the strategic focus?	Internally focused, new product development, new account development, market share growth; customer relations addressed by marketing department.	Externally focused, customer relationship development, profitability through customer loyalty; employees are customer advocates.

Strategic Questions	Product-Centric Approach	Customer-Centric Approach
How is performance measured?	Number of new products, profitability per product, market share by product/ sub-brands.	Share of Wallet (SOW) of customers, customer satisfaction, CLV, customer equity.
What is the management criteria?	Portfolio of products.	Portfolio of customers.
How is selling approached?	How many customers can we sell this product to?	How many products can we sell to this customer?

Source: Adapted from Denish Shah, et al., "The Path to Customer Centricity," *Journal of Service Research* 9(2): 113–124.

Texas Instruments is another company that successfully adopted a customer-centric approach. When it was using a product-centric approach, it was constantly having financial pressures and increasing customer frustration. The company could not attract new customers and was losing existing customers. The management was unhappy and attempted to improve results by focusing on customers. They introduced a Customer Loyalty Bootcamp program, which focused on three major areas:

- More time was spent with customers.

- Metrics that reflect customer satisfaction were created to understand the needs of customers.

- Special programs were designed to bring in a cultural change at Texas Instruments.

The payoffs of applying this program, which focused on a customer-centric approach, included the following:

- Marketing gains for three consecutive years

- Efficient and timely services

- Better understanding of customers

As this example shows, companies are changing their focus from the product-centric to customer-centric approach to improve profitability.[3]

For a firm to be customer-centric in its approach, interactions between the firm and the customer, between customers, and between firms are essential. In the current scenario, the timely and efficient management of interactions within an organization is recognized as a major source of competitive advantage. We define these interactions in aggregate as *interaction orientation.* Interaction orientation helps firms develop organizational resources for successful management of customers. Although firms may be following a traditional product, sales, or a market orientation, a compelling need currently exists to evaluate the feasibility of adopting interaction orientation. Interaction orientation is at the center of the customer-centric approach. Whereas the product-centric approach focuses on product orientation and sales orientation, the customer-centric approach focuses on market orientation and interaction orientation.

Firms have gradually moved from a product-oriented approach to an interaction approach. Initially, firms were product-oriented, and the manager's focus was on making superior products. Then, a selling-oriented approach (with the focus less on the quality of the product and more on the sales interaction itself) became popular. The belief of selling-oriented firms was that aggressive selling and promotional campaigns could lead to higher profitability. The concept is practiced more aggressively with goods that customers do not think of buying, such as insurance. The concept of a market-oriented approach gained popularity in the mid 1950s. Focus shifted from products to customers, and products were designed according to customer needs. Managers were concerned about finding the right product for their customers. Finally, the focus has moved to an interaction-oriented approach, wherein customers are an integral part of the marketing strategy of the firm. The inputs from customers are collected and treated as a firm resource. Table 14.2 shows the different approaches.

Table 14.2 Marketing Approaches and Characteristics

Firms	Key Characteristics
Product oriented[4]	Consumer will choose products that offer the most quality, performance, and innovative features.
	The product is viewed as a source of business for the firm.
	Manage a portfolio of products.
	Transaction oriented.
	Customer-to-customer linkage is not strategically important.
	Customer data is considered a control mechanism.
Sales oriented[5]	Sales efficiency and effectiveness is the focus.
	The relevance of product/market is of secondary importance.
	Pushing the product is more important than creating the product.
Market oriented	Marketing activities are conducted for a firm's customers.
	The customer is viewed only as a source of business for the firm.
	The strategic importance of customer-to-customer linkage is not recognized.
	The need for coordination is considered limited to the functional departments within a firm.
Interaction oriented	Marketing activities are conducted with the customer.
	The customer is viewed both as a source of business and as a business resource for the firm.
	The strategic importance of customer-to-customer linkages is recognized and included in the customer empowerment component.
	The effect of the network economy on the strategic importance of managing and coordinating outsourced production and service is recognized and included in the interaction response component.

Firms can take a few steps to improve their interaction at different levels:

- Firms can improve their interaction with customers by capturing individual customer transactions and by improving supply-chain logistics.

- Firms should enable customers to obtain information freely, exercise choices, praise or criticize the firm/product/service, and even participate in designing the product/service.
- Marketing should be an activity that is measured and analyzed at the individual customer level. The components of interaction orientation are as follows:
  - **Customer concept.** It is the belief that the unit of every marketing action or reaction is an individual customer. Wells Fargo is an example of an organization that believes in the customer concept. It has continuously invested in technologies that help maintain real-time visibility of the firm's customers. According to Danny Peltz, Executive Vice President, Wells Fargo, these efforts have resulted in increased customer involvement compared to the competition and an upward trend in revenue, transaction volume, and services per customer.[6]
  - **Interaction response capacity.** Interaction response capacity is the degree to which a firm can provide successive product, services, and interaction experience based on the previous feedback by a specific customer (and all other customers). Boeing is an example of a firm that believes in the concept of interaction response capacity. For its airline customers, Boeing's rapid response center handles technical problems that arise outside of normal business hours. The center uses interactive video, the Internet, and telephone systems that seamlessly allow access to people and data across multiple sites.
  - **Customer empowerment.** Customer empowerment refers to the extent to which a firm allows its customers to do the following:
    - Connect with the firm and design the nature of transaction
    - Connect and collaborate with each other by sharing information, praise, and criticism about a firm's product and services

    IBM supports Linux, for example, to provide more customer choice (especially appreciated by customers who want to avoid expensive, licensed software). Hewlett-Packard encourages online peer-to-peer service, and the

rich information that the members of this online community provide helps HP raise its overall service efficiency. These examples demonstrate that IBM and HP recognize customer empowerment as a strategic activity.

- **Customer value management.** Customer value management refers to the extent to which a firm can quantify and calculate the individual customer value and use it to reallocate resources to customers who will add higher value in the future. IBM has developed sophisticated techniques to assess the future customer value of its institutional customers. This focus on customer value management has helped IBM improve profitability in the U.S. market over the past few years. Figure 14.1 illustrates the process of interaction orientation. Antecedents are factors that affect the level of interaction orientation in the firm. These factors can be moderated by customer-initiated contacts and competitive intensity. Customer-initiated contacts provide vast information about each customer's needs and wants and help firms interact with customers to design a customized product/service for them. Competitive intensity forces firms to differentiate products/services from competitors by providing more offerings (not by keeping interaction with customer in mind). Firms with a high level of interaction orientation avoid falling into these pitfalls. By avoiding these pitfalls, firms can increase customer satisfaction, positive word-of-mouth, and acquisition and retention of profitable customers.

Firms that are adopting interaction orientation are able to attract and retain the most valuable customers. Also, they can keep competitors away from their customers because of the customers' heightened attachment to the firm. Thus, customers are developed into a skilled resource for the firm; they help the firm acquire new customers by referrals, word-of-mouth, and so on. The firms also start exhibiting superior aggregate-level business performance, by dynamically maximizing the profit function for a firm, at every stage of activity and across all customer segments. The firms can develop a dynamically shifting portfolio of

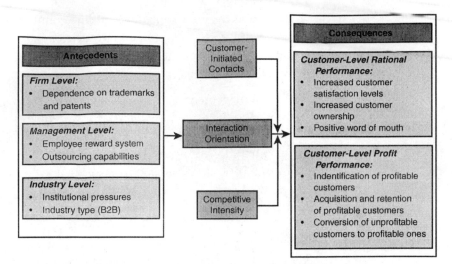

Figure 14.1 Interaction orientation: Antecedents and consequences

Source: Adapted from V. Kumar and Girish Ramani, "Interaction Orientation and Firm Performance," forthcoming, *Journal of Marketing*. Printed with permission from the American Marketing Association.

product and services. They also develop the ability to foresee customer response and plan marketing activities for longer time horizons.

Firms that are not adapting interaction orientation to a sufficient degree face issues such as these:

- Obligation by the firm to continue serving a large base of unprofitable customers

- Uncontrolled proliferation of negative word-of-mouth

- Customers directing competitor's attention to the firm's vulnerable areas

- Inability to plan for the future

- Poor marketing accountability, leading to lower profit and lower returns on marketing investments. Firms such as IBM and American Express have successfully adopted the interaction orientation. Their endorsement of practices consistent with the elements of interaction orientation and recent business performance demonstrate the managerial significance of an interaction orientation.[7]

People Dimension

Although the successful adoption of a customer-centric marketing approach and the interaction orientation helps firms to navigate the business dimension of organizational challenge, it is equally important to address the challenges in the people dimension. For successful implementation of a customer relationship, initiative, certain steps should be taken to deal with any reluctance to change (as is typical in the people dimension):

- **Generate awareness of the need for change.** Firms can do this via relevant and specific communication with employees.

- **Create a desire to participate and support the change.** Firms can achieve maximum participation by communicating the initiative's effectiveness and potential benefits.

- **Disseminate knowledge about how to change.** Firms can do this by creating channels of communication and sharing information in a transparent way.

- **Enable stakeholders to implement the change on a day-to-day basis.** Firms can do this by authorizing employees to interactively respond to customers.

- Reinforce to keep the change in place. Firms can do this by following up with the management and employees frequently to discuss the initiative's progress (including any benefits derived from such). After sorting out organizational issues, firms might face implementation challenges related to any customer relationship management (CRM) initiative. Therefore, successful implementation depends on firms understanding data-driven factors, on accountability in execution, on transparency in execution, and on understanding the metrics dashboard.

Implementation Challenges

When dealing with implementation challenges, managers have to focus on the following four factors: data-driven factors, transparency in execution, accountability in execution, and metric dashboards. The following sections explain each of these factors.

Data-Driven Factors

Data collection from a relatively large customer group is a tedious and expensive task, and therefore the implementation of a CLV framework in B2B and B2C scenarios presents a great challenge for organizations. The organizations that sell through intermediaries find it impossible to gather data from customers because they are not in direct contact with the end customers. To develop a customer-level strategy, the following four data characteristics are essential:

- The data should be at the customer level.

- To derive the drivers of profitability, the data should contain all the transaction information (including Past Customer Value [PCV], recency, frequency, and contribution margin).

- The longer the span over which the data is collected, the better. At the least, firms should collect data for two or three years.

- Marketing touch information should be included in the data. The data should include all the marketing touch methods used (direct mail, email, and so on) and the date each touch occurred.

After collecting data with these characteristics, firms can develop a customer-level strategy to aid manager decision making.

Transparency in Execution

A well-known telecommunication company was planning to introduce a new CRM initiative. The initiative included the formation of special groups (12 to 16 people from customer interactive, marketing, and sales departments), who were to be responsible for providing users the required inputs during the implementation of the CRM initiative. However, the management decided not to communicate the initiative to its internal and external users until the implementation was near completion. Therefore, the management failed to generate awareness and the desire to participate among the users. By the time management was ready to train the internal and external users, 50% of users said they knew nothing about the initiative and were not enthusiastic about undergoing training. As a result, the initiative was not implemented for another four months, and the company registered a huge loss of $800,000.

CRM initiatives should be well communicated to both internal and external users. Even the slightest discrepancy should be communicated so that errors are eliminated.[8]

Accountability in Execution

In another example, a global publishing company attempted to launch a CRM initiative. It established a special "communications" group that remained active throughout the entire implementation of the initiative. The group even started a Friday "paper" memo to update all internal and external users as to the latest developments. But, when it came to CRM application training, who would receive the training first became a point of conflict. This conflict led to a delay in the implementation of the CRM initiative. The company could have avoided this problem by empowering a group to implement the initiative. Such a group could have still kept users updated, but could also have ensured a smooth training process (and thus a timely and successful implementation of the CRM initiative).[9]

Metrics Dashboards

Organizations create metrics dashboards to identify and implement key performance measures of a customer to help management track and monitor customers for the effective allocation of resources. Traditionally, metrics that reflected the success of product-centric firms were, for example, share of hearts, mind, and markets; and product and portfolio management metrics. However, the shift to a customer-centric approach has necessitated an emphasis on forward-looking metrics, such as Customer Lifetime Value (CLV) and Customer Spending Score (CSS).

Share of Hearts, Mind, and Markets

These metrics try to depict the true picture of key factors in market share, market concentration, and customer satisfaction. The metrics try to identify the correlation between variables behind market share, and try to explore measure of awareness, attitude, and usage, which are major factors while making a decision to select one brand over another.

They are designed to measure how well the firm is doing with its customer. Some metrics used to evaluate success in the market are the Boston Consulting Group (BCG) matrix and revenue market share.

Product and Portfolio Management

These metrics provide the optimum solution to the following questions:

- What will be the sales from a new product?

- Does the launch of new products affect the sales of existing products?

- What are the true needs of customers? Is the company able to deliver products and services to cater to those needs?

They are used to determine the sales forecast for new products, growth projections, and compound annual growth rates (CAGRs). These metrics also study the impact of sales of new products on the sales of existing products. Commonly used metrics are volume projections, CAGR, cannibalization rate (percentage of new product sales taken from an existing product line), and brand equity metric (tracking the value of brand).

Customer Profitability

These metrics measure the performance of individual customers. They keep track of changes in the number of active customers and the ability of the firm to retain them. They also allow firms to identify the profitable and nonprofitable customers, and therefore reallocate resources (proportionate to the level of customer profitability) to profitable customers to improve revenue. Commonly used metrics are number of customers, RFM, and CLV. CLV is a forward-looking metric that predicts the future behavior of customers and helps the firm design marketing spending to acquire new customers and retain profitable existing customers.

As stated in the IBM example, IBM shifted from a customer spending metric to a CLV metric in a pilot study. The key steps involved in implementing the CLV framework include the following:

1. The firm rank ordered its existing customers to decide which customers to target and which ones to ignore. The ranking was done using the CLV score.

2. The next step was to identify the high-value customers by understanding their specific characteristics and then develop a unique marketing effort to capture those customers. This also helped the firm to identify future profitable customers.

3. The firm decided on its optimum contact strategy for these highly valued customers, in terms of type and frequency of communication.

4. The firm then used a purchase timing model and a choice model to isolate different time periods when these customers were most likely to buy various products/services.

Table 14.3 shows the revenue generated by different metrics for IBM customers, with the CLV metric providing maximum revenue.

Table 14.3 Revenue by Different Metrics for IBM Customers

% of Cohort (Selected from top)		Using the first 30 months of data to predict the next 18 months of purchase behavior			
		Customer Lifetime Value	Customer Spending Score (CSS)	RFM	Past Customer Value
15	Average Revenue	30,427	21,789	22,622	23,542
	Gross Value	9,184	6,659	6,966	7,185
	Variable Costs	107	114	110	104
	Net Value	9,077	6,544	6,856	7,081

The reported values are in dollars (expressed as a multiple of the actual numbers) per customer and are cell medians.

Figure 14.2 shows the reallocation of marketing touches and contacts using the CLV maximization framework.

The net result of using CLV was therefore higher revenue and higher value in 2005 versus 2004 for the No Touch in 2004 but Touched in 2005 group of customers. If the revenue increase is about $12,700 per customer across categories, for about 1,511 customers (for the No

STATUS QUO

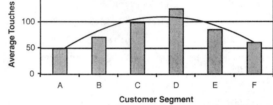

RECOMMENDED

Figure 14.2　Reallocation of marketing contacts

Source: V. Kumar, Rajkumar Venkatesan, Timothy Bohling, and Denise Beckmann, "The Power of CLV: Managing Customer Value at IBM," forthcoming, *Marketing Science.*

Touch in 2004 but Touched in 2005), the total increase is about $19.2 million. Among the customers who were touched in 2004, the CLV-based model recommended touching about 24,000 customers in 2005. The average revenue for this set of customers is at least $14,058. This results in a total revenue contribution of more than $300 million (after accounting for the direct marketing expenses). So, the CLV-based model recommendations did not miss out on identifying existing sources of revenue, and they identified new sources of revenue. Figure 14.3 shows the incremental revenue and new business due to the implementation of the CLV-based strategy.

In other words, although the challenges appear to be formidable, they are surmountable, as shown in the IBM example.

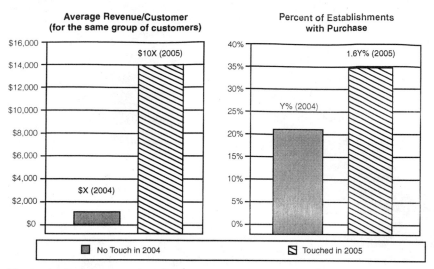

Figure 14.3 Incremental performance by adopting CLV framework

Source: V. Kumar, Rajkumar Venkatesan, Timothy Bohling, and Denise Beckmann, "The Power of CLV: Managing Customer Value at IBM," forthcoming, *Marketing Science*.

Conclusion

As the example with IBM shows, the organizational and implementation challenges common within most firms are not insurmountable. However, to stay at the leading edge of customer management, firms need to continue to work toward collecting information at the individual customer level. Firms can overcome many of the obstacles they face by better understanding their customers, interacting with their customers, and valuing their customers. Adopting the Interaction Orientation can help marketers maximize profitability for the firm and also gain credibility within the organization—thereby making these organizational challenges easier to overcome.

Endnotes

1   V. Kumar, Rajkumar Venkatesan, Timothy Bohling, and Denise Beckmann, "The Power of CLV: Managing Customer Value at IBM," forthcoming, *Marketing Science.*

2   *Ibid.*

3   www.destinationcrm.com/articles/default.asp?ArticleID=4269&TopicID=10

4   Philip Kotler and Kevin Keller, *Marketing Management,* 12th Edition (Prentice Hall, 2005).

5   *Ibid.*

6   www.bea.com/contents/news_events/white_papers/BEA_WellaFargo_ss.pdf

7   V. Kumar and Girish Ramani, "Interaction Orientation: The New Measure of Marketing Capabilities," forthcoming, *Journal of Marketing.*

8   Barton Goldenberg, "Successful CRM: Getting the People, Process, and Technology Mix Right," 2002, at www.informit.com/articles/article.asp?p=26256&rl=1.

9   *Ibid.*

15

The Future of Customer Management

Relevant Issues

- How has customer management evolved over the years?
- What are the different approaches to customer management?
- What is the future of customer management?

The evolution of customer management has been gradual over the years. Firms initially started with individual customer management and looked at individual needs, but then moved on to mass marketing and tried to target the entire market. Over the years, these firms realized that to gain a competitive edge, they need to concentrate on segmented customers, and now more so on individual customers. Coca-Cola is a company that has gone through this cycle of evolution. It has experienced an entire cycle of customer management since its inception in 1886. In the initial years, also referred to as the "first phase," the competition was low, and competitors could enter the market easily. Coca-Cola wanted to stimulate progress by making itself a national brand by means of national distribution and brand pulling power. To achieve this, the company launched a sales force that catered to the needs of each and every customer (that is, provided customized services). The sales force and their national campaign made Coca-Cola the most powerful brand in the history of marketing. In the "second phase," with the entry of competitors such as Pepsi, the market became stiffer, and price competition emerged. Coca-Cola targeted entire-market customers and adopted marketing strategies to cater to the needs of these customers to gain a price advantage. This strategy helped them reduce production cost so as to gain a price advantage.

Mass-media advertisement is the lowest common denominator appeal, designed to speak to as many potential customers as possible. Coca-Cola was soon known as a brand that is perfect for anyone, anytime, anywhere. The reach derived from this strategy was achieved, but by sacrificing knowledge and awareness of individual needs. During the "third phase," Coca-Cola went back to market-segmentation strategies and segmented customers based on demographic and psychographic factors. Slowly, the attention moved toward individual customers. The company philosophy was to know each and every customer, to know them intimately and know them well. Salespersons or sales managers kept a tabulated record of daily purchases. Thus, a record of what each customer was doing and, more important, a record of what he was *not* doing was always available. That was the pulse of business—and the only way to feel the pulse of the entire business at one time was to know each and every customer. These records enabled managers to intelligently analyze and to describe and prescribe remedies. Coca-Cola thus made a full circle, reverting to marketing strategies for individual customers, with which it started off.[1]

Customer management (CM) changes (definitions and use) do not constitute merely an evolution in business practice, but a revolution. Specific factors lead to this conclusion:

- The reason why companies invest in CM has changed. Traditionally, companies implemented CM strategies to reduce cost and to make CM more efficient. Today, however, CM strategies are implemented to retain loyal customers and to help businesses grow their revenue and profit.

- An increasing number of companies approach CM as a means to an end, not an end in itself. Managers have learned how to successfully implement CM strategies in lucrative business scenarios, set reasonable expectations for returns, and evaluate and understand new business opportunities that will arise.

- How CM is perceived has changed. Initially, companies relied on software that used the traditional backward-looking metrics to manage customers. Now, however, managers use the forward-looking metrics (which are customer-focused and customer-centric strategies) to manage customers.[2]

- Sophisticated analytics now exist to take advantage of available data. This makes CM a more lucrative business initiative for firms because of its ability to produce accurate predictions.

Figure 15.1 shows the various stages of the CM evolution. The figure shows three customer groups and four marketing strategies. The customer groups have evolved from individual customers to entire-market customers to segmented customers and then back to individual customers. Four marketing strategies implemented during this evolution are one-to-one, mass marketing, campaign based, and interactive marketing. These four strategies are aligned with these three customer groups to efficiently manage the respective customer groups. In general, firms started with marketing strategies for individual customers and followed with mass-marketing strategies for entire-market customers to gain a price advantage. After attaining these advantages, they reverted to segment and individual-level CM to gain a competitive edge, as was the case with Coca-Cola. Currently, firms are adopting interactive marketing strategies to help them gain competitive efficiencies in executing customer-level strategies in the market.[3]

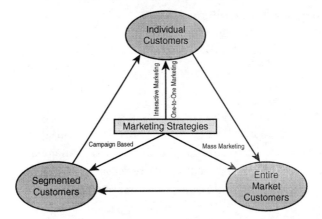

Figure 15.1 Evolution of customer management: Aligning customer groups with strategies

Customer Groups

During the evolution of the CM strategies, customers were mainly targeted in three basic customer groups: individual customers, entire-market customers, and segmented customers.

Individual Customers

In this group, each and every customer is treated individually. It is an approach that concentrates on providing products and services to one customer at a time by identifying the customer's needs and wants and then meeting those individual requirements. It aims to provide the customer with services/products over a period of time so that a lifetime relationship can be developed. The individualization of interaction is an important component in building customer loyalty. Better returns on investment are expected as a result.

Entire-Market Customers

Here, the entire market is targeted. The marketing strategy involves marketing of a product to a wider audience. The idea is to broadcast a message that will reach the largest number of people possible. For example, Henry Ford applied the concept of entire-market customers in the automobile industry. His Model T was conceived and marketed as a "universal" car, one that would meet the needs of all buyers. By adopting mass-production techniques and eliminating optional features, he was able to reduce costs and sell his product at an affordable price. Ford viewed his product as being the only one that consumers needed.

Segmented Customers

This group can be defined as a group of customers that helps the firm better understand a customer, its likely direction, and its potential reaction to products. Such an understanding helps managers to make decisions while anticipating expected future returns, product requirements, response to competitive threats, and other strategic issues.

Segmented marketing analysis allows managers to view the customers at an acceptable and sometimes intuitive level of aggregation. Common practice finds customers segmented along certain management realities of running the business: existing or historical partner channels, and product or marketing campaign features. Many marketing-segmentation schemes that were used were based largely on the origination channel or reflected product types. Coke has introduced different flavors over the years to segment customers based on product types. It has different products targeting different segments: PowerAde for athletes, Coca-Cola Zero for those who like calorie-free drinks, Full Throttle for students, and so on. Others reflect geographic locations of customers or branch locations, which can be tapped to reflect a variation in local market conditions.[4]

Market segmentation started as early as the 1920s. General Motors used market segmentation in the 1920s when it produced different models for different groups of customers to compete with Ford. Pepsi made a series of attempts, beginning in the 1930s, to successfully enter into Coca-Cola's market share through changes in products and targeted promotion strategies. In the 1940s, television provided a powerful tool for both new and old companies to reach segmented customers. By the 1960s, market segmentation had surpassed mass marketing as the primary approach.[5]

Marketing Strategies

Four main marketing strategies are implemented to target these customer groups.

Initially, one-to-one marketing was implemented to target the individual customers. Gradually, firms' focus shifted to a larger customer base, and the entire market became the target group. Mass-marketing strategies were used to target the entire market. This marketing strategy was for the mass audience, and the message was to reach out to as many people as possible. Campaign-based marketing strategies were used to target market segments. The focus of firms again shifted to individual customers. As firms got a deeper understanding of their customers, marketing strategy changed from transaction-based to interaction-based marketing. Therefore, most of the firms are now following marketing strategies targeted at either segmented customers or individual customers.

Aligning Marketing Strategies to Customer Groups

There are four possible alignments between marketing strategies and customer groups: one-to-one marketing and individual customers; mass marketing and entire-market customers; campaign-based marketing and segmented customers; interactive marketing and individual-level customers. The following sections discuss each alignment.

One-to-One Marketing and Individual Customers

Customer strategy began its journey with one-to-one marketing to the individual customer. This was feasible because of the availability of a single product for a smaller audience. One-to-one marketing is a widely used marketing strategy that focuses on individual customers. It is an integrated approach that combines all major departments of an organization: marketing, sales, production, distribution, finance, and so on. It recognizes the fact that the lifetime values of loyal customers who make repeat purchases far exceed those of fickle customers who constantly switch suppliers in search of options and other deals. In other words, organizations provide tailored products to meet customers' needs, thereby making comparative buying difficult for customers and changing their focus from price to benefits.[6]

Apart from the benefits just described, other benefits of one-to-one marketing include the following:

- The cost of retaining a loyal and profitable customer may be higher than the cost of acquiring a new customer, but it may be worth it.

- The knowledge of an individual customer is very precise; therefore, products and services can be more accurately targeted.

- Satisfied and loyal customers (even though they might not be that profitable) can provide excellent references and referrals.

- It helps convert prospects into customers, increases revenue, and builds brand loyalty.

- It helps an organization differentiate itself from competitors.[7]

Harrah's Casino used one-to-one marketing to the individual-level customer management to gain competitive advantage. To stimulate loyalty, it introduced a loyalty-based Total Reward program that rewarded customers with compensations. The reward program sought to gather information about customers and use it to customize the company's marketing program for each customer. The data collected helped Harrah's to keep track of its customers' preferences and thus develop marketing plans accordingly.[8]

Mass Marketing and Entire-Market Customers

As product proliferation occurred and the number of customers increased, firms had to resort to mass marketing. Marketing products to a large audience is referred to as mass marketing. Mass marketing is the best strategy to target an entire-market group. Traditionally, mass marketing has focused on radio, television, and newspapers as the media used to reach this broad audience. Exposure to the product is maximized by reaching the largest audience possible. In theory, this would directly correlate with a larger number of sales. The approach results in a single marketing plan with the ideal mix of four Ps: price, product, place, and promotion strategy for the entire market.

Firms generally use mass marketing to target an entire market because

- It expands volume through lower prices.

- It reduces cost through economies of scale that are achieved by high volume of output.

Mass marketing began around the 1880s, with the introduction of the railroad and the telegraph system.

Manufacturers such as Quaker Oats, Proctor and Gamble, and Eastman Kodak used refined mass-production techniques to establish consistent product quality so that they could mass market their products. Sears and Montgomery Ward developed a mass-marketing niche through mail order. The grocery retailer A&P, on the other hand, established its mass market through private branding and the systematic operation of multiple stores.[9]

Campaign-Based Marketing and Segmented Customers

Campaign-based marketing strategy is often used to supplement segment marketing. It evaluates market performance and then sets the business objectives. The firm proposes making complementary offers to segmented customers to encourage them to maintain their loyalty to the firm. Figure 15.2 explains the functioning of campaign-based marketing.[10]

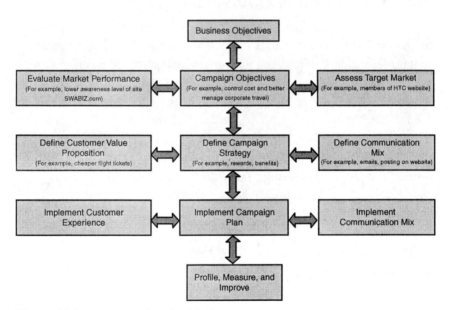

Figure 15.2 Campaign-based marketing process

For a business to grow, managers need to market the products via valuable marketing strategies. By developing marketing campaigns based on the process described in Figure 15.2, managers can keep a record of the creation of new customers from the segmented market and monitor the retention of existing customers. For example, managers can see how much sales have increased because of the new customers during a particular campaign and how many loyal customers made a purchase during the same campaign. (For example, consider the IBM study described in Chapter 14, "Organizational and Implementation Challenges." Of the total profit of $19.2 million, 40% came from incremental purchases of the existing customer, whereas the remaining 60% came from purchases of new customers.) By doing this, managers can check the efficiency of a firm's financial investment.

Southwest Airlines adopted campaign-based marketing to improve the awareness of an online feature its company provided. The business travel site SWABIZ.com was relatively unknown to most customers. SWABIZ provides unique benefits for companies seeking to control costs and better manage corporate travel. With the goal of increasing visibility and ticket sales for SWABIZ, Southwest Airlines combined with Spur Digital and launched a marketing campaign. They integrated a program that utilized email and the HTC (Houston Technology Center) website to promote a campaign for its members. Leveraging HTC's access to its member base, Spur developed a three-month campaign to promote SWABIZ to HTC members. Results from the campaign were convincing, increasing revenue, brand awareness, and brand loyalty.[11] Figure 15.2 provides a sequential flow of the process followed by Southwest Airlines to target segmented customers.

Interactive Marketing and Individual-Level Customers

Currently, firms are adopting interactive marketing strategies for individual customer management. Interactive marketing refers to a trend whereby marketing has moved from a transaction-based effort to conversation- and interaction-based marketing. Interactive marketing is the ability to address the needs of each and every customer, remember what the customer demanded, and address the customer in a manner that illustrates that managers remember what he/she wanted.

Firms that adopt the interactive marketing approach make an assessment of individual customers, including their needs, wants, and ways and means of communication. This assessment includes lifetime value and profitability. It establishes a department that identifies the necessary components and interfaces for delivery of products/services to the customer. Firms try to find appropriate ways to integrate different strategies to the new strategies adopted. Also, they integrate different organizational components. They encourage interaction within the organization and with customers to build trust, encourage collaboration, create demand products/services, create positive referrals, and so on. The department also appoints monitors and measures the impact of any change in the firm's consumer base. Then, it adapts to the changes so that market opportunities can be exploited.

The benefits of adopting an interactive marketing strategy include the following:

- Those customers who acquire the various interactive technologies are more affluent and attach a greater value to their time. They will pay for responsive service and for having their particular needs met.

- Sales conversions increase because of increased customer confidence, and buy-in is induced (through which a number of different product benefits are interlinked).

- Customers can have access to comprehensive product information to address a wide range of needs.

- By linking with other companies' delivery mediums, one company's products can be cross-sold to another and the linking reciprocated.[12]

Firms such as IBM and American Express are successfully adopting interactive marketing strategies. Their endorsement of practices consistent with the elements of interaction orientation and recent business performance demonstrates the importance of the managerial significance of an interactive marketing.[13]

As mentioned in Chapter 1, "Introduction," the path to profitability for a typical firm begins with acquiring customers and giving them a richer experience so as to increase their loyalty toward the firm's products/ services. This leads to higher retention and enhanced revenue. But, in the current atmosphere, CM has taken a reverse path. In this book, we have discussed how the reverse path can be followed. In other words, it pays to identify profitable customers first and then create a sense of loyalty and satisfaction in them.

Are Some Firms Taking the Practice of CM Too Far?

Although CLV can be used as a metric to manage customers, it is important not to go overboard with it. The following examples might help to get a perspective on whether certain actions taken by a few companies might have any long-term harmful consequences.

Recently, Sprint Nextel decided to dump 1,000 of its 53 million customers for calling its customer service too often (because customer service calls cut into profits). For example, for a typical wireless subscriber who spends about $55 per month, a firm can make about $24. In addition, it costs about $2 to $3 per minute to service a call to a customer service representative. If a customer service call exceeds 8 to 12 minutes per month, the firm does not make any money from that customer. Similarly, AT&T canceled service to customers who make most of their calls in the roaming mode. Verizon canceled service for customers who exceeded 5GB of data usage per month on its network. It is apparent that telecom firms evaluate the profitability of each customer, and firms such as Sprint Nextel, AT&T, and Verizon "fire" their customers for not being profitable.[14]

ING Direct is an online bank with more than 6 million customers. It shuts down the accounts of more than 3,000 to 4,000 customers each month because these customers need a lot of hand-holding, and that costs the firm. This six-year-old firm will not be able to offer higher interest rates to its customer if it is not able to contain its costs.[15]

It is true that in wireless and banking firms, about 20% to 30% of the customers give 100% of the profits, and the bottom 20% actually induce losses for the firm. The middle 50% or so typically break even. So, a majority of the up-sell/cross-sell marketing strategies are aimed at the middle group to make them profitable.

Is firing customers a good strategy? Given that the cost of acquiring a new wireless customer ranges between $300 and $350, telecom firms typically make a profit only after the first year of service. Therefore, considerable thought and computation have to go into making the decision to fire a customer. For example, about 50% of all wireless users in the United States made a call to their customer service department. Among these customers, 42% contacted their providers with billing issues.[16] If the origin of the problem is with the telecom service provider, calls related to resolving these issues should not be factored into the customer profitability computation. It is paradoxical that the firing of customers is happening even when these firms are losing customers in large numbers every month.

It is also true that a customer received 30 unsolicited telemarketing calls from Sprint over a few months trying to up-sell/cross-sell. How is Sprint able to justify this behavior when it fires other customers for making too many calls? The answer may lie in the potential profitability of the customer (that is, the CLV). For example, consider the airline industry. They know that their most profitable customers are the elite frequent fliers, the ones who buy many profitable goods and services; and it's these customers who are supposed to receive perks, but the perks are not guaranteed. Although these customers are profitable, they may get fewer free upgrades and may deal with less-accommodating agents if they are too demanding or obnoxious.

In summary, a better way of practicing CM in the future is to clearly state the benefits for each customer based on his or her level of service. Then, give the customer the option to add a higher tier of service for some additional fee. This way, both the firms and the customers can coexist because the focus is now on profit, loyalty, and satisfaction (in that order). Maximum CLV is possible if customers and firms are able to interact and understand each other well.

Taking Your Company to the Next Level of CM

Firms are trying to step up the ladder of customer evolution, as shown in Figure 15.3.

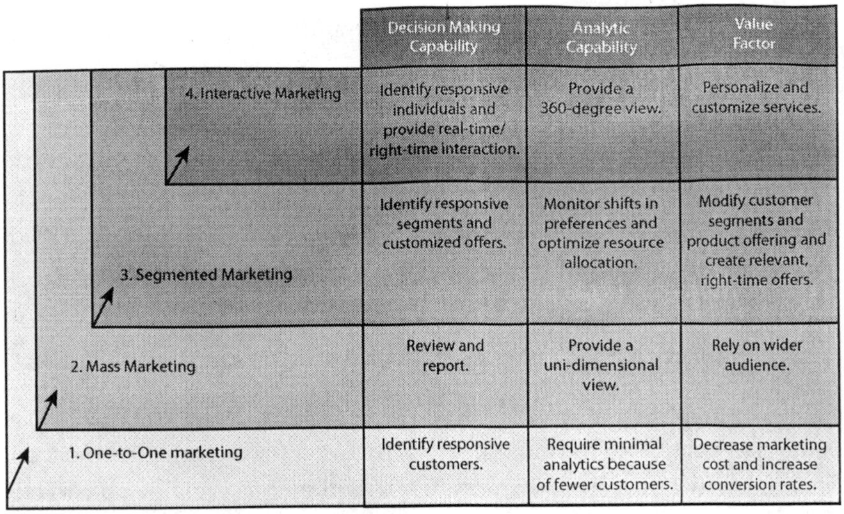

		Decision Making Capability	Analytic Capability	Value Factor
4. Interactive Marketing		Identify responsive individuals and provide real-time/ right-time interaction.	Provide a 360-degree view.	Personalize and customize services.
3. Segmented Marketing		Identify responsive segments and customized offers.	Monitor shifts in preferences and optimize resource allocation.	Modify customer segments and product offering and create relevant, right-time offers.
2. Mass Marketing		Review and report.	Provide a uni-dimensional view.	Rely on wider audience.
1. One-to-One marketing		Identify responsive customers.	Require minimal analytics because of fewer customers.	Decrease marketing cost and increase conversion rates.

Figure 15.3   Hierarchy of customer evolution

Source: Adapted from Ron Swift's CRM presentation.

Providing customized products and services makes customers more loyal to firms and hence increases customer retention. Firms can also further increase the product's attachment to the customer by processing their feedback and suggestions and trying to incorporate those changes (that is, use interactive marketing targeted at individual customers). That would give customers a sense of attachment to the product and induce loyalty, which thereby would lead to increased retention. Another advantage of interactive marketing is the possibility of generating positive word-of-mouth, the ability to cross-sell, and so on, all of which would help firms to increase profit immensely. Many firms have started adopting interactive marketing, and in the future this level of customer management will be followed widely.

Today, it takes anywhere from 30 days to 1 year for a firm to obtain a 360-degree view of a customer or to reverse the path of profitability. A firm that is able to use this view takes some time to determine the right actionable information in the right format for each customer interaction in the contact center. In the future, can a firm take this marketing action within a day (or perhaps even the instant a customer walks in)? Do we have the right systems in place to effectively control and capture all relevant customer data? Are we indexing and categorizing the captured information so that we can find a relevant solution quickly and easily?[17] If we have the right information system, the data can be processed in real time, and relevant information for the ideal marketing strategy can be provided instantly.

Therein lies the future of CM, where you have a marketing plan for each and every customer, to make him even more profitable as soon as the purchase information is updated.

Conclusion

The continuing evolution of CM is made possible as we understand the interactive relationships that develop between firms and customers and customers with other customers. Firms will increasingly be able to customize marketing messages to larger target audiences based on the customer's expected response and the customer's value to the firm. By following the CM strategies previously discussed, firms can reduce overall marketing costs, increase overall customer response rates, and, most importantly, increase overall customer and firm profitability. Therein lies the future of CM— where you have a marketing plan for each and every customer with the goal of making each customer more profitable.

Endnotes

[1] www.businessweek.com/chapter/tedlow.htm

[2] www.crmproject.com/documents.asp?d_ID=3780

[3] Girish Ramani and V. Kumar, "Interaction Orientation: The New Measure of Marketing Capabilities," forthcoming *Journal of Marketing.*

[4] www.strategicanalytics.com/articles/2003signals_segmentlevel.php

[5] www.answers.com/topic/mass-marketing

[6] www.managingchange.com/onetoone/overview.htm

[7] www.managingchange.com/onetoon/benefits.htm

[8] www.icmr.icfai.org/casestudies/catalogue/Marketing/Harrah.htm

[9] *Ibid.*

[10] www.davechaffey.com/Internet-Marketing/C4-Strategy/
Internet-marketing-strategy-process/

11 http://www.spurdigital.com/web-marketing-resources-from-spur-digital/resource/
article/case-studies-southwest-airlines-online-partner-marketing-campaign-103.html

12 www.managingchange.com/sim/benefits.htm

13 Girish Ramani and V. Kumar, "Interaction Orientation: The New Measure of Marketing Capabilities," forthcoming *Journal of Marketing*.

14 http://tech.msn.com/news/articlecnet.aspx?cp-documentid=5120444&GT1=10240

15 http://articles.moneycentral.msn.com/savinganddebt/consumeractionguide/areyouabadcustomer

16 http://tech.msn.com/news/articlecnet.aspx?cp-documentid=5120444&GT1=10240

17 www.crm2day.com/library/EEpFZkEpyVcNuPJAiA.php

Index

loyalty. *See also* attitudinal loyalty;
  behavioral loyalty
    brand loyalty, 195
    brand value and, 189
    profitability and. *See also*
      Customer Lifetime Value (CLV)
        behavioral loyalty versus atti-
          tudinal loyalty, 93-94
        customer segmentation, 95-98
        linking in loyalty
          programs, 103
loyalty instruments (CLV driver), 64
loyalty metrics, 24-25, 29
    compared, 79
    CLV (Customer Lifetime Value),
      36-40
        calculating, 40-55
    PCV (Past Customer Value),
      34-35
        drawbacks to, 36
    RFM (Recency-Frequency-
      Monetary value), 30-32
        drawbacks to, 36
    SOW (Share of Wallet), 32-33
        drawbacks to, 36
loyalty programs. *See also* loyal
  customers
    effect of, 16
    evolution of, 107-110
    framework for, 99
        attitudinal loyalty, measuring
          and cultivating, 102
        behavioral loyalty, building,
          99-102
        loyalty and profitability,
          linking, 103
        two-tier rewards strategy,
          103-106
    history of, 12-16

maximizing CLV with, 79-80,
  93-110
profitability and, 11-12
reasons for failure, 23-24

M

market orientation, 254
market segmentation (in customer
  management evolution), 270-271
    campaign-based marketing
      strategies and, 274-275
marketing
    communication. *See*
      communication
    decisions, stopping investment in
      loyal customers, 25-26
    efforts by loyal customers, 20-21
    optimizing direct marketing
      expenditures, 205-206
marketing actions (CLV driver), 61
marketing contact frequency (CLV
  driver), 64
marketing cost (M), calculating
  Customer Lifetime Value (CLV), 48
marketing resource allocation
  strategy (maximizing CLV), 80-81,
  113-124. *See also* communication
marketing strategies (customer
  management evolution), 269-272
    advantages of interaction-based
      marketing, 278-280
    aligning with customer groups,
      272-277
Marks & Spencer's, 14
Marriott, 14
mass-marketing strategies, 128, 271
    entire-market customers (in
      customer management
      evolution) and, 273-274

multiple channels
    benefits of, 163-164
    communication via, 170-172
    research shoppers and, 164, 166
myths about loyal customers
    debunking, 22-23
    lower cost of service for, 18-19
    marketing efforts by, 20-21
    price sensitivity of, 19-20

N–O

net present value (NPV),
    calculating, 45-46
Nokia, 187-189

one-time purchases with add-on
    products/services, calculating
    Customer Lifetime Value (CLV), 55
one-to-one marketing strategies, 271
    individual customers (in
        customer management
        evolution) and, 272-273
operational efficiencies, customer
    relationships versus, 2
opportunity cost from customer
    attrition, 145
optimizing direct marketing
    expenditures, 205-206
overcommunication, risk of,
    116-117

P

P&G (Proctor & Gamble), 223, 274
Pareto principle, 6
passive word-of-mouth
    marketing, 21
PCV (Past Customer Value), 24,
    34-35
    drawbacks to, 36
people dimension (implementation
    challenges to CLV-based
    framework), 259

Pepsi, 271
portfolio management metrics, 262
predicting
    customer attrition, 147-150
        hazard models, 151-154
        logistic regression model,
            150-151
        statistical issues, 154
    customer purchase behavior, 129
        accuracy, lack of, 130-132
        joint-probability strategy,
            132-137
        sample size, 131-132
    Customer Referral Value (CRV),
        228-230
    purchase sequence. *See* purchase
        sequency prediction strategy
        (maximizing CLV)
preventing customer attrition, 147
    intervention strategy, 155-161
    predicting churn, 147-154
price discounts, 178
price premium behavior, 195
price sensitivity of loyal customers,
    19-20
probability of active customers,
    44-45. *See also* joint-probability
    strategy (purchase behavior
    predictions)
Proctor and Gamble (P&G),
    223, 274
product availability, 176
product categories (cross-selling
    strategy), 138-141
product-centric approach, changing
    to customer-centric approach
    business dimension of, 251-253,
        255-258
    people dimension of, 259
product characteristics (CLV
    driver), 61, 70